LONDON TO TOKYO

SR Scholarly Resources Inc.
Wilmington, Delaware · London

SCHOLARLY RESOURCES, INC.
Wilmington, Delaware

Reprint edition published in 1973
First published in 1942 by Hutchinson
   & Co. Ltd., London

Library of Congress Catalog Card Number: 72-82112
ISBN: 0-8420-1405-5

Manufactured in the United States of America

129658

SIR JOHN TILLEY, G.C.M.G.

LONDON TO TOKYO

BY

The Rt. Hon. SIR JOHN TILLEY, G.C.M.G.

Lately His Majesty's Ambassador to Brazil and Japan

WITH 13 ILLUSTRATIONS

HUTCHINSON & CO. (*Publishers*) LTD.

LONDON : NEW YORK : MELBOURNE

MADE AND PRINTED IN GREAT BRITAIN AT
ST. ALBANS BY *The Mayflower Press* (of
Plymouth), WILLIAM BRENDON & SON, LTD.

To

MY WIFE

LIST OF ILLUSTRATIONS

CHAPTER I

HAVING ONE DAY AGREED TO WRITE THIS VOLUME OF MEMORIES, I READ with consternation the following day this sentence in Miss Dorothy Sayers' book, *The Mind of the Maker*: 'The writing of an Autobiography is a dangerous business; it is the mark either of great insensitiveness to danger or of an almost supernatural courage.' Nevertheless I start with no consciousness of any intention to write words which will bring down wrath or obloquy on my head.

I am not anxious to say very much about purely personal matters, but I take it that some background is required for any form of memoirs. I therefore begin by recording the fact that I was born on January 21st, 1869, into what I can only describe as a complicated family. My father, John Tilley, had been married three times, one child eventually surviving of each marriage. His first wife was Cecilia Trollope, a sister of Anthony Trollope; his second wife was her first cousin, Mary Anne Partington; his third wife was my mother, Susanna Montgomerie, who was his own first cousin once removed. Relationships were therefore almost inextricably mixed.

My mother died when I was eleven, but her house, Annick Lodge, in Ayrshire, was a second home for me for many years after her death. Her grandfather, Alexander Montgomerie, who was brother to the twelfth Earl of Eglinton, bought this place, near Eglinton, at the end of the eighteenth century. It was called Greenvale; but finding to his disgust that his neighbours began to address him as 'Greenvale' he changed the name to Annick Lodge, which he hoped would bring them back to the use of his family name.

Annick Lodge seemed to me as a child, and still seems to me, almost perfect as a home. The house stood on the banks of a brown river where once the monks of Kilwinning had a mill; the river, before a mill dam was made a mile or so further down, had a few salmon, so I was told, and still had trout to give a fisherman uncle and a fisherman butler a little sport. There was an avenue of great beeches along one bank below the house, by which one came first to a bathing pool, and then to the rapids. We sometimes had a flat-bottomed boat, but it had difficulty in travelling over the shallow places. The river valley opened out in front of the house to give room for what in England would be called a small park, and on the brae top to one side was the big garden: on the other side of the river the banks and braes only left room for a narrow walk.

The core of the house was a tower with walls six foot thick in which, in the fifteenth century, the monks lived; there were three big rooms one above the other; then, perhaps fifty years later, another room was added on each floor: in the eighteenth century someone converted the tower into a gentleman's house by adding big cellars, a small dining-room and drawing-room on the first floor, and bedrooms above. When my great-grandfather bought the place at the end of that century he added a charming Adam front with wings: the main part of this addition contained a hall, a fine staircase, and four large rooms; this left a tiny courtyard in the middle of the house, and then he filled up a gap with more rooms, and he and his son erected servants' quarters in various directions. At the end of the stone-floored servants' hall were two large cupboards which served as sleeping places for his men-servants. As a result of all this the house was a network of passages and steps and large and small staircases which somehow or other seemed remarkedly attractive.

In the hall was a great gilt Buddha brought back by a naval uncle from some war in China. Much of the furniture and china had been my great-grandfather's and therefore of an excellent period.

I remember being told that at Eglinton, his brother's home, the Chippendale furniture was banished to the servants' quarters in the early nineteenth century to make room for something more modern. Eglinton is no longer inhabited, but I am glad to think that one relic in particular survives elsewhere. This is a small figure of St. Benet, the Patron Saint of the Setons. The Montgomeries are Setons in the male line, and the sixth Earl of Eglinton, who was the first Seton Earl, brought his Patron with him. When the house was rebuilt early in the nineteenth century, St. Benet was built up stone by stone till he reached the roof, where he presided over the place for a hundred years or so. He was not, I believe, the founder of the Benedictines, but a north country saint called St. Benet Biscop, though why the Setons adopted him I cannot say. He figures as their Patron Saint in Scott's *The Abbot*.

The twelfth Earl of Eglinton was succeeded by his grandson, afterwards known as the 'Tournament' Earl. He was then a boy, and my grandfather was for many years heir presumptive. When he became engaged to my grandmother he was tersely described to my other grandmother, Mrs. Tilley, as having 'plenty of blood but no money'; but he and his wife lived up to their position by always posting to London instead of taking the coach; to Mrs. Tilley's mind a shocking extravagance.

In the early part of the nineteenth century, and still more so in the eighteenth, Scottish families did not stray very far, either in search of society or in search of husbands and wives, consequently Ayrshire was pervaded with my mother's relations, Montgomeries, Boyles, Fergussons, Hamiltons and Oswalds, who between them owned a considerable share of the county. My great-grandfather and his brothers were brought up at Coilsfield, their home until the elder succeeded to Eglinton. Coilsfield has attained some celebrity from the fact that Robert Burns was enamoured of their dairy-maid, 'Montgomeries' Peggy' as the poet more romantically styles her. He refers indeed in his poems more than once not only to

Peggy, but to her employers, whom he describes as a soldier race 'who strode along.' They were not, I fear, always very amiable to their neighbours. My eldest uncle having sold Annick Lodge, a younger brother and sister then moved to another part of the county, wishing to die and be buried in Ayrshire. Unfortunately they discovered that the old burial place went with Annick Lodge, and the purchaser was determined to be buried there himself. This caused considerable dispute and commotion in the family, and in the end room was left in the grave for the two Montgomeries, but a neighbour observed of the newcomer that the poor man would never have been so anxious to be buried among all those Montgomeries if he had known how disagreeable they could make themselves. This suggests a horrid scene in the churchyard, but among their own family the Montgomeries, in my experience, were full of kindness and affection.

Among the families to whom they made themselves disagreeable were the Cuninghames, with whom they had a feud lasting for several centuries so bitter that mutual murders were not uncommon; of these Cuninghames my future wife was one, so that my ties with Ayrshire have been well confirmed.

To go back to my father. He was a posthumous son, and his father had been born in 1768, a hundred years before myself, while my mother's father, uncles and aunts were all born also in the eighteenth century, so that I was altogether out of my generation.

My father joined the Post Office service in 1829 on the nomination of Sir Francis Freeling, the then Secretary, who was a friend of his mother's. He had to pass some form of qualifying examination, which was conducted by Sir Francis himself in the presence of his daughters. In 1839 my father was made Surveyor of the North of England, and in that year married Cecilia Trollope. He settled at Penrith, and as his district included Northumberland, Cumberland and Yorkshire, a great part of his life at that time was spent on coaches. My father's great friend while he lived in Cumberland, and indeed afterwards, was Sir George Musgrave of Edenhall. Sir George was decidedly of the old school. When my father went to congratulate him on his son's engagement he was very angry. "Congratulate me because my son is going to marry a pawnbroker's daughter." "Surely not," said my father. "I understood the father was a stockbroker." "What, pray, is the difference?" asked Sir George.

My father and his wife brought their families with them, for old Mrs. Tilley and old Mrs. Trollope both came to live in the neighbourhood, though the latter was not very happy there. She once took my father to call on Wordsworth, but he insisted on waiting outside, and when she came out she said he had done well, for the poet was most disagreeable.

In 1849 my father became Assistant Secretary of the Post Office, and Secretary in 1864, having married my mother in 1861. Anthony Trollope was my godfather, and I remember him very well, with his somewhat shaggy appearance and boisterous laugh.   On one occasion he wrote to say that he would look in next day for lunch: anything would do for him; a crust of bread and a scrap of cheese.   My half-sister (his niece) and I arranged in a small back-room a table covered with a grubby kitchen cloth, smeared with grease and mustard; and on this we set the tail end of a stale loaf, some mouldy bits of cheese, and a jug of water.   When Uncle Tony arrived my sister led him to the feast, explaining that as she knew he would be in a hurry she had everything ready.   He looked at the table with loathing, but when my sister said: "Well, that is what you asked for, but if you have changed your mind there is some more lunch in the dining-room," he fairly roared and hugged her like a bear.   A little later, while I was away at school, he came to dinner one night; after dinner my sister read "Vice Versa" aloud to him and my father, also a great laugher. Uncle Tony roared as usual; suddenly my father and sister noticed that while they were laughing he was silent: he had had a stroke from which he never recovered.   I do not think he ever heard me say my catechism, but I once wrote to him from my private school to tell him, with an eye to the main chance, that I had won second prize in a spelling bee, a form of entertainment then rather popular.   He replied, sending me half a sovereign, but alleging, I still believe untruly, that in my letter to him I had spelt night with a k.

My father was a man of fine character, and equally fine presence and manner.   He was apt to inspire awe among those who worked with or under him, and I gathered that those who worked over him, as Postmasters-General, were not always exceptions to the rule.   Meeting the Austrian Ambassador, Count Deym, at Belvoir, my father said: "You know the Duke was for six years my master."   "On the contrary," said the Duke of Rutland, "Sir John was mine."   The Postmaster-General, however, was not expected to interfere very much in the work of the office in those days. This is in contradiction to what seems to be now the general supposition. Ministers are often blamed because they leave too much power in the hands of the permanent officials, the implication being that things were done better in the past.   In some offices no doubt, such as the Foreign Office, the Minister ruled as well as reigned, but in many others it was not so.   In the course of Mr. Gladstone's first administration Lord Emly was appointed Postmaster-General.   Mr. Gladstone sent for my father and said: "You must just do the best you can with him."   My father used to say that the great Stores originated with him.   What happened was that one of the Post Office staff came to him and asked if they might use a large cupboard outside his room for storing tea, which the clerks were combining to buy on some economical system.   That was the small beginning of the Civil Service Stores.   One other story of a new departure at the Post Office. Owing to the death of an old Mr. Creswell, the postmastership of Gibraltar, an important post, had become vacant.   In due course some of the higher officials came to my father's room and asked whether he had considered the choice of a successor to Mr. Creswell. "Certainly," he said, "I propose to appoint his daughter, Miss Creswell. She has really done the work for some time and done it very well." The others objected that he could not appoint a woman. "Why not?" he asked. "There is surely no law on the subject." "Well," they said, "no law, but it would be very difficult." My father turned to his Private Secretary and said: "Bring me a bit of paper." Taking the paper he wrote: 'Appoint Miss Creswell Postmaster of Gibraltar. John Tilley.' "There," he said to his friends, "it's done; it was not difficult at all. What made you think it would be?"

From such account as I have given of my family it will be seen that in childhood my lines fell almost entirely among those who, from my point of view, were elderly. What effect this had on me I do not pretend to say, but I presume that it had some effect.

From a preparatory school at Thorpe Mandeville in Northampton-shire, which sometimes figures in the delightful books of Eric Parker, I took a scholarship at Eton and spent six happy years in College there. In these days it is common to find writers in the Press urging that the time has come for Eton to 'share its advantages' with boys from the elementary schools. What these writers have in mind I find it difficult to understand. What there is good in the organization of the school as regards teaching (and I believe that organization is at the present time quite excellent) can be adapted to any other school. The buildings, apart from historical interest, are not by any means such as to be beyond the reach of local education authorities. The 'advantages of Eton,' as seen by parents, lie largely in the standards set by the boys themselves and in the fact that their children will find their friends' children there. If any great number of boys from elementary schools were sent to Eton by the local education authorities, either those boys would turn into average Etonians, which is not, I imagine, what the theorists in question want to see, or, alternatively, the present type of Etonian would disappear and the supposed advantages with him. Another difficulty with things as they are in elementary or senior schools is that the standard of education for boys entering the school would have to be considerably lowered, for I do not believe that it is true, as often alleged, that the elementary schools yet turn out boys who would put their contemporaries from private schools to shame. I speak as having had a good deal to do with schools under the control of local education authorities. It would, of course, be practicable to take quite a small number of elementary or 'senior' schoolboys into each of the public schools as a preliminary to the establishment of County Boarding Schools, for which we ought to work. The number of boys thus taken in would be a minute proportion of the whole, but the arrangement might help to make boarding schools popular with parents who have not hitherto thought of them. What we want is surely diversity, not uniformity, of type.

It is difficult to believe that, in what is so constantly described as a free country, parents who wish to do the best they can for their children, often at the cost of much sacrifice, will in the future be forced to accept the education provided by the State whether they like it or not.

The headmaster during most of my Eton life was the great Warre. I was up to him, in Head's division for my last two years and for four terms (halves, properly speaking) was in sixth form. The point about this that often occurs to my mind is that in all that time I never, as far as I can remember, ever had any conversation with Warre of any sort excepting such as arose out of lessons, or my duties as sixth form præpostor. We took these duties by turns, a week at a time, one of them being to collect the victims who were to appear before the Head in Chambers at twelve. Those who were to be swished were bidden 'to stay'; the others were told that the headmaster wished to see them after school. During these interviews the præpostor stood behind the Head's chair. On one occasion Bill Llewelyn had been summoned. He was a charming person, a member of the XI, and admirable in all respects, as may be read in Gibb's *Cotswold Village*. His offence was a very minor one, for which he was given fifty lines to write out. That settled, he smiled at the Head and wished him many happy returns of the day. The Head merely grunted. I suppose he was a very shy man, even on his fiftieth birthday.

People sometimes criticize the size of Eton on the ground that the Head could know so few of the boys. I do not think there is much in this. It is only in quite small schools that time would allow of the headmaster acquiring any practical knowledge of all the boys. The best tribute to Eton that I have ever come across appeared in a letter, to *The Times* it must have been, in the shape of a casual reference to 'Eton, that happy place'.

My last half at Eton, the summer half of 1887, was much occupied with the glories of Queen Victoria's Jubilee. We carried out, under Warre's direction, a successful torchlight procession at the Castle which has often been described: there were other excitements, and some of us were given places in the Abbey. As a matter of fact, we did not see very much as we were high up in a gallery above the nave, but we looked down on the Queen's Procession, and my most vivid memory is of the rustling of the leaves of the service papers as that enormous congregation punctiliously turned them over. It was like the sound of a rushing wind.

In October of that year I went up to Cambridge, having secured one of the Eton scholarships, which were a much richer prize in those days than they are now, when free lodging, free dinners and free commons no longer form part of the emoluments.

Here I hasten to protest that on going up to King's I did not come under the influence of Oscar Browning. I had nothing to do with him. I say this more emphatically because in a recent obituary notice of E. F. Benson in *The Times* it was stated that on going up to King's he came under the influence of Oscar Browning, Walter Headlam and Charles Waldstein. Benson was in my year and I knew him intimately. We were in the opposite camp, for there were unfortunately two camps, to Oscar Browning. Moreover, Walter Headlam, though a great friend of ours, was only a couple of years older and did not begin to lecture till, I think, our last year. Waldstein, though very much older, was a friend, but we saw little of him at that time. Possibly Benson saw more of him later on when he 'did' archæology after taking his degree.

If anybody exercised any influence over us it was M. R. James, of whom we did see a great deal. His character, learning and habits generally have been too often and too well described for me to try to do so again here. Very nearly all the friends of whom, while I was up, he was the High Priest are, alas, dead; Marcus Dimsdale, Walter Headlam, Lionel and Francis Ford, Ted Sanderson, E. F. Benson, A. J. Bather, Alfred Martineau, George and Gerald Duckworth and Robert Norton. They were a delightful set of men. Of course, in theory there should be no sets in College: there should be universal love and brotherhood; perhaps in some distant epoch there may be, and rights and lefts will be indistinguishable; in fact, the other day at the quincentenary celebrations at King's I heard it said that the millennium had already arrived. In my day one possible cause of dissension was that we were all (by hypothesis) clever; no one was admitted unless he was a candidate for honours. My half-brother, who was a Fellow, once said that we should be so much better if we had a few stupid men among us.

The only unusual occupation which I had at Cambridge was that of Assistant Editor, and for a short time Editor, of the *Cambridge Review*. We were considered to publish rather solid reading and did not go in much for bright and forward ideas. We did indulge once in a series of anonymous letters to lecturers, criticizing, sometimes severely, our masters and pastors. Of these I contributed one addressed to the great Jebb which was subsequently reproduced in a *Book of the Cambridge Review*. My advice to Jebb was that he should learn to act, for he read his lectures without looking up from his notes. I observed that he might have said 'at a certain hour on certain days I shall be reading to myself my edition of the Philoctetes, so far as it at present goes; if any members of the University choose to come' and look on or listen, they may do so.' I went on, 'It is possible that half the members of your class would not recognize you if they met you in the street, for they never see your face, unless they catch a glimpse of it as you enter the room.' I advised him to go to J. W. Clark, then famous as the high protector of the A.D.C., from whom he might pick up some valuable hints. I thought that after that he would collect a much larger audience, and suggested the market place with a 'bema' in the centre for himself as altogether suitable for so great a classical scholar.

One of the features of the *Review* was the publication week by week of the University Sermon. Some of the preachers were by no means anxious to hand over their manuscripts, having views about copyright which did not assort with our custom. It was sometimes my lot to appease them.

One of the recalcitrant prelates was Archbishop Thomson of York, but the Master of Trinity to whom I appealed kindly bade me come to the Lodge after breakfast to interview His Grace. It was with great trepidation that I found myself standing in the hall with a somewhat disgruntled Archbishop towering above me.

I thought of this scene a good many years later when my wife and I were calling on Sir William and Lady Whittall, the great figures of the English Levantine Colony at Moda, opposite Constantinople. When we had been there some time Lady Whittall suddenly exclaimed to her husband: "By the way, there is that Archbishop waiting to see you."

In those days King's Chapel and its music was, as it still is, one of the notable features of Cambridge, but in my day it was compulsory for King's men, unless they were nonconformists, to attend a certain number of services, and the Chapel, which after all was intended for them, was seen to be fulfilling its proper function. I cannot believe that attendance did them harm, it probably did them good; now that attendance is not compulsory the sprinkling of surplices that one sees is somewhat doleful in its sparseness. I have had two shocks in my life in regard to King's Chapel which I may record here. Once, long after I had gone down, I was staying at Cambridge, and coming out of Chapel I met on the threshold Sir Clement Hill, who had been for many years a colleague in the Foreign Office and was then Member for Shrewsbury. He asked me if I knew the place and what there was to see. I made various suggestions, to which he replied: "Yes; but is this Chapel worth seeing?" I had believed King's Chapel to be known in all the corners of the world. Years later again I met Sir Charles Trevelyan at a ceremony in Bury St. Edmunds. The Trevelyans and their relations the Macaulays are a very great Cambridge family. I told him that I was just off to Cambridge for the inauguration of the great new organ in King's Chapel. "Very interesting," said he. "Have they had no organ at King's up to now?" Perhaps if ever he sees this story he will say that he was merely trying to abate my pride.

Many of the King's Dons of those days have figured in Benson's novels under various thin disguises; Oscar Browning being obvious to everyone who knew Cambridge. One was J. E. Nixon, a great classical scholar, but a quaint-looking figure in a black morning coat, pot hat, dark glasses and a black kid glove concealing the loss of a hand. He gave musical parties for undergraduates and, according to Benson, when excited by the music 'tore off his hands and went at the piano with his stumps'. There was Ropes, who under the name of A. R. Reed made a name as a writer of musical comedies, and was to us remarkable for a straggly red beard and the fact that he had shot off his own finger when intending to shoot the bed-maker who called him in the morning and whom he mistook for a burglar. There was also Churton, a clergyman who had a name to conjure with among missionaries, one of whom coming to Cambridge during a holiday set out with enthusiasm to call on him; but Churton, seeing a stranger entering his room, fled into an inner room; the stranger following, Churton fled back through a third door and out of his rooms, so that the missionary had to give up in despair. Another remarkably shy man was Mozley. He was supposed to be afraid of dogs: at any rate if, when he emerged into the Court, anyone whistled he fled back to his rooms. I have watched E. F. Benson performing this trick with great success. As someone sang at a King's 'Combi': "Here's to the health of our friend Mr. Mozley. He will run to his rooms if you watch him too closely." He had held a Fellowship for many years and was entitled to rooms, but I cannot remember that he attempted to teach anything. Walter Headlam, as I have said, was a great friend of ours. He was a magnificent scholar and a delightful companion. He was no athlete, but he took suddenly to riding and equipped himself beautifully: unfortunately he was not, I suppose, fitted by nature to be a horseman. I shall never forget going down towards the back gate of King's and seeing Headlam coming along the Backs on his hired steed at a very slow amble; suddenly he began to wobble in his seat and presently fell off. I have frequently seen people thrown off, but I do not recollect ever seeing anyone else absolutely fall off.

I have already referred to Oscar Browning and my concern at the possibility of being described as having come under his influence. I am not thinking of his political principles which, though he stood for Parliament as a Liberal, would not seem from his manner of life to have been extreme, or of his supposedly progressive ideas, but of his general character which did not in my opinion, any more than in that of the former headmaster of Eton, Dr. Hornby, fit him to be either a guide, a philosopher or a friend for youth.

The King's Dons were naturally not by any means all queer. The Senior Tutor, George Prothero, the historian, was not only learnèd and cultivated, but a man of practical wisdom and great charm. He left King's to become Editor of the *Quarterly*. The Junior Tutor was my brother, Arthur Tilley, who had won both the Newcastle and the Tomline scholarships at Eton for classics and mathematics respectively, had been 2nd classic in 1874 and later achieved a great reputation by his books on the history of French literature. During one vacation he and I made a delightful tour in France to visit places in which as a student he was specially interested. Paris, Arles, Montpellier, Toulouse, Albi, Carcassonne, Bordeaux (to see Montaigne's Château), and Argelès in the Pyrenees, Poitiers, Angers, Amboise, Blois and back to Paris. I thus acquired what may be called a good framework for knowledge of France. Most of these places were then outside the beat of ordinary tourists: the hotels were designed for French and not for English travellers and the people at the tables d'hôte were nearly all French. We stayed in Paris at the Hôtel St. Antoine in the Rue St. Roch, a thoroughly French hotel, but with a considerable clientèle among Cambridge Dons, to whom the proprietor, M. Bélard, was a sort of family friend. We dined on Good Friday with some French friends of my brother's who gave us a splendid *dîner maigre*, including lobster and some kind of waterfowl, and maintained that, heretics though we were, we could not fail to profit spiritually by such a meal. We met hardly any English people during the tour, but an exception was William Bridgeman, who was travelling in charge, so to speak, of Lord Chelsea. Bridgeman held for a term or two an Eton mastership, the prelude in various cases to fame of other kinds. Bridgeman became a cabinet minister, Rowlatt a judge, Inge the greatest of modern deans, Hugessen, as Lord Brabourne, a considerable figure in the City, and no doubt other instances could be found.

During my last year at Cambridge my father, through Sir James Fergusson, a relative of my mother's, then Under-Secretary at the Foreign Office, had my name put down on Lord Salisbury's list of candidates for the Foreign Office. A nomination for the examination thus became possible but was not actually promised, and we were told that my place in the Tripos might carry weight. In the book on the Foreign Office published by Sir Stephen Gaselee and myself I said something about this system of nomination, and some critic complained that I had not said just what the system was. I do not believe there was a system. The mere fact of a nomination being required no doubt created a certain amount of mystery and deterred people from thinking of the Foreign Office for their sons. In much later years I have found that long after the abolition of any qualification for the diplomatic service in the shape of private means, some people still persisted in thinking that the necessity for private means existed and abandoned the idea of the service for those in whom they were interested. I may add here that, in my experience, it takes many years for the public to grasp the fact that administrative or other reforms have taken place, and they continue to complain of abuses which have long disappeared; this is notably true of the alleged idleness of the Civil Service, which was held up to scorn until the time that people began to complain that the Civil Service was too busy.

The 'system' of nomination had, therefore, much less in it than was supposed. I believe that no one who could be vouched for, and who had a creditable record at school and University, stood in any danger of being refused a nomination. There was, however, another barrier in the fact that a first-rate knowledge of foreign languages was required and made it necessary for young men to spend some considerable time abroad after leaving school, so that the education of candidates was apt to be an expensive matter; especially as the limits of age were from nineteen to twenty-five and the vacancies few, so that the young men who failed might find it difficult to find an alternative profession.

At the time when I made up my mind to try for the Foreign Office, Ancient Greek was an optional subject for the examination as well as Italian and Spanish. The obligatory subjects were Arithmetic, Handwriting, Orthography, English Composition, Précis Writing, French,

German, Latin, General Intelligence and Geography. The optional subjects included History of Europe to be read in two specified books, Constitutional History equally taken from specified books, and the languages mentioned. Before I had a chance of competing, first Greek was cut out and Russian put in, and then Political Economy and Shorthand were made optional subjects, the latter being Lord Rosebery's idea.

The principles on which these changes were made I consider altogether heretical, as indeed in later years they came to be regarded by Lord Lansdowne. A young man who took a first class in the Classical Tripos at Cambridge was likely to have better brains than one who could only offer modern languages learned colloquially; at any rate he ought not to have been put at a disadvantage by comparison with one who had never been to a university and had spent his time after leaving school in a French or German family. It might, of course, be that the latter was a brilliant specimen, but the way chosen was not the right way of attracting brains, and the examination was planned on the erroneous theory that a boy's education should be adapted to his intended walk of life. It is on this theory that some people still wish to see boys who are likely to work on the land taught nothing but the most elementary subjects, on the ground, for instance, that geography is not requisite for a boy who will never leave his native country, or that a knowledge of French will not help him to plough a straight furrow. The idea of including shorthand in our examination was doubtless based on the unconscious expectation that we should for ever do, as juniors then did, nothing but the most routine work.

Having taken my degree my next business was to improve my French, which was moderately good, and my German, which was almost nil.

For the former purpose I went off to spend three months with a Curé de campagne near Tours, traditional home of the best-spoken French. He lived in a good-sized village named St. Martin le Beau. The Presbytère was a bungalow, L-shaped and having its long side at right angles to the road, from which, like so many French villages, it was shut off by a high wall. My first recollection of it is that on my opening the gate a small flock of goldfinches flew across the garden, and being my favourite bird I regarded their welcome as a good omen. I may say at once that M. le Curé was of no help in regard to ornithology; if I asked him the name of any small bird he replied: *"C'est un pinson"* (a chaffinch); if I would not have this: *"Alors c'est une pèce"* (a hen chaffinch, or so he said). He had an old housekeeper and they made me very comfortable, the Curé being somewhat of a gourmet, the local wines good and the house well kept. He had had other English lodgers who wished to learn French, but he was somewhat ingenuous about education. My brother, who discovered him, had said that I wished to learn to write French correctly. The Curé took this to mean that I wished to learn to form my letters correctly and spell correctly; he was vague about style. His own education, like that, I take it, of all French priests, had been purely professional, in the

Petit Séminaire followed by the Grand Séminaire. His stipend from the French Government was nine hundred francs a year: the rest of what we should call 'his living' came from payments for Masses and other religious services, which could not have been a great deal. He had, I believe, some private means and I suppose possibly some help from diocesan or other such funds. Most of his colleagues lived very simply indeed. Apart from Masses one small source of income depended on an Altar of Ste Rose de Lima in his Church. Ste Rose apparently cures skin diseases, and fairly often there was a ring at the bell and someone left two sous for an Évangile to be said before the altar. When there was a certain accumulation of sous, M. le Curé went to his church and repeated the proper number of Évangiles. He was ingenuous about other matters besides literature: for instance, he professed a horror of witches, and when in our walks we met an old woman who was reputed to be a witch and to do a great deal of harm in the neighbourhood by her spells he would turn to the other side of the road, make the Sign of the Cross, and mutter something about "*les mauvaises femmes.*" I do not know what his ideas about the Church of England may have been, but I gathered what was the impression he left on other people by some questions put to me by a friend of his. We went to take *déjeuner* with the Chasublier in Tours. This gentleman's wife tackled me on the subject of religion: "*C'est que vous ne croyez pas en Jésus Christ.*" "*Oui, madame,*" I replied. "*Autant que vous.*" "*Je me trompais donc, c'est que vous ne croyez pas en la Sainte Vierge.*" "*Oui, madame, ma religion ressemble beaucoup à la vôtre.*" But the Curé here broke in and changed the subject violently before I could disturb his friend's mind unduly.

In politics the Curé was a Conservative: somewhat inclined to the Legitimists—that is, to the party who looked up to the Comte de Chambord as Henri V. The only political action on his part of which he told me took place when General Boulanger was to the fore. He and a local friend went into Tours and brought back, carefully concealed, a quantity of the General's proclamations. At dead of night the friend shoved these papers under all the doors in the village, with the result that at the forthcoming election of deputies one and all voted for Boulanger, who was not even a candidate. The Mayor, himself a Bonapartist, got into much trouble on this account with the Government, who blamed him for allowing such a thing to happen in his Commune. The Curé told me that in the first years of the Third Republic the priests had a very bad time. If he went about his parish, thinking perhaps to call at some farm, the farmer would shout to his wife: "*Apporte mon fusil que je tue ce corbeau.*" A brother priest, however, felt during the Franco-German War that he had got his own back. An angry soldier shouted at him: "*Pourquoi est-ce que tu restes ici?*"; answer: "*Pour vous enterrer demain.*"

My Curé's ideas of his own religion must have been almost as elementary as his ideas about mine. We were once hurrying to the station to catch a train: on the way we met a man in evident anxiety, who stopped us and said: "*Vous êtes Monsieur le Curé de St. Martin le Beau n'est ce pas?*" I thought to myself that it was probably a case of Extreme Unction. Without any hesitation my friend answered: "*Non, monsieur: le presbytère est là bas. Je pense que vous trouverez Monsieur le Curé chez lui.*" As we hurried on the Curé turned to me and said: "*Maintenant vous voyez comme ma religion vaut mieux que la vôtre; demain j'irai chez M. le Curé de Dyeres: je ferai ma confession at tout sera fini.*"

Here is another tale of the manners and customs of the neighbouring priests. At some little distance from us, funds had been collected to set up a village Cross. There was to be a great gathering for the Benediction, at which ceremony the Archdeacon of Amboise was to officiate. After the service there was a *déjeuner* at the Presbytère at which the Archdeacon was in the place of honour, and I, almost the only lay guest, at the end of the table. As the Archdeacon sat down a cheerful tune broke out from nowhere in particular, much to the mystification of the guests. Presently it turned out that some sort of musical box had been concealed in the chair and was set off by the impact of the Archdeacon's person. I cannot conceive this happening at any vicarage in this country.

I once attended with the Curé another very much larger *déjeuner* in his own village given on the occasion of a wedding. There must have been a great waste of money, for the parties did not belong to rich families; a great deal of good local wine was drunk, and songs were sung, but as some of these turned on the Chambertin of the Abbé or some such topic, my friend removed me rather hastily from the scene.

The Mayor, to whom I have referred, owned a pleasant château outside the village, but only came there for short visits. We went to lunch with him also, and although he and his family were Parisians and anxious to be polite and hospitable they obviously looked on me as a strange sort of creature. The Mayor was perturbed at finding that I wore knickerbockers and stockings; surely the calves of my legs must get wet when it rained. His son, who had learned a little English, tried to arrange his sentences according to English grammar: "*J'ai vu vous hier*" instead of "*Je vous ai vu*," and was nearly incomprehensible. Madame had done her part by providing some plum cake which she had obtained with some trouble from Paris, being under the impression that it would remind me of home.

We were always very particular about titles; no one, if it could be avoided, was addressed by name. It was always "M. le Maire, M. le Curé, M. le Chef de Gare." Our neighbour, M. le Curé d'Athée, who was a contemporary of my friend, and had been at the Seminaires with him, once in a moment of exuberance exclaimed: "*Eh bien! Augeron.*" My Curé pointed out to me afterwards that he had quickly repressed this unpardonable lapse of courtesy: "*Qu'est-ce-que vous dîtes M. le Curé.*"

Of the higher dignitaries of the Church I saw nothing, although I heard a good deal of Monseigneur Meignan, the Archbishop of Tours. He was aggrieved at not having been made a Cardinal, and made up for this as far as he could by wearing a 'Soutane Rose', that is a near red cassock instead of a strictly purple one. Later on he did receive his Hat. Nor did I hear much of politics, apart from the Boulanger episode, and the iniquities of the Freemasons, who were looked upon by clerical society as the enemy; the schoolmasters and mistresses, who were state officials, seemed to be mostly in that camp, and among other crimes taught the children never to salute anyone, least of all the priests, or even old Madame de Champchevrier, who, as her name suggests, was or had been the great lady of the district. The crime was the greater in France, where salutations are much more insisted upon than here.

After three months in France I was sent off to spend a year in a German family at Dresden. The family, as a matter of fact, consisted of only two: an old Prussian lieutenant-colonel and his Saxon wife, who was much younger. Though Saxon by birth she was thoroughly Prussian by pre-dilection and spoke with contempt of the fear of the Prussians shown by the Dresdeners in 1866. Some girls of her family had been obliged by their parents to wear their two best dresses night and day all ready to flee into the forest, or its equivalent, as soon as the Prussians approached, but the family woke up one morning to find that the Prussians had come in with the milk.

Saxony in those days had its own king, King Albert, and a very good one. He had no children, and the only other members of the Royal Family were the king's brother, Prince George, and his sons and daughters. The eldest of these, the last king of Saxony, was considered rather wild in his youth, and his wildness had become public property owing to the fact that when walking in the park with his father a large dog belonging to his favourite actress rushed up and fawned upon him.

I had various teachers at Dresden, but the one of whom I saw most was a young schoolmaster, with whom I took long walks in order to acquire practice in French and German conversation. He used sometimes to tell me the latest jokes about the Kaiser, such as his nickname of *der Reise Kaiser* (the travelling Emperor) and the change of *Heil dir im Siegerkranz* to *Heil dir im Sonderzuge* (the special train instead of the crown of victory); but the point which I specially remember is that any remark of this sort was made in a whisper, or where there was no possible chance of being overheard, as all liberals lived in dread of a prosecution for *lèse-majesté*. A good many years later, but well before the Great War, I remember similar precautions being taken when I was dining with a friend at a restaurant in Berlin. It is no new thing for Germans to live in terror of the police.

Living with this old couple I saw few young Germans, but I do recollect the pride with which a young cadet told me that at some family reunion he had managed fifteen mugs of beer. The chief excitements of our life were the theatre where we had an *abonnement* and an occasional *Kaffee klatsch*, or tea party. All the same the Colonel habitually described his wife as a *Vergnügens-Crocodil*, a crocodile for pleasure, poor thing. Their flat was furnished with extreme simplicity, partly no doubt for want of money, but the old man was ready to denounce anything in the way of luxury; "*Ach! dieser luxus*," and his wife talked with envy of a friend's flat in which there were thick carpets. As in France everyone was spoken of by titles if at all possible; not only *Frau Oberst-Leutnant* (Mrs. Lieut.-Colonel) but *Frau Leutnant* and *Herr Landesältester*, this being a friend who seemed to be something like a deputy-lieutenant; but the climax came in a letter from the mother of one of my teachers who was too ill to give me a lesson: it was signed *Helene Oberzollrathswitwe Gottschald* (Chief-Customs-Councillor's Widow).

There was naturally no anti-English talk, seeing that the Colonel and his wife and several of the friends of whom they saw most lived by taking in English lodgers. Indeed, Dresden was full of English and Americans and I heard my own language wherever I went. The enemy was France, many of my acquaintances having lived through the Franco-Prussian War. Although these people were civil and friendly to me and other English people, it does not follow that their sentiments were very different from those which came to expression in 1914 and 1939; many people talking and writing about foreign countries and their pleasant experiences there seem to overlook the fact that individuals in all countries refrain as far as possible from quarrelling with their bread and butter. Hotel keepers, shopkeepers and so forth are not fools. Another similar mistake often made, as it seems to me, by travellers is to ascribe all sorts of virtues to the country people, who are believed to be far more hospitable and friendly than people in towns. One reason for this is that country people from the nature of their work and their way of living are easy to get at and easy to engage in conversation. You cannot stop strangers in Piccadilly and chat with them, or knock at a door in a London street and hope to be offered a cup of tea, whereas on a country road you have the natives more or less at your mercy.

So far as politics were concerned, though I heard little about them, my acquaintances were all, or professed all, to be good Conservatives, and my Colonel's wife, who actually was one, nearly had a fit when in her little box at the theatre George Duckworth, who was then lodging there, said in a loud voice: "*Aber Frau Generalin, social Demokrat wie Sie sind.*" She was only a Mrs. Lieut.-Colonel, but even a General's wife would have been terrified at being spoken of in public as a Social Democrat.

As I associate St. Martin-le-Beau with goldfinches so I associate Dresden with redstarts, which were always to be seen in the Grosser Garten.

A vacancy had occurred in the Foreign Office while I was in Dresden, but I could not then have passed in German or Spanish (which I also learned at Dresden from a German). When my German year was over I

B

had to go to Scoones, the crammer, who for years had prepared everybody, I believe with not more than one or two exceptions, for the Foreign Office and the Diplomatiç Service. The work which we did with Scoones illustrated the fallacious ideas with which the scheme of the examination had been drawn up. History taken from four books could obviously be crammed, nor was précis writing much better. I do not think any of us actually took shorthand for the examination, certainly I did not. When my first chance of an examination came, which was in 1893, I was already twenty-four, and there was only one vacancy for the Foreign Office and that vacancy I was so fortunate as to secure. Only one of the candidates did not come from Scoones, and he, thanks to the system of marking, got no marks at all: about as complete a failure as it is possible to conceive.

As I said before, the possibility of having to wait till one was twenty-four was a severe deterrent to many possible candidates, and in the case of the Diplomatic Service there was the further barrier of a financial qualification, in the shape of an undertaking that the candidate could rely on a private income of £400 a year. The Diplomatic Service, except for Ambassadors and Ministers, was very badly paid. Taking an Embassy at random from the Foreign Office list of 1890 I see the following salary figures: Secretary of Embassy (a man with thirty-two years' service) £850 and £150 house rent; Second Secretaries £435 and £315, these two having respectively fourteen and nine years' service and the latter being a man of thirty-three; and these were living in one of the most brilliant European capitals and expected to take a prominent place in society. The Third Secretary had £150 and an allowance of £100 for having passed an examination in Public Law. Attachés were unpaid. There were six of them in the Service who had all had two years' service, and one had taken history honours at Oxford in 1885. The junior member of the service was twenty-five. Even in the Foreign Office there was a small class with salaries of £100, whereas in the offices of the other secretaries of state the worst salary was £200. The senior man among the junior clerks—whose salaries rose to £600—had twenty-two years' service and his salary must have been about £400. In spite of all this there were in both branches of the service a number of men of marked ability and much common sense.

CHAPTER II

AT THE BEGINNING OF MARCH, 1893, I TOOK UP MY POST IN THE FOREIGN Office, after first being presented to Sir Philip Currie, the Head of the Office. I was assigned to the Eastern Department, which dealt with the affairs of the Near and Middle East, including Russia, the Turkish Empire and

Egypt. In those days there was the sort of feeling about the departments of the office that there is about the different houses in a school and the colleges in a university. Each had its own characteristics. The Eastern Department thought highly of itself socially and was a little 'superior'; the African Department was more rugged in its virtues, the Western Department rather more *fainéant*, although in each department there were individuals, such as Eyre Crowe in the Western, who by no means answered to this description. Our Chief was Frank Bertie, afterwards Ambassador at Paris during the Great War, who died as Lord Bertie of Thame. He was decidedly one of the able men of the office; although, as things were, he had had little chance of proving it. He was a man of picturesque appearance, fine grey hair and a ruddy face, much given to the most Rabelaisian types of conversation, very kind by nature but apt to explode with anger now and again. 'The Bull' was the excellent nickname with which he was baptized in Paris, and he was pleased with it himself. He once came into my room during the war and told me of some *lâches* (a word much in our mouths) which had occurred in the Paris Chancery; he had gone in and told them that if such a thing happened again he would toss some of them: they had no idea, he declared, that he knew of their name for him and were much out of countenance.

Our hours of work were curious. The early boy in the department came at eleven. Someone else was expected to come at twelve and the others about twelve-thirty. After one was definitely late. Bertie himself came at one, having had *déjeuner* at home at midday. We hoped to get away about seven, but were often kept till eight, or later, by telegrams, or the despatch of the bags for Constantinople or St. Petersburg, or by the requirements of the Secretary of State coming back late from the House of Lords. There were in my experience two types of Juniors, one who lamented that he had been going out to dinner but got on with his work, the other who lamented that he could not get on with his work because he was going out to dinner. This difference of lamentation, as everyone knows, persists in all sorts of situations in the course of one's experience.

Next to Bertie was Eric Barrington, who had been Lord Salisbury's Private Secretary, most efficient in that capacity and altogether charming. Then there was Conyngham Greene, later on to be Ambassador to Japan; Tower, who ended as Minister at Buenos Ayres; Fairholme, a great linguist who resigned early on account of his health and lived to be eighty. Tyrrell, now Lord Tyrrell; Jolliffe, now Lord Hylton; Robert Norton; Theo Russell, late Minister at The Hague; and Johnny Ford. Russell and Ford were both sons of ambassadors. One or two of these were away when I arrived and one or two left soon: our usual complement was about nine.

The work of us juniors was purely routine: we deciphered telegrams and 'blued' on a sort of jelly copies of these telegrams for various people beginning with the Queen. She always had to have the first and blackest copy, as she was annoyed if the telegrams were not easily legible. We became experts in the various codes employed and I can still remember some of the commoner groups of figures used. We copied by hand all the despatches which were being sent to our Missions abroad, and in fact all the letters which emanated from the department as well as numerous other documents, sometimes of portentous length, which were required for one purpose or another. Very bad for the handwriting. There were only two typists in the office, who worked mainly for the Secretary of State himself. The 'second division' clerks had no part in the work of the political departments, which was all regarded as more or less secret. The filling and tying up and sealing of the bags, done at the latest possible moment which enabled the messenger to catch his train, was always the cause of stir in what Fairholme called the hive. Then there was the despatch of the 'pouches' sent to Cabinet Ministers with the latest telegrams and confidential papers. Occasionally there was a shortage owing to the slackness of a Minister in returning his pouch; his supply was cut off for a day or two: he complained and wanted more pouches to be provided, but Lord Rosebery backed us up and said he would have no more 'hostages to fortune' going about the country. There was also the care of the archives for the current and the past year: letters had to be docketed and have p.p. (past papers) attached to them before being sent in to Bertie; the papers done with at the end of the previous day had to be put by. If a paper was missing Bertie was apt to come into the 'third room' with a smart pair of gloves on and hurl all the papers out of a cupboard into the middle of the room, 'just to learn us to keep them properly'; the gloves because he thought the papers might be dusty. One new boy having thoroughly learned his duties, as he thought, came early, and having docketed all the letters that had arrived at once put them neatly away in their proper places so that for a day or two we had a deceptively idle time.

We were rather like schoolboys, but my feeling is that we were efficient; there was no nonsense about sticking to any particular hours or any particular duties; much of our work was doubtless rather rough and ready, but it was intelligent. We were not in awe of our superiors; there was no question of saying 'Sir' to an Under-Secretary, or 'Mr.' Bertie, or anything of that sort; we were on equal terms. As a matter of fact, when, some years later, second division clerks were admitted into the Foreign Office, the same habits, I am glad to say, continued to prevail. There was no nonsense about addressing them, or expecting them to address us, as Mr. Smith or Mr. Jones, though I believe such ideas were held in some Government offices.

Even abroad in those days it was only Ambassadors who were addressed as 'Sir' by their staffs. I remember Bertie coming into the third room and saying: "What do you think? Pomposo" (a mere Minister at a European Court) "makes his Chancery call him Sir." Now, Sirs are broadcast in all directions.

Though the work was routine our days were not dull: news often came of important events; there was a good deal of well-informed talk, much, or at least some, of the correspondence made interesting reading, and there were a good many lighter intervals when there was a lull in the work. Visitors, including diplomats on leave, were by no means infrequent, though we did not, as had been the habit in past years, give them drinks. Now, I fancy, the head of a department in the Foreign Office would be astounded if he found an idle young gentleman or two chatting in an official room.

Apart from the regular staff we often had an honorary Attaché as clerk: the present Sir Harry Verney was for some years a popular junior in the Eastern Department; so was the present Lord Clarendon; but a year or two later the then head of the department refused a duke as being perhaps difficult to deal with.

Although the Foreign Office and Diplomatic Services were then separate in theory, in practice men were constantly changing from one to the other, temporarily or permanently. Of those mentioned above, Green, Tower, Jolliffe, Russell and Ford were really diplomats; Tyrrell and Norton were clerks, but had just been abroad for a time. There was plenty of knowledge of the world.

Bertie's own work, at the age of fifty, consisted mainly in minuting on the papers put before him the appropriate directions for having them printed, copied and so forth and seeing that everything was complete before passing them on to the Under-Secretary, to be by him sent to the Secretary of State. The Under-Secretary occasionally had a few remarks to make, but practically all the executive work of the political departments was done, and had always been done, by the Secretary of State himself. Apart from the official despatches the Secretary of State carried on a private correspondence with our Representatives at the more important posts, and these letters were a considerable source of difficulty to the office, since we often did not see them, and they were taken away by the Secretary of State when he left office; consequently the official knowledge of what was going on was incomplete.

Lord Rosebery was a popular chief and intended to be so. He, and he only, in my experience, once went all round the office and saw what people were doing; he occasionally asked some of the staff to stay with him at Mentmore, though there was some annoyance shown when one man who had been at Eton with him addressed him in his reply as 'Dear Rosebery,' and he arranged that a junior in each of the big embassies should send him a regular letter full of gossip. He was always ready to uphold the office when called upon and, what was more important, his foreign policy was much firmer than had been expected of a Liberal Minister and therefore admired by his staff.

After a year in the Eastern Department I was transferred to the Far Eastern Department, and there made my first, though distant, acquaintance with Japan as a world power. The China-Japan War, and the rapid success of the latter, first made the world realize that Japan was to be reckoned with among the powers. This was only twenty-six years after the restoration of the Emperor to power and the adaptation to Japan of modern principles of government. The abolition of the ex-territorial rights of foreigners was also negotiated in 1894.

Remarkable as this sudden rise to power seemed to the whole world I am inclined to think that Japan was given credit for a greater feat than she had really accomplished. China had long been familiar to Europeans not as a powerful country but at least a vast country with a remarkable civilization. Japan was thought of as a little country, and the mere fact of perpetually speaking of 'little' Japanese makes people unconsciously assume that they must have wonderful qualities to compensate for their small size. China, however, was really rotten. Japan, even then, was big enough to support a powerful army and navy, and her victory did not really imply that she was on a level with the Great Powers. Much the same argument applies to her success some years later in the war against Russia. Japan only touched the fringe of either of those two countries, but her victories there gave, as I afterwards learned at Constantinople, a spur to the pride of all Oriental nations.

After the war some of the Powers obliged Japan to modify her peace terms, and Great Britain by not joining in this pressure laid the foundations for her future policy of alliance with a country which seemed to be her Asiatic counterpart. A good deal is often made, at least in speeches, of this similarity of position. How often have we heard references to the friendship between the two island empires, a phrase which seems to bring us a little closer than the talk of traditional friendship which we apply by turns to nearly all the countries of the world. I believe very little in these friendships; I doubt whether any substantial proportion of the people of any country cares two straws about the people of any other. The relations between the United States and ourselves, although often unduly idealized, are of a different nature.

After the China-Japan War, the famous Chinese statesman Li-Hung-Chang came to London. He was then an old man, and either on that account or for reasons of dignity he was carried up the great staircase at the Foreign Office in a chair. I well remember seeing the chair stop half-way up in order that an attendant might wipe Li-Hung-Chang's nose.

That staircase was the central feature in those days of many splendid parties in honour of the Queen's birthday. I particularly remember one at which Cardinal Vaughan, a most imposing figure in his scarlet robes, stood near the head of the staircase receiving the homage of his co-religionists. I also remember another party at which there was a terrible question as to the respective precedence of the Prince of Bulgaria and the Austrian Ambassador. The Prince having been asked to take Lady Salisbury in to supper the Ambassador retired in dudgeon to some distant corner, leaving his chair vacant. Lady Salisbury went after him, reproached him for not taking her in to supper, and brought him triumphantly back.

At another party I noticed Lord Acton, almost my contemporary, with a fine star on his breast. Stopping to look at it I found that the only word of the legend visible was 'Og'. I asked if this was a Bashan order, but he replied with some asperity that it was a Danish order, the oldest in Christendom, and that Og was Danish for *and*.

Here for a few pages I would leave the Foreign Office to talk a little about holidays. Some part of these was devoted to hunting, not very professionally, with Lord Eglinton's hounds, and were productive of a great deal of enjoyment and amusement. The country is of mixed character: stone walls in the north, a good country in the middle and the beginnings of hills in the south; Ayrshire forming a long narrow strip along the coast. There were no big fields, but a fair number of hunting people of all classes, happily, from the county itself and generally a sprinkling of soldiers from Glasgow or even Edinburgh. Lord Eglinton hunted four days a week and the hunt was generally popular and very successful. The Master, like others, had his trials: for instance, when a very young soldier told him with pride that he had ridden the whole way with the foremost hound, disregarding all danger signals (really indicating sown grass).

Surely in Ayrshire there was a greater variety of sport obtainable (not for me!) than in almost any other county in England or Scotland; hunting, grouse, pheasants, salmon, polo, yachting, racing, famous golf at Prestwick and elsewhere. In those days there were only two or three courses, now there is a series all along the coast; where holiday-makers were unknown there are now huge holiday camps, and all the towns and villages along the sea have grown prodigiously. Ayrshire seems to me nowadays to have lost its reality, and become merely a playground for Glasgow and other cities: just as many towns abroad, in Italy for instance, where one sees and hears foreigners all round one, cease to be real and approximate to the White City.

Most delightful of all the Ayrshire houses which I frequented was my cousin's, Dick Oswald's, house at Auchencruive, on a high bank above the river Ayr. The Ayr, with grand trees on its further banks, made the beauty of Auchencruive, but behind the house was a vast lawn which was another great feature of the place. Another and different feature was the stables. In his hey-day, when I was a boy, Dick was a member of the Four-in-hand Club and had ten grand blue roans, which were well known in London: there were also generally from ten to twenty hunters, for not only was he very keen himself but his wife, Maude Oswald, was recognized (for instance, in the Duke of Portland's Memoirs) as one of the finest women riders of the time. It is odd now to think that when we went from Annick Lodge to Auchencruive we drove four miles to the station, went by slow train to Prestwick, a distance of some eight miles, and drove out three miles to Auchencruive: the whole journey of about fifteen miles (twelve by direct road), taking the best part of two hours from door to door.

Auchencruive had been built late in the eighteenth century by Mr. Richard Oswald, whose wife was my aunt (with several greats). He was a London merchant and an M.P. who was employed by Lord Shelburne to negotiate the Treaty of Independence with Benjamin Franklin acting for the United States; the idea being, rather strangely for that age, that a plain business man could do the work better than the statesman or diplomat who would normally have been employed.

I have an account book, kept by his clerk in copperplate handwriting, which shows the daily small expenses at his office in Philpot Lane and his house in George Street, Hanover Square. Nathaniel Steptoe, his man-servant, is to have £12 a year and no vails. Mention is made of a suit for the black boy, of the dreadful mistake by which two bottles of sweet wine were placed on the table, of the sherry sent round the world and of the hen lost from George Street for the return of which two shillings was paid.

Among the pictures at Auchencruive, now turned into some kind of agricultural college, were a portrait of Mr. Oswald's friend and adversary, Franklin, and a fine full-length portrait of Mrs. Richard Oswald by Zoffany. Mrs. Oswald is seated under a tree, and the story is that Zoffany put in a portrait of Mr. Oswald, in the background, but was obliged to paint it out again to satisfy Mr. Oswald's bashfulness. Dr. Williamson, in his book on Zoffany, has turned Mrs. Oswald over to the Oswalds of Dunnikier and credited her with all sorts of relations that she never possessed. The picture is now in the possession of Lord Lee of Fareham.

In 1894 and 1895 I spent some weeks with my father and sister travelling, one year in France and the other in Germany and Austria. The French tour was the more interesting. We went to the South-East, Bourges, Nevers, Le Puy, Clermont Ferrand, Mende and the Gorges of the Tarn. The latter is now a much advertised and highly developed excursion. In 1894 it was almost unknown. Starting from the tiny village of Ste Enimie, we four (my sister had an elderly maid with her) expected to have a boat to ourselves. The proprietor, however, begged us to take with us a French doctor from Arras who would have no other chance of making the excursion. The doctor was a very silent person with no visible luggage but a small paper bag. We started about six in the morning and stopped at ten for lunch in a small riverside inn at Lamalène. The doctor took a roll from his bag, which accounted for half its contents. After lunch we were delayed in the inn by a thunderstorm. A small crowd of women who had been washing their linen in the river took shelter in an outhouse of the inn, where they amused themselves by plastering each other with mud. At every clap of thunder they crossed themselves and said a prayer, and then picked up the mud again. We got to our destination in the evening after a long and reasonably exciting voyage over the rapids and through beautiful scenery, which could not expect to escape the tourist hordes much longer. Next morning we saw the doctor going off to the station with his paper bag, now containing, we imagined, only his toothbrush.

At Mende the hotel was full, but the manager found two primitive rooms for us in the town. My sister woke next morning with a headache, said she must have a cup of tea (one took tea, also soap with one then) and sent out her maid for milk. The maid could not speak a word of French, but was a determined woman, and seeing a man carrying two pails suspended from his shoulders like milk-cans she compelled him, in spite of his protests, to follow her. Arrived at the hotel she fetched a jug, ordered a pail to be opened, and found pig-wash.

Somewhere in that part of the country we had a long drive during which I sat beside the driver. He talked about the *escargots* for which the district was famous. I told him that I was not very sure what an escargot was. "Were there none in England then?" he asked. I admitted there were not. "*Mon Dieu! Quel pays,*" was his verdict. I had never thought of England in terms of snails before, but I was suitably crushed.

In 1896 my people had a house at Lynton on the face of the hill, and I put in four or five days with the staghounds, in one of which I had a three hours' run and saw the death of the stag.

In 1898 my father died at the age of eighty-five. He told me that he had had a very happy life. After leaving the Post Office he busied himself with all sorts of local government and philanthropic work in London. He was nominated as an Alderman for the first London County Council, but like most Conservatives was not elected. *The Times* deplored the loss of his great administrative ability. He was eminently just, generous, humorous and resolute.

About a year after my arrival in the office I had the good luck to become Spanish Translator. Apart from French, which was supposed to be common knowledge, all letters and papers reaching the office in foreign languages were translated by three of the clerks who had passed an examination—competitive if necessary—in German and, respectively, Spanish, Italian or Russian. Actually documents in Russian and other Slavonic languages were rare, and each of us acted for a week at a time as translator of all the Romance and Teutonic languages, assuming, as someone said, 'knowledge by official grace.'

Besides much Spanish and some Italian I did at times a great deal of Portuguese and Dutch, some Scandinavian languages and occasionally Greek; having recourse to the help of the British Museum if absolutely necessary. In case this statement should be thought to be arrogant, let me say that knowledge or understanding of languages is far from being always a sign of great talent. It might almost be described as a knack, and I have more than once warned people not to take a recruit into their businesses merely on the ground that he knew this or that language and without due regard to his brains.

Being Spanish Translator it came about that I was called upon in 1898 to do a great deal of the translation required for the preparation of our case in the Venezuelan Arbitration proceedings.

The Arbitration arose out of long-continued disputes between Great Britain and Venezuela over the frontier line between that country and British Guiana, in the course of which we had threatened force. The great importance of the question arose, not from the extent or value of the territory in dispute, or the misdeeds of Venezuelan authorities, but from the fact that the United States Government chose to regard our action as an infringement of the Monroe Doctrine. The language used by President Cleveland and Mr. Secretary Olney in demanding that we should submit the question to arbitration bordered on the warlike, and relations between Great Britain and the United States underwent considerable tension.

After some protests Lord Salisbury agreed to an arbitration, but not before one of his despatches, at a critical moment, had been placed by our department in the bag for Shanghai instead of the bag for Washington. There had been the usual rush to get these bags off in proper time, but this might not have been accepted as an excuse if Lord Salisbury had not been in a philosophical humour and merely observed that things had gone wrong all along with these negotiations.

Many of the papers which I translated were of the sixteenth and intervening centuries, discovered in various libraries and collections of archives by Mr. Reddan, an Irishman who had previously been a Vice-Consul in Venezuela. He was a tremendous enthusiast on the subject of the boundary, almost stone deaf and decidedly odd.

An Agent was appointed to deal with the diplomatic side of the negotiations, this being first Michael Herbert and then George Buchanan, our Chargé d'Affaires at Darmstadt, to whom I was appointed secretary.

The arbitration proceedings were to take place in Paris, in a hall at the Quai d'Orsay, and the whole party when we arrived in May, 1899, made a most imposing array.

The British arbitrators were Lord Russell of Killowen, then Lord Chief Justice, and Sir Richard Henn Collins, afterwards a Lord of Appeal. The Counsel were the Attorney General, Sir Richard Webster, afterwards also Lord Chief Justice of England; Sir Robert Reid, afterwards Lord Chancellor; S. A. T. Rowlatt, afterwards a distinguished Judge; and George Askwith (the late Lord Askwith) and himself famous as an arbitrator. The Diplomatic Agent, as I have said, was George Buchanan, later Ambassador at St. Petersburg when the Great War broke out. The Colonial Office was represented by C. A. Harris and Everard im Thurn, later Governors of Newfoundland and Fiji respectively. There was also Frank Webster as Solicitor, taken on because the Attorney General, his brother, said he could not possibly go into Court without a solicitor, which reminded me of *Alice in Wonderland*.

Lord Salisbury is supposed to have said afterwards that never again would he have half the bar and a crowd of officials living at the country's expense in Paris. The American Arbitrators were Chief Justice Fuller and Mr. Justice Brewer; and there were two or three Venezuelans present, including their Minister. The latter attended the sessions with a marmoset concealed about his person, which bewildered us all by its squeaks, as for some time we supposed them to emanate from some mysterious bird.

The Attorney General's opening speech lasted for twelve days, and the opening Counsel for the United States went one better: the others took only a few days each. The Attorney General assembled as many of the party as he could at 7 o'clock every morning to go through the aspects of the case which would come before the Court at the next sitting. I was not wanted for this confabulation and rode in the Bois instead. In the evening we often bicycled with the Attorney General and after that there were frequent banquets and many smaller dinner parties. Delcassé, the Minister for Foreign Affairs, attended one or two of the banquets and made a most favourable impression. He was afterwards sacrificed at the behest of the German Emperor in 1905 for taking too strong a line in regard to Morocco.

On other evenings we did a good many theatres and music-halls; including one at which Yvette Guilbert sang with her usual sang-froid extremely startling songs, to the great admiration of one of our party who had brought his wife, and not knowing a word of French commented particularly on Yvette's modesty. We also heard a good deal of anti-English sentiment, and talk about Fashoda and Major Marchand, *qui malgré les Anglais a planté notre drapeau* and that sort of thing. This Anglo-French incident, arising in 1898, was settled with comparative ease by the firmness of the British Government; but we were decidedly unpopular in Paris and were to be more so when the Boer War broke out later in the year. I learn from the Cambridge Modern History that in order to avoid any more disagreeable talk about Fashoda the name of the place was changed to Kodok. There may be lessons to be learned from this device.

While we were in Paris a new Government was being formed, and there was the usual bickering about places in the Administration. I heard a man of my acquaintance, whose father-in-law was a candidate for office, telling his wife that the new Prime Minister *"s'est conduit envers ton père d'une façon infâme."* French political life was certainly never very worthy of admiration, and officialdom throughout the country was much too prevalent.

The President of the Republic was M. Loubet, who did not inspire great respect; although I believe most respectable. We once went to a garden party at the Élysée, at which thousands of guests were present: we passed through a series of rooms in one of which stood the President and Madame Loubet, of whom little notice seemed to be taken. He was a great farmer at his house in the country, and a music-hall song described his arrival there on holiday, when all the sheep exclaimed: '*Bonjour Monsieur Loubé-é-é-, bonjour Monsieur Lou-beh-eh-eh.*'

Once when we went to the races at Longchamps we found the stand practically empty, except I believe for the Duchess Grazioli. On the previous Sunday royalist malcontents had attempted to assault M. Loubet and Paris society was too nervous of another incident to show itself. In England, probably, in such circumstances the stand would have been overcrowded.

Among our favourite restaurants was Laurents in the Champs Élysées, where the Embassy juniors had a table reserved in the middle of the day and a *prix fixe déjeuner*. I made friends with the head waiter, Charles, whose comments on Paris society were sometimes amusing. On one occasion, seeing Count Boni de Castellane looking in through the window, he told me about the Castellane family: the two brothers, the Marquis de Castellane and Count Boni, were not too well off. "*Alors, il leur a fallu refaire leur blason, et l'un est parti en Autriche et l'autre en Amérique.*" They both married heiresses as Charles had intimated, but the expression '*refaire leur blason*' pleased me.

I cannot leave Paris without a tribute to George Buchanan, very charming, very modest, very able, very courageous. He proved himself in St. Petersburg. His wife, Lady Georgie, was delightful also. They had come from Darmstadt, where they watched over the Grand Duke and Grand Duchess on behalf of Queen Victoria, and no doubt gathered from the crowds of royalties and their suites who thronged the place a great deal of useful information about European politics. Such posts of observation no longer exist, the public liking to think that its servants are always hard at work in an office.

In a letter written soon after his return to his post Buchanan says: 'We spent Wednesday in the bosom of the Russian Imperial family, Emperor, Empress, three Russian Grand-Dukes, Prince Nicholas of Greece and our Grand-Duke and Grand-Duchess. We lunched, played tennis and dined *en famille* as if we had known each other all our lives.' Three weeks later he writes again: 'We have been doing nothing of note with the exception of giving a small dinner to the great Mouravieff (the Russian Foreign Minister). He made himself very pleasant and by the end of dinner he and my wife agreed that they felt that they had known each other all their lives. . . . I tried my best claret in Mouravieff's honour and found it excellent.' Buchanan had also been talking about the South African war to a German officer who had been Military Attaché in London and was 'one of the few Germans who has any sympathy for us.'

In another letter written just after he had reached Darmstadt he speaks of the 'terrible dullness of the inhabitants of the Residenz Stadt,' and ends: 'We miss you very much and I can never be grateful enough to you for all your help and assistance at Paris.' Actually I did little but copy out reports.

Lord Russell seemed to me then, and still seems, one of the few really great men that I have met. He was a dominating personality and inspired awe in many people, but I found him very kind. Once when we were back in London I went to lunch with him and Lady Russell. There were two portraits of him by Sargent in the house and he asked me which I liked best. I told him, and he said: "Well, most people like the other; they say I look as if I were saying 'damn'; my wife agrees with you, but then you and she have known me when I was not saying 'damn'."

Sir Richard Webster, our leading counsel, was a very good man, in every sense of the word good, most amiable but with a restricted sense of humour. Sir Robert Reid was emotional and I once took a walk with him in the Champs Élysées. He, a very big man, stopped to put a struggling beetle carefully on its feet again, an action which I thought characteristic. He also told me that he was determined not to open his mouth on the subject of South Africa, where war was on the verge of breaking out, until he had read all the papers official and otherwise. I said: "But you will read them in order to see how wrong the Government is." "Perhaps you are right," he replied.

Some years later, when Buchanan was on leave, he and I dined with Reid, now Lord Loreburn, and found ourselves in the midst of the fine flower of the Liberal party: our host, who was Lord Chancellor, Campbell Bannerman, John Morley, John Simon and Mr. Winston Churchill, a new recruit, being made much of by his new friends. Campbell Bannerman impressed me as a lazy person, stretching himself out almost at full length after dinner: also as stuffing at dessert like a schoolboy. I met him again at dinner with the Kay Shuttleworths, where my impressions remained much the same, though his political friends professed to find him in splendid form.

With Everard im Thurn I made great friends and during a week's vacation in the middle of the proceedings we went off together on a bicycling tour in the Jura. There, as elsewhere, I saw the undeveloped beauties of France. At le Pont we stayed in the remarkably dirty hotel, paid two francs for our dinner and two francs fifty for our rooms: now I believe there is a splendid hotel and all facilities for winter sports. I find a letter from im Thurn, written on his way to Ceylon, where he was to be Colonial Secretary, in which he recalls this tour. He tells me that he had just acquired the art of free-wheeling. 'It would have been a splendid thing that day you and I came down the long slope of the Jura. How I wish we could have another ride.' He was, by the way, by no means proficient at bicycling when we came to Paris, and one day in the Bois his bicycle ran away with him down the *allée réservée aux cyclistes* and shot him, a very big man, straight into the victoria of an indignant French lady. We had no accident in the Jura and greatly enjoyed the hill scenery, climbs not too severe for our purpose, and extremely primitive accommodation.

Of my friends Sir Sidney Rowlatt and Sir Alexander Harris I will only say that they are most happily still with us and going strong.

I should add that the President of the Tribunal was a Russian lawyer of international repute, M. de Martens, and that one of the American justices, Mr. Brewer, combined with judicial acumen an evangelistic spirit which prompted him to distribute tracts to any of the party whom he might meet out of court, and a tendency to conviviality which, when he was carried out through the hall of our hotel, filled the ladies with consternation. He could also spit into the fire from a great distance.

The great Arbitration ended in an almost complete victory for us. This was most satisfactory as it proved that we had not, as Mr. Olney had accused us of doing, grasped at territory to which we had no right. It was still more satisfactory that our relations with the United States fell back into their proper orbit. That more than a dozen or so of the people in either country knew what the trouble was about I do not believe.

Having returned to London early in October, 1899, and having much leave due to me, I thought the time had come to make an Italian tour. I stopped in Paris for a day or so on the way, and had a glimpse of the great Exhibition of which I seemed to have formed a poorish impression. The British Pavilion was closed because of the rain! Presumably the authorities were afraid of the mud, and in my diary I note that the only interesting part of the German Pavilion was shut also.

In the course of the day I travelled by the newly opened underground railway. The stops were so brief that one had to spring in and out with great agility, and all the French women screamed loudly as they did so.

Apparently my opinion of the Exhibition was not peculiar to myself, for I note that in the train going south my companions were all Italians returning dissatisfied from the Exhibition.

In Italy I followed a more or less stereotyped route, spending a fortnight in Rome. There I was lucky enough to attend a service in St. Peter's at which Pope Leo XIII was present. He was carried in, a frail white figure, on the Sedia Gestatoria amid tremendous shouts of *"Evviva il Papa Rè,"* which took me by surprise. At some moment of the service the Pope left his seat to proceed to the Altar, whereupon an old peasant beside me shouted in ecstasy *"Anda, Anda."* The Pope was actually walking.

Buchanan had just arrived in Rome to take up the post of Counsellor of Embassy and I did many of the sights, including a delightful bicycling ride into the Campagna, with him and Lady Georgie.

From Rome I went on to Naples, Amalfi and Castellamare, seeing the temples of Paestum on the way. Nothing in Italy gave me more pleasure than gazing at those temples and the sea which could be seen through the ruins.

As it happened, the Chamberlain family were making much the same tour at the same time: Mr. and Mrs. Chamberlain, her mother and Austen. Great interest was taken by the Italians in the visit; also by a German on his honeymoon with whom I made acquaintance. He asked me who the members of the party were, and when I told him exclaimed: "*Er muss doch ein guter Mensch sein, wenn er mit seiner Schwiegermutter herumreist.*" ("He must after all be a good fellow if he travels about with his mother-in-law.") Going towards Milan I found myself in the same compartment with Austen near the front of the train. The rest of the family were in a compartment at the back of the train. At Milan Station, when our train for some reason drew up not alongside the platform but on a further line, this family arrangement created remarkable confusion. There was a great crowd on the platform and those in front cried back and those behind cried forward, for both in front and at the back was an Englishman with an eyeglass and white buttonhole corresponding exactly to their expectations and each party ran to see what the other party was gazing at.

I came back to the Foreign Office at the end of the year to serve in the Consular Department, where the work was mainly administrative. The Consular Service had gradually grown up on no particular plan. As my chief was fond of reminding people, appointment to a Consulate or Vice-Consulate was an individual affair, carrying no right to promotion or transfer to any other post, although such transfers were in fact quite common. The posts were filled after a qualifying examination by nominees of the Secretary of State, and the last appointment of that kind was made a year or two after this. The happy person was Colonel Brookfield, a man of fifty, who had been Conservative M.P. for East Sussex for a good many years and had had some financial reverse. He had commanded a Yeomanry battalion in the South African War and had claims on the party.

Well-known instances of men who had been pitchforked into Consulates in the past are Beau Brummel and Sir Richard Burton. Occasionally young men who had failed for the Diplomatic Service were given Vice-Consulates, and even in recent days this precedent has been followed, but as a result of the placing in the examination.

My chief in the Consular Department, William Cockerell, was by no means fond of innovations of any kind, his favourite motto being *Quieta non movere*, but he regarded himself as a sort of father to the Consular Service, and its members were assured of a friendly and sympathetic welcome when they came on leave. He was, as a result, very popular, and this in itself was a most useful thing, for some Diplomatic and Consular officials, and I believe officials from distant places depending on other departments of State are apt to complain that when they come home they can find no one to whom they can unfold either their troubles or even their news. Everyone is too busy; which sounds a better excuse than it really is, for it is good business to keep up personal relations between those at home and those abroad and time ought to be made for it.

Lord Salisbury, though he did not cultivate the society of the staff at home—by doing which he would perhaps have gained but little—kept in touch with the more important of Her Majesty's Representatives abroad by private letters, as I have already said, and also I believe by inviting them to his house. Lord Rosebery did the same, but I think the practice has gradually diminished.

After returning from Italy I still had some leave due, which I spent in Ayrshire, hunting three or four days a week. Then came the usual London round, dinners and other parties over which gloom was cast by the South African War. The Government were violently attacked, as other Governments have been since, on the ground that they did not foresee the Boer resistance, did not send men out soon enough, selected their Generals badly and so forth. On February 1st George Wyndham made a speech in defence of the Government which, I was told by Ronnie Hamilton, his father, Lord George Hamilton, thought one of the finest he had ever heard. A few days later, calling on the Kay Shuttleworths, I was told by Miss Kay Shuttleworth, who had heard it, that it was thrilling.

At a dinner party, also at the Kay Shuttleworths, about this time I met Lord Kimberley, our former Chief. He said in the course of conversation that if he were offered his life again he would only take it on condition of never being a boy; he had been very nervous, which made him miserable, but later cured his nervousness by taking resolutely to hunting. He thought himself very lucky to have had so good a start in life as "My merits could not have been very evident."

I saw Diamond Jubilee win the Two Thousand Guineas in the spring of 1900, and in the summer spent a week-end with Admiral and Mrs. Fanshawe, where I met a young naval officer named Pound who impressed me as 'full of life and good sense.' Among other friends whom I saw from time to time was Oliver Borthwick, then working for his father's paper, the *Morning Post*. I had met him first in Paris with the Buchanans; Lady Georgie's brother, Lord Bathurst, having married Oliver's sister. I found him a delightful companion and have always thought that his early death was a great loss.

CHAPTER III

IN 1901, ON SEPTEMBER 7TH, I DID THE BEST THING I HAVE EVER DONE by marrying Edith Cuninghame, daughter of Sir William Cuninghame of the Ayrshire family to whom I have already referred; a Crimean V.C. who, after leaving the Army, had been Member for Ayr Burghs. To her, by right, this book is dedicated.

Very soon after our wedding we went off to Lisbon for a month or two on official business, I having been sent to search in the archives there for documents bearing on the Boundaries of British Guiana. This time the

Lift to right : E. Monson, G. H. Fitzmaurice, I. Lambton, Hon. P. Ramsay, G. A. Lloyd, R. H. Hoare, J. A. C. Tilley.

SAO PAULO RAILWAY
The Serra

trouble was with Brazil, but the affair was not on the same scale as that with Venezuela.

We went out by Royal Mail; but in a very different sort of boat to the palatial liner which carried us to and from Brazil in later years. However, by whatever boat one arrives, the Tagus is always a joy, and in those days a visit to Portugal might be considered an exciting novelty.

From the windows of our hotel, the Braganza, we had a splendid view across the estuary to the country beyond, and even in November we could usually sit at breakfast with the windows open to admire it.

We had a large bedroom and a small dressing-room opening off it, on the opposite side to the windows. One of the first things that happened was that a gale got up and, the bedroom windows being open, blew the dressing-room window opposite out into the street. The next thing was the ordering of a bath, bathrooms being still in the dim future. A hip bath on four legs was brought in and placed in the middle of my wife's room. The bath was tepid, whereas she wanted it hot. I asked in my best Portuguese for something *mais coquente*, more hot. A can was brought and poured into the bath, leaving it as tepid as before. I reiterated my *mais coquente* and the same thing happened. When the bath was overflowing we gave it up. What I had asked for no doubt was not hotter water but more hot water, but my Portuguese conversation was not good enough to disentangle the problem.

My work in the library was interesting, but the management was a good deal less businesslike than it doubtless is to-day. The librarian allowed me to range about by myself very much as I liked, while he sat and smoked cigarettes and dropped cigarette ends to the imminent danger of the Archives.

In my report I said:

'I was provided with a chair and table close to the rooms in which the Colonial Archives are kept. I was encouraged to smoke and found the cigar and cigarette ends on the floor an easy way of calculating the length of my stay which lasted three weeks.

'Your instructions were that I should search for any records which might exist of the Expeditions or alleged Expeditions of Portuguese officers in the years 1639, 1670, 1725, 1727, 1736 and 1740. I give a list of the documents examined; these included *papeis de Serviço*, which amounted to about seventy bundles some four or five inches thick chiefly consisting of papers of two or three sheets laid flat. Many of these papers had originally been inclosed in coverers, but the latter being torn it was impossible to say in most cases which was coverer and which inclosure; consequently as the papers had no docket, it was necessary to examine almost every sheet separately . . . to find the account of an expedition which took place in 1737 it would be necessary to look through each of the bundles for (probably) 1735–38

C

and 1739–42, as the despatches of the different Governors are not kept separately.'

In fact it was like looking for a needle in a haystack. However, I did find one good account of an expedition which took place in 1738 that was of considerable importance, and I brought back with it copies of a large number of other papers, which were more or less useful.

Mr. Harris of the Colonial Office, in acknowledging the report, says: 'I consider the big Belforte document quite worth the trouble of the journey.'

As I spent most of each day in the library I had no time to see anything of Portugal outside Lisbon, but I liked the place, and it is pleasant to think that after some vicissitudes the country is now in such admirable condition. Once when passing through Lisbon on my way to Brazil some sixteen or seventeen years ago, a friend on board, who had gone into exile during the monarchy, told me that he regretted the revolution when he saw the state into which the country had fallen. If he were alive now he would be happy.

We saw the King Dom Carlos and Queen Amélie one night at the theatre. Either as a matter of etiquette or of preference, for they were not supposed to be on very good terms, they sat in separate but adjoining boxes, and left in separate carriages, each drawn by four mules with crimson harness.

The play that night was performed by an Italian company, the star performers being a Signor Zacconi and his wife. I do not remember what it was about except that a baby was thrust down a hole in the middle of the stage, so it must have been somewhat lurid. When we left Lisbon by train a little later we went first to Madrid, where we knew no one except some of the Embassy staff. Consequently we were somewhat embarrassed on leaving our sleeping-car to find ourselves the centre of an enthusiastically welcoming crowd. They had mistaken us for Signor and Signora Zacconi. As an Ambassador arriving at a new post I might have been well enough pleased, but as it was I was relieved when the Simon, or Simons pure, emerged from the train in their turn.

We found an excellent second-hand furniture shop in Lisbon and there bought for eleven milreis (about a guinea, I suppose) a delightful Worcester dessert service of twelve plates and three dishes, with a border of salmon pink and gold gilt and a crest in the middle; the crest being a hand cutting a bunch of grapes. I imagine this service, originally no doubt much bigger, was made for an English wine merchant and left behind when English people hurriedly departed, possibly during the Napoleonic wars.

When we got home we found the service to be of the very best Worcester period, but on taking it to someone at Christie's were told that the crest made it practically worthless for sale purposes, which has always seemed to me odd.

We had not time to make many Portuguese friends, but one lady at least called on us and left a card bearing her name: 'Donna Maria Teresa de M. Mascarenhas Valdes Pinto da Cunha', which is long enough for anyone. An English lady living in Lisbon, who was a recent bride, told us that many Portuguese ladies called on her when she first arrived and, in accordance with custom, she had presently to ask them to a tea-party. Her trouble was that it took such a terribly long time to address the envelopes, which one can well believe if their names approached that of our friend in length, and when one remembers that each name had to be prefaced, though in an abbreviated form, by *Illustrissima, Excelentissima Senhora*. Though we did not know many Portuguese in Lisbon we knew them in Rio and as colleagues elsewhere and have found them commonly very charming people. Few foreigners in London have had so much social success as M. de Soveral, so long Portuguese Minister and a close friend of King Edward VII. I did, however, once have something like 'words' with him when I objected that a Portuguese version of some agreement did not coincide with the English; he escaped by saying that it was Colonial Portuguese.

I doubt whether many people in this country, apart from history students, realize how great a part the Portuguese played in the fifteenth century in the discovery of the world as we know it, especially in the time of Prince Henry the Navigator. I believe they were a more virile people than the Spaniards and deserve better of historians; the greatness of Spain, often vaunted, being a little difficult to disentangle from the greatness of Charles V as Lord also of the Empire and the Low Countries.

To-day, Portuguese immigrants in Brazil who come and go between the two countries are generally excellent workers.

As a race they have no doubt been affected by the strain of black blood due to the importation of slaves in the middle ages, but if nations have the government they deserve, this particular nation evidently has great merits.

When we were in Lisbon the Administration was slack and little progress had been made even in the most ordinary matters. When we dined out with some English friends not long after we arrived the deficiencies of the street lighting were only too obvious, and even inside the house we had difficulty in finding our way upstairs to their flat by the light of a candle placed on the bottom step of the staircase.

We came home from Lisbon by land, spending a week at Madrid on the way. Hotels in Madrid were not of a very superior kind, but a friend at the Embassy had secured for us in one of the best what he believed to be the only room which could boast of a fire.

The great attraction of Madrid to most travellers is the Prado Museum, with its marvellous collection of Velasquez pictures, as well as those of other Spanish artists, and these we thoroughly enjoyed. We also 'did' Toledo and the Escorial, the latter as bleak a place as one could find anywhere and in that respect well worthy of Philip II. I am not sure, however, that it was as bleak in his day, for in the course of years trees have been recklessly cut down and the appearance of the country doubtless changed.

I went out one evening to the theatre. I have no recollection of the play except that it was historical, but I do have bitter recollections of the length of time which it occupied. Supposed to begin at nine-thirty, the curtain rose at ten, and after each act there was an interval of a good half-hour; I got back to the hotel at one, having seen only two acts.

The British Ambassador at the time was Sir Mortimer Durand, who had been there rather more than a year. Lady Durand told us that in that time they had never been invited to a private house, and had only once and by accident attended a private party—one which happened to be taking place at a house where they were leaving cards.

Back in England, we spent our leave hunting a little, with my wife's aunt and uncle, the Alan Penningtons, in the Quorn country. Alan Pennington was a famous figure in the hunting-field. As a boy he had been in the Navy and served in the Crimea; then he had a few years in the Rifle Brigade and the rest of his life had been given up to hunting. Mrs. Pennington, too, had been one of the very best ladies in the hunting field, but had nearly given it up after some forty years of it. Alan Pennington made a habit of saying just what came into his head, and by long custom was licensed to do so, but I believe in the Holderness country, of which he had once been Master, it was long remembered against him that he had said there was certainly a good deal of grass on the railway embankment if not elsewhere. The Penningtons were then in some trouble about servants, the kitchen-maid having left 'because they did not eat enough for titled people.'

In the following year, 1902, the great event was of course the coronation of King Edward VII. I watched the procession from a seat near the Abbey and afterwards lunched in the House of Commons with Mr. Akers Douglas, who had just been appointed Home Secretary. Mrs. Akers Douglas told me that she had known nothing about the appointment till she saw a mounted policeman waiting to escort them to the Abbey. Their eldest son, now Lord Chilston, was one of the party; he had been my best man, and has been and is, if he will allow me to say so, and will I hope always be, one of my best friends. My chief recollection of the party, however, is not the luncheon itself but the coronets hanging on pegs outside the rooms where peers were lunching, very much as if they were schoolboys' caps.

At the end of that year I was made Secretary to a Committee appointed 'to enquire into matters concerning the Consular Service.' The Chairman was Sir William Walrond, long a Conservative Whip, and besides him and Lord Cranborne there were two members destined to become famous in their respective ways, namely Mr. Bonar Law, then a junior member of the Government whose ability was beginning to be noticed, and Sir James Mackay, afterwards Earl of Inchcape. The latter took the leading part on the Committee and was mainly responsible for the Report.

The Committee found that

'The General Consular Service as it at present exists offers no attraction to capable young men. It is not a properly constituted or graded public service, and offers no definite prospect of promotion to those who enter it, for men who are new to the service may be given appointments over the heads of others who have been there for years before them.

'The Committee strongly recommend that the present system of nomination and age limits for the General Consular Service should be abolished, that admission into that service should be by limited competition, and that the age for admission should be from twenty-two to twenty-seven; these limits will enable candidates to compete who have had both a University and Commercial training.

'Evidence has been submitted to us tending to show that the most successful British traders have no desire to invoke the assistance of our Consuls and that they consider themselves able to obtain much more useful information for their business than the best Consul can supply.

.   .   .   .   .

'The Committee suggest that great advantage would result if young men trained in commercial houses could be induced to enter the Consular Service. Such men would speedily get into touch, and would be in sympathy, with the Commercial communities of the place at which they were appointed to reside.'

As subjects of examination the Committee recommended French and German, ability to express points clearly and correctly in writing, arithmetic, commercial geography, political economy, British mercantile commercial law. The Report ended with very civil remarks about myself. The Committee seem to me, as I look back, to have been somewhat misled by wishful thinking, besides falling into some heresies.

A young man who has done well at the university and then had some years experience of business would doubtless make a good Consular official; but can we expect to get him? With the qualifications expected of him he will, after four or five years experience in business, probably see before him much better openings in London than in the Consular Service, where he would as a matter of course spend a good many years in foreign provincial cities, possibly in hot and not very exciting countries. Moreover, as I said in relation to the Foreign Office and Diplomatic Service, not many young men like, as a rule, or are able, to wait so long before beginning their professional life.

In speaking of heresies I am thinking of the examination subjects, which are largely 'cram' subjects. I do not believe that so far any better way of testing candidates has been discovered than competition based on a liberal education at school and university, unless it be by plain unadulterated selection by a strong committee. The recommendations of the Committee were duly accepted and their scheme remained in force till after the Great War, but I cannot recollect that we got any candidates with business experience.

In April, 1903, my wife and I took a short holiday in Holland. In that then peaceful country it was astonishing to find ourselves in the midst of a General Strike. I wrote to a relation from Amsterdam:

'The strike does not hurt us much except that the street cleaners have struck, which makes the streets less pleasant than usual for walking about; the lamplighters have also struck, but some did go round yesterday accompanied by soldiers with fixed bayonets. All the railway stations are occupied by soldiers, which looks exciting, and when we went to the restaurant at Haarlem station we found it full of soldiers' beds, while a party of dragoons with their horses were picketed in the booking office at the station here.'

I recollect also seeing a crossing-sweeper squatting on the pavement to eat his lunch while a soldier stood guard over him. I believe the strike was eventually settled with no serious trouble. We had unfortunately chosen a bad moment for bulbs, the early flowers being over and the tulips not quite out, but such as there were made a fine show.

In November of that year I was appointed Secretary of the Committee of Imperial Defence, and held that position till the following June, when as a result of the Esher Committee a regular office was established with Sir George Clarke as secretary. The Prime Minister, Mr. Balfour, was chairman of the Committee and took the deepest interest in the work. What struck me also was the complete supremacy which he exercised over his colleagues. They included the Secretary of State for War and the Chief of the General Staff, the First Lord of the Admiralty and First Sea Lord, the Directors of Naval and Military Intelligence, Lord Roberts, and other Cabinet Ministers whose departments happened to be concerned; sometimes the Chancellor of the Exchequer, sometimes the Foreign Secretary or Secretary of State for India, once or twice Lord Curzon when he was on leave from India, and once or twice a Canadian Minister.

Mr. Balfour was by no means always impressed with his colleagues' success in grasping the situation under discussion. "It did not seem to me," he said one day, "that any of them saw the point at all." He himself took endless trouble to study the questions which were coming up for discussion, and afterwards to see that my minutes accurately reproduced the decisions reached.

For some time before the Dogger Bank incident there had been much tension in our relations with Russia, and I ran between Lord Walter Kerr, the First Sea Lord, and the D.M.I., Nicholson, who professed astonishment at the pacific attitude of the Admiralty.

I was struck by the competence of Mr. Arnold Forster, as Secretary of

State for War; he was enthusiastic about his work, and I note that he was at the same time markedly deferential to Mr. Balfour.

It was my business to circulate papers to the members, and I had occasional difficulties when they declared that they had never received these papers. I assured Mr. Balfour that I had duly placed those for Cabinet Ministers in their Foreign Office pouches. "Of course you did," he said reassuringly; "do you suppose Ministers ever look at those papers when they get them?"

I note at the end of January that Mr. Balfour looked haggard and worn. He told me afterwards that he was overwhelmed with business, and in the busiest week of the year, after the Cabinet had sat all Saturday, Monday and Tuesday, he had had to go off to Windsor. Shortly afterwards he was down with influenza, which perhaps had more to do with his depression than work. Lord Roberts ascribed this attack to the 'fearful hot baths' Mr. Balfour takes, 'and sits in them ever so long.'

Lord Roberts himself was a charming man to work for; extraordinarily simple and friendly, as for that matter was Mr. Balfour himself. But then they were permanently great; it is the people who attain a brief period of office and then disappear again who are, in my experience, apt to be a little self-important while their greatness lasts.

The work of the Defence Committee naturally did not permit of my taking notes of what passed, as it was all what is now called very hush-hush, but many of the arguments turned on the blue-water theory and the belief in our practical immunity from invasion was strongly held. Alas!

One casual remark of Mr. Balfour's made in the midst of this pressure of work sticks in my mind: he said the Liberals when they came in would be astounded at the increase in the Prime Minister's work since they were last in office: he did not see how the Prime Minister could ever again be in the House of Commons.

In March of this year I see that we were dining with Sir Thomas Sanderson, and met the Italian Ambassador, M. Pansa. He told us that when he was at Constantinople he had formed a nice little income, for such purposes as the upkeep of the garden, out of abuses which he stopped but did not report to his Government. I take it he was not a very brilliant negotiator, for Lord Lansdowne once described him as 'spending an hour kicking round one turnip.'

My term as Secretary to the Committee of Imperial Defence came to an end at June, 1904. My appointment was only temporary, and the work only occupied a few hours of the week; the summoning of meetings, attendance on those occasions, circulation of papers and preparation of minutes, with occasional correspondence with the members and sometimes acting as messenger between them. I was well aware that Lord Esher's committee was recommending that the Committee should be taken much more seriously in future and that there should be a regular full-time secretary, or secretariat, a post for which only a soldier could possibly be qualified.   However, Mr. Balfour's method of communicating to me the nature of their proposals was characteristic though possibly designed to let me down easily in case I should have any aspirations to the new post.

He came into my room, which I shared with another Foreign Office man, saying that he supposed I knew all about the Esher Committee's proposal. Officially I knew nothing and I replied accordingly.   "Well," he said, "it seems there is to be a regular secretary and I believe it is to be a man called Clarke or something of that sort: I believe he is a major."   Seeing that Sir George Clarke (afterwards Lord Sydenham) was himself a member of the Esher Committee, in whose work Mr. Balfour was deeply interested, it was obviously inconceivable that he did not know all about Sir George.

I remember hearing that after the war, when Mr. Balfour ceased to be Foreign Secretary, he came in to the Private Secretary's room and said: "By the way, I expect you have heard that I am leaving this office, and am going to be Lord Privy Seal."   Actually he had been appointed Lord President of the Council.   This vagueness, I think, was entirely assumed.

The next two years passed very quickly.   I note one echo of the Venezuelan Arbitration: for in May, 1895, some of those associated with that episode were invited to dine with the West Indian Association, the guest of honour being the former Attorney General, by now Lord Alverstone and Lord Chief Justice.   We had a magnificent dinner, and now in 1941 the menu looks astounding: nine courses with a sorbet in the middle to revive our appetites.   The real feature of the dinner was the fruit, and I believe the object was not only, or perhaps not so much, to do honour to us as to introduce West Indian fruit to the notice of the public.   On the back of the menu appears this legend:

The fruit has been specially obtained for the occasion from the West Indies and includes the following:

Red Bananas	Apple Bananas
Oranges	Grape Fruit
Pine Apples	Star Apples
Naseberries	Mangoes
Limes	Shaddocks

All this on the top of the nine courses.   My chief recollection is the beauty of the Red Bananas; and I suppose that most of these fruits made no greater impression on the mind of the public than on mine, for few of them have become favourite.

CHAPTER IV

IN THE SUMMER OF 1906 WE DECIDED THAT THE TIME HAD COME TO TAKE a turn of service abroad. For this purpose I had to effect a temporary exchange with a member of the Diplomatic Service, and I happened at the critical moment to receive a letter from Errington, now Lord Cromer, proposing just what I wanted. These exchanges were typical of our British love of making odd rules and then getting round them. The qualification supposed to be required for entering the Diplomatic Service was a private income or allowance of £400 a year; for the Foreign Office there was no such qualification. Exchanges between the two services were constantly being made, some temporary and some permanent, and no questions, so far as I am aware, were ever asked as to whether the income of the Foreign Office clerk came up to standard, or whether he had any at all. Sir Charles Hardinge, now Lord Hardinge, was all in favour of exchanges and encouraged me to go to Constantinople, for which I have always been grateful. I was moreover to go as First Secretary and Head of the Chancery, a position of some responsibility, and attractive in spite of a gloomy letter from my predecessor, Charles Marling, who said that I should be most unhappy, that the Ambassador had his own views about the appointment and, in any case, wanted someone who would stay for years. He added that the climate was bad for children, and that only a rich man could live comfortably there. All these predictions and warnings were completely falsified. The Ambassador, Sir Nicholas O'Conor, was most cordial and kind; living was cheap rather than expensive, the climate suited us very well and we were remarkably happy.

British relations with Turkey in 1906 were largely concerned with the Sultan's treatment of his Christian subjects, Armenians in Asia Minor and Greeks and Bulgars in Europe, especially Macedonia.

In various treaties the Porte had undertaken to put an end to the long continued ill-treatment of the Armenians, but with no serious intention of doing so. Massacres continued and the culminating point was the organized massacre in Constantinople itself which was carried out in 1896. This brought home to the Powers more vividly than massacres in distant parts of the Empire the horrors that were being regularly perpetrated.

In the two years that I spent at Constantinople it was the Macedonian rather than the Armenian question with which we had to deal, and various plans were put into execution for European supervision of the Administration and the establishment of an European gendarmerie. It must be borne in mind that the Turks in Europe were not, for the most part, themselves tillers of the soil, and had not really settled down in the country. They were a conquering race living on the country and treating the Christian population as a subordinate race, more or less after the German style of to-day. To the stray traveller they often appeared to be delightful people with good manners and dignified behaviour. The Turkish soldiers, too, looked like good-natured rough country-men. "*Comme ils sont bons,*" the Apostolic Delegate said to me once, surveying the guards outside the Mosque where the Sultan was performing his devotions. I thought, and think, that his praises were probably quite undeserved: these 'good fellows' would doubtless have been quite ready to ill-treat Armenians or other suitable natives at any time.

As to the Sultan Abdul Hamid, no one ever suggested that he was good, or had any virtues at all. He had a sort of cunning and showed some degree of skill in playing one Great Power against another. He was also rather good at giving the soft answer which turns away wrath and sometimes allowed himself a little sarcasm. One instance of the soft answer tactics was what was known in Diplomatic circles as the *coup de montre*, which meant pressing into someone's hand his father's watch as a token of his real esteem and affection. An instance of his sarcasm was his habit of occasionally, in the midst of a lecture by the British Ambassador on his general mismanagement, inquiring about the present state of Ireland. This came well home to Sir Nicholas O'Conor, who was an Irish Roman Catholic.

Another feature of the Macedonian situation was that apart from the misgovernment of the Turks there was bitter hatred between the various Christian races themselves, Serbians, Greeks and Bulgarians. Guerrilla bands were constantly carrying on operations against each other, and some of the Greek Bishops and Priests were among the ringleaders. 'This notorious prelate' I recall as the term applied to one of the more prominent Greek Bishops.

Meanwhile the position of foreigners was still regulated by the so-called 'Capitulations,' the particular treaty with England having been made in the seventeenth century. The theory was that the foreign Powers had capitulated to a merciful Sultan; the fact was that the Powers compelled the Porte to allow foreigners to live under the jurisdiction of their own diplomatic, judicial, and Consular officers, and under their own laws. Consequently there was a considerable European population, especially at Constantinople and Smyrna, living in comparative ease and comfort in spite of the misgovernment by which they were surrounded. At the same time foreigners were by no means popular in Constantinople, and we were discouraged from going to Stambul, that is the Turkish quarter across Galata Bridge, without a kavass, as the Embassy guards were called. Also we were advised to carry revolvers if we rode into the country. There was always a chance, we thought, of an attack on the Embassy, and humorous plans were laid for its defence, including an arrangement for the O'Conors' governess to pour boiling sealing-wax on the crowd below.

The Sultan allowed no social communication, or as little as possible, between Turks and foreigners of any position. Only once while I was there did any of the Turkish Ministers dine at the Embassy, the exception being the special occasion of a visit by the Commander-in-Chief in the Mediterranean. Once or twice a few of them attended the larger Entertainments. The Embassy ladies were allowed to call on two or three Turkish ladies in their respective harems, and one progressive Turkish lady was sometimes allowed to visit European ladies. This was Madame Turkhan Pasha, whose husband became Foreign Minister after the Revolution. Once we lunched with Reshid Pasha, the Sultan's brother-in-law.

When I speak of the Sultan discouraging intercourse between Turks and foreigners I mean Turks literally: we were allowed to associate with the Sultan's Christian subjects, Greek, Armenian and notably Syrians. In fact with some of the more villainous of the latter we were on quite good terms, and they occupied positions of greater power and responsibility than most other Christians.

I am told that something like this was the position in Russia before the war, except that there were fewer exceptions to the ban.

The Sultan's chief instrument of government appeared to be the spy system. There were spies everywhere. The chief spy, Fehim Pasha, drove about in an open carriage lined with coloured satin, and created terror on his appearance in the bazaars, not so much because the shopkeepers expected to be arrested as because they expected him to demand their finest wares as a free gift. After the Revolution he was torn to pieces by a mob in some place on the Asiatic side to which he had fled. Two spies were constantly on watch in a semi-basement opposite the Embassy gates, their eyes about on a level with the pavement, to see who went in and out. At Therapia, on the terrace where we found a house for our second summer, we shared a spy with two other diplomatic families. He spread his blanket there at night and by day was useful in picking up the toys which our children dropped out of the window.

Another striking feature of the administration was the universal corruption. The highest officials did not exactly take bribes openly but withdrew with their visitor into some inner apartment where matters were settled. One method followed in less elevated circles was for an official to place his expected visitor's file at the bottom of a great heap of papers. If the visitor asked when his long-standing business or complaint would be dealt with he was shown the extent of this heap. Something passed into the official's hands and the file then appeared a little higher up; something more passed and finally the file might rise to the top.

One more explanation I would add. The Sublime Porte was an office; the Foreign Office was located there. It corresponded in fact to Downing Street or the Quai d'Orsay. I say this because writers sometimes endow it with a sort of personality to which it is not entitled.

Having given perhaps a somewhat sinister presentation of the Sultan, I might for the sake of impartiality quote a few words of an article which appeared in a local paper on one of His Majesty's birthdays.

L'allégresse est générale en ce beau jour: elle est dans toutes les maisons, dans toutes les villes, dans toutes les provinces, comme dans tous les cœurs, sur l'immense territoire de le Turquie. Si son peuple l'aime, jamais Souverin a-t-il mieux aimé son peuple. C'est sous le règne de ce Glorieux Monarque que la Turquie aura pris le merveilleux essor qui en fait une des grandes puissances de l'Europe.

That is not my conception of the Sultan, but it is obviously fair to quote it.

Now I go back to our own personal doings. We started from London at the end of August, 1906; spent a day in Paris, arrived at Marseilles the following morning and went on board the French boat *Equateur* which was to take us to Constantinople.

Our first excitement was the appearance on board of a party attired in what might be described as ancient oriental fashion. The party consisted of a man and two women, one carrying a baby. A French lady described the man as looking like a *Christ décroché* and the women as dressed *à la Sainte Vierge*. The man wore a short tunic and a sort of toga: the women also wore a sort of toga of purple over green. We discovered eventually that the man was English, and the women one Greek and the other English. They were on their way to the man's home on Mount Hymettus. What we did not know was that one of the women was destined to become well known as Isadora Duncan, the dancer who died in 1927, and whose memoirs were sufficiently stirring. Looking back it seems odd that she of all people should be dressed *à la Sainte Vierge*.

In the evenings on board we were entertained by a party of French priests, going out to the East as missionaries; they gave us comic songs, recitations and imitations of rockets exploding.

We reached the Piræus on September 3rd. Alban Young, from the Legation, met me and took me for a drive to Phalerum. He directed the driver by poking him on one side or the other with his umbrella, explaining to me that he had learned so many languages in the course of his career that he could not be bothered to start again with Greek. The chief thing that impressed itself on my mind, and for that matter on my person, was the prodigious quantity of dust. Next day we were at Smyrna, when we first made acquaintance with the common objects of the East. On the morning of the 6th we awoke to find ourselves at Constantinople. It was too dull a day for us to have a good view, but anyhow we were busy transferring our family and luggage to the Embassy launch which was to take us up the Bosphorus to Therapia, where the Embassy had its summer quarters.

We had hoped to go straight into a house, but there was not one vacant at the moment, so we had to be content with the hotel, from which we presently went backwards and forwards to Pera, the foreign quarter of Constantinople, to find a house for the following autumn and winter.

These journeys were made by the crowded steamers which plied up and down the Bosphorus. On returning to the hotel my wife found it necessary always to take off most of her garments and have them well shaken from the balcony to get rid of the fleas and other creatures which she had collected on board. When we came back to Therapia the following summer we had some trouble in bringing back all the furniture we needed. One article left behind was a baby's bath. Being myself in Pera one day I volunteered to bring the bath back with me. A Kurdish *hamal*, or porter, brought it to the landing-stage for me, but when I was not looking he deserted me so that I had to carry the bath on board myself. This would have been quite all right if one of the Sultan's Syrian Ministers had not been on the boat, seen me coming, and made low salaams to which I had to reply as gracefully as I could with a bath in one hand and an umbrella in the other.

In my diary I comment on the gardens of the Therapia houses, which were charming with a great tangle of flowers, though roses had but a short life there.

On the 14th the Ambassador left for England on leave, the whole staff and many of the British Colony seeing him off. We went down the Bosphorus in the Embassy launch with some grandeur, but the trail through dirty streets from the landing-stage to the station, with dozens of hamals carrying bits of luggage, was not impressive. This mixture of pomp and squalor was thoroughly characteristic of the country.

After the Ambassador and Lady O'Conor had gone we went off to look at the house we had taken in Pera. On the way we crossed Galata Bridge for the first time and admired the wonderful variety of costumes and the other usual sights.

The house stood high and commanded a splendid view across the Bosphorus to the mountains and the Asiatic side of the Sea of Marmara, including Mount Olympus. On the slope which occupied the foreground were Turkish houses with two or three minarets to break the outline. The house was approached by a cobbled road full of great holes in which the street dogs lay, nursed their families and licked their sores. They were mostly friendly animals. We hired the house from a Mr. Jones; to make up we subsequently hired a house at Therapia from His Beatitude Paul Peter XII Sabbaghian, Patriarch of the Armenian Catholics.

Before we left Therapia for the winter season in Pera we had a great deal of amusement one way or another; and so far as we were concerned the best part of it was the riding in the forest of Belgrad and elsewhere. I had a most sturdy white pony, bought from Percy Loraine (lately our Ambassador in Rome), and named by him Creamstealer (*Kaimakchalan*) after a snow-capped mountain in Macedonia. The pony's only vice was shying. This was too much for the colleague to whom I eventually resold him and who wrote that after returning from rides side by side several times they had finally been obliged to part.

We duly carried revolvers when we rode, but I only once came even near to using one. I was riding alone in the forest when a scoundrelly looking Kurd rushed out from among the trees and ran after me: he put his hand on the pony's quarters; as unconcernedly as I could I gave the pony a prick and we cantered out of the man's reach. Presently he reappeared round a corner and followed with greater determination. I thought the moment was coming to use my revolver and felt in my pocket for it; then I observed a big gate in front of me and the Kurd now rushed past me to open the gate and earn a penny.

On another occasion my wife and I with two or three other ladies and a young attaché rode over to the Black Sea shore for a picnic. While the ladies prepared lunch I took a stroll and met a soldier, purporting no doubt to be on guard over something. He seemed suspicious of us and I thought was going to be disagreeable; but he only asked "*Hareminiz varme?*" ("Is this your harem?") when I hastily replied "yes," hoping the ladies could not hear or follow the conversation. He appeared to be quite satisfied.

Part of the attraction of our rides, both in the Therapia season and in the spring when we rode out from Pera, was the variety of flowers and flowering shrubs, the fine trees, those especially on the Asiatic side, and the birds, from an occasional eagle, to kites, storks, and brilliant king-fishers with deep red breasts, and other small birds. The views of the Bosphorus and the Black Sea were enchanting. The sight of a long line of storks returning in the spring to Constantinople from their winter quarters was fascinating.

Among the foreign colleagues who sometimes rode with us was Count Limburg Stirum, lately Dutch Minister in London, whom, with Countess Stirum, I hope we may claim as lifelong friends. He is one of the finest, if not quite the finest, linguist I ever met, and could carry on a conversation with three people in three different languages—a very difficult feat.

Of our own staff the Counsellor and Chargé d'Affaires in the Ambassador's absence was George Barclay; the others were Macleay, Loraine, Pat Ramsay, Rex Hoare and Edmund Monson, who all eventually became Ambassadors or Ministers. The honorary Attachés were George Lloyd, already with a reputation for brilliance, and tremendously keen about all Near Eastern affairs, and John Lambton, later Earl of Durham. Lamb was first Dragoman, to be succeeded presently by Fitzmaurice, whom I saw lately described as 'the great Fitzmaurice.' Cator and Piggott were the Judges of the British Court, Surtees Military Attaché, and Roger Keyes, who in two years only appeared once for a few days, Naval Attaché.

The Turkish fleet was hardly worthy of his attention. It lay mouldering in the Golden Horn. Once Fitzmaurice and some friend did notice a sentinel keeping careful guard over a warship lying alongside the quay; Fitzmaurice said something to the man about the importance of watching over this valuable ship, and the man, pleased, at once replied that there was indeed a valuable crop of potatoes growing on the deck which was somewhat exposed to thieves. This state of things did not, at any rate at once, disappear with the advent of the Young Turks during the following year. One of my former colleagues wrote to tell me that Admiral Gamble, who was lent by us to the new Turkish Government, was aghast to find a sentry diligently protecting a nice little cabbage garden made in the mud at the bottom of one of His Imperial Majesty's ships.

George Lloyd, whom I have mentioned among the staff, was a brilliant young man, but a little disgruntled in the Embassy because he fancied that the Ambassador did not properly appreciate his talents. Sir Nicholas, in fact, treated him as he would have treated any other Attaché, whereas Lloyd was somewhat consciously at the beginning of a great career.

At the end of September we went to our first Selamlik. The diplomatic body, or a good many of them, assembled in a building overlooking the Mosque where the Sultan performed his Friday's devotions.

From the windows we watched his arrival and departure between a lane of troops, his carriage followed by a small and perspiring body of elderly aides-de-camp. In the 'Loge,' as it was called, we met for the first time many of our colleagues, among the most attractive being Marquis Imperiali and his wife, who later on were very popular at the Italian Embassy in London. The German Ambassador, Baron Marschall Von Biéberstein, was a famous figure in the East; he too was afterwards Ambassador in London, also Foreign Minister.

The Sultan looked, I thought, 'old, grizzled and Jewish.'

About the middle of October the Embassy moved to town. Luggage of all sorts was moved by bullock cart, the archives by a native carriage. Pat Ramsay and I accompanied the archives on our ponies: a terribly slow business, as any sort of carriage takes a long time to cover some fifteen miles on a shocking bad road. I see in my diary that our furniture took eight hours and I suppose the archives took three or four.

We bought a good deal of furniture for our house in the Bit Bazar (louse Bazaar) extraordinarily cheaply and soon settled down. We were never tired of our view of the Bosphorus. In the garden of one of the small Turkish houses below us I once saw from our balcony two Turkish women chatting in their garden: suddenly they saw me, a man, and hastily flung their petticoats over their heads in order to veil their hair. An upside down idea from our point of view.

Our household consisted of an English manservant, nurse and lady's maid, a Greek cook and kitchen-boy, an Armenian washerwoman, and Hamza, a fine-looking Albanian Moslem boy who was what, in modern English, would be described as a house-parlour-boy. The native servants lived together in peace and amity, except that at the outset there was some rivalry between Greeks and Armenians, who slept out, as to the possession of a straw mattress swarming with vermin which we found in the house and hastily threw out.

Hamza was not very industrious and easily satisfied in the matter of sweeping and dusting, but we had not much furniture and on the whole he served us very well. One of his duties was the delivery of letters, which was complicated by the fact that he could not read. Therefore, having been told verbally to whom the letters were addressed and more or less where the addressees lived, he went to the nearest of the houses, asked the servant to pick out the right letter and direct him to the next. Letters were generally addressed very simply—'Mrs. Tilley en Ville.' If there was a local post I never heard of it and it is probable that the Sultan would not allow such a thing.

So far as Europeans were concerned this did not much matter as there were not a great many of us, and everybody knew, or knew about, pretty well everyone else. Anyway, the numbering of the streets was a chancy business. Reuter's agent who had lived for some years at a No. 13, complained once that there were two houses numbered 13 and his letters consequently went astray. He was asked to choose another number and chose No. 8.

This gentleman had been in Constantinople at the time of the Armenian massacre and told me quite gravely that when Armenians whom he knew personally were seen escaping through the streets of Pera he found it quite difficult to get them to stop and give him a coherent account of what was happening.

We had, by the way, no serious massacres to deal with, but the Armenians were always apt to have an unpleasant time. One pastime of the Turkish soldiers was to catch Armenian women and put cats in their drawers. This must have been exceedingly disagreeable, but I am afraid we took it rather flippantly. I, as head of the Chancery, had a drawer in my writing-table to which Fitzmaurice had a key. In this drawer I put any papers which I wanted him to see, and if they dealt with what Sir Nicholas called 'cogglesome' questions I would tell him that there were cats in his drawer.

I do not think Macedonian Greeks or Bulgars suffered in this particular way, but the Turkish soldiers had a habit of stopping peasants in the road and getting on their backs for a ride. This, of course, was in their lighter moments.

I began now to take Turkish lessons and eventually passed a somewhat elementary examination in Turkish conversation. My teacher, Euripides Stavridi, a Greek as his name shows, taught most of the secretaries: he also acted as translator to the Porte. Once, having received no pay for some years, he decided to withdraw from this appointment. After he had been away six months some officials came from the Porte to beg him to return, and his father also pressed him to do so as he feared that, being Christians, they might otherwise get a black mark against their name. Stavridi went back and was led to a room where papers were stacked up to the ceiling. He asked what they were. They were the papers received in various foreign languages during his absence, none of which had been translated.

TOKYO EMBASSY STAFF

LADY MARY DORMER   W. J. DAVIES   R. M. TILLEY   MRS. HILL   LT.-COL. L. HILL

Author   SIR HAROLD PARLETT

CHUZENJI—" LARKS " RACING

He took me once to a variety entertainment at a small theatre. We went immediately after dinner; at twelve-thirty, a Turkish comedy began, but at one-thirty when the curtain fell on the first act I came away. This was worse than Madrid.

Another evening some of us went to S. Sophia at the hour of evening prayer, and watched the scene from a high gallery. The men were most fervent in their prayers, while children ran races and called and whistled to each other wherever there was a vacant space. The drive home was a little nerve-racking I thought, as our two carriages had to make their way through a huge crowd of men leaving the mosques, who made their feelings about foreigners quite unmistakable.

One day that autumn we dined with Adam Block, the British representative on the Council of the Debt, who had formerly been first Dragoman of our Embassy. He told us of a conversation between the Ambassador and Tewfik Pasha, then Minister for Foreign Affairs: this conversation, unlike so many, proved extremely amicable, the reason being that their Excellencies were talking on different subjects. At last Block laughed so much that he had to stop them.

Tewfik was Ambassador in London after the revolution, but I do not think his command of French could have been very great. I went to the Palace with Barclay when he presented his credentials to the Sultan as Minister, after Sir Nicholas O'Conor's death. Barclay stood facing the Sultan at a distance of a few feet, Tewfik behind the Sultan, Fitzmaurice behind Barclay, I behind Fitzmaurice: an arrangement reminiscent of a rouge at Eton football. Barclay having made his short speech the Sultan replied. He mumbled something for a minute or two in Turkish and Tewfik had to translate it. "*Sa Majesté Impériale dit qu'il est très content de vous voir et—chose—et—chose.*" More mumbling from the Sultan and Tewfik began again: "*Sa Majesté Impériale vous assure, M. le Ministre, que chose, et qu'il espère chose.*" I fancy the Sultan really said nothing and Tewfik was unable to invent. Hence all these 'choses.'

On November 12th there was a night Selamlik, the Sultan's procession being headed by torches; the surroundings of the Palace, Yildiz Kiosk, were brilliantly illuminated and so were many of the ships on the Bosphorus. Altogether a beautiful sight.

Here is a note about Turkish luncheon parties. A great friend of ours, Miss Hughes, was lady-in-waiting to the Khediveh Mère, the mother of the Khedive Abbas. We asked her about *Iftar*, or lunch: she said the Khediveh did not stay long but left her guests to go on eating for an hour or two more. Another European lady told us that she once went to *Iftar* with the Grand Vizier's wife, and was five hours at table, being stuffed with tit-bits all the time and only a drop of water to drink.

The only experience of that sort which we had was when we and Mrs. Barclay went to lunch with Reshid Pasha. We had alternate Turkish and European courses, seven of each. I don't know how many hours the meal

D

lasted, but fourteen courses in an Oriental house would be bound to last a good many.

Here are some extracts from my diary:

On November 17th we went to the Baisemain ceremony at the Dolma Bagché Palace. The Sultan stood in the same sort of position as the King at a levée, in a magnificent hall with no furniture but a golden throne. The high officials filed past him bowing, but the Sheik ul Islam ran forward to kiss the hem of his cloak. In accordance with etiquette the Sultan prevents this by pulling the cloak away: this was done three times. This from our point of view made a somewhat comic interlude. Another was provided by an Attaché of the German Embassy, who, being at the back of the crowd of onlookers, stood on a chair to see better. The Sultan spotted him and sent a chamberlain to make him get down. I was pleased about this because at a dance at the German Embassy at Therapia, where Mrs. Barclay for some reason danced with the wife of the Swedish Minister, Baron Von Marschall, terribly shocked, sent this same attaché to stop them, saying "*Es schickt sich nicht.*" ("It is unbecoming.")

After the first few grandees had saluted, kissed the sacred scarf held out for them by a high official and backed away, the Sultan seated himself on the throne and received a large number of officers, and then priests, only rising when he wished to be specially civil. The priests wore garments like dressing-gowns, of green, purple or brown, embroidered with gold, and white and gold turbans.

In the evening of that day we gave our first dinner-party in town, and I was glad to find that Barclay, who was an epicure, approved of our cook's performance, although there was no lobster. During a previous term of service at Constantinople his cook had orders to furnish a lobster for dinner every day. Not a good régime.

A few days later Captain Brian Molloy, the King's Messenger, and George Lloyd came to lunch. Molloy told us that he had been hauled over the coals at the F.O. for bringing a bag too many home; that is, one more than appeared on his waybill. He argued that it was much better than bringing one too few. This excuse was dismissed as frivolous, so he said that the truth was that the biggest bag had had a little one *en route.*

On the 26th we dined with one of the Syrian Ministers, Nedjib Pasha Melhamé, to meet M. Étienne, a former French Minister of War, whose visit was being a good deal advertised. I observed that at dinner everyone seemed 'rather distrait and anxious as if they expected someone to be either arrested or bombed, but no one was.' But for this note in my diary I should not have thought that in those days bombs were a form of horror to worry us much.

A few days later we paid the visit to the Whittalls at Moda, of which I have spoken. They were indeed Patriarchs and had about sixty grandchildren, all of whom, we were told, came every day to pay their respects to their grandparents.

October 7th. I note that in the course of my ride I met a man with a vulture for sale. It was tucked comfortably away under the man's arm and apparently quite peaceful. I do not know whether vultures make good pets.

Next day we were taken by one of the experts in Byzantine history round the ancient Walls of Constantinople: we were to do that round often again and always found it full of interest, our pleasure being only marred by the carcasses of horses which were deposited outside one of the gates. Even without having read all Gibbon one easily dreams of the glories of Byzantium. The 'Walls' was then more or less an all-day excursion. We left our house quite early in an *araba* tied together with string, or so it appeared, were rowed up the Golden Horn and then walked some miles along the Walls, had a picnic lunch half-way, picked up another *araba* on the far side of Stamboul and so home. Now one does the whole thing in a car in an hour or so, which makes it less, and not more, agreeable.

The friend who had escorted us round the Walls told us a tale of Fuad Pasha, who was Governor of Kadikeui (on the outskirts of the town) at the time of the Armenian massacre. Fuad was told by the Sultan that the massacre was to begin at Kadikeui. He said nothing, but when a boatload of men with clubs arrived off the quay he sent down an A.D.C. to say that if those men landed he would blow their brains out. Result, temporary disgrace of Fuad, but after six months the Sultan sent for him for a chat of reconciliation. As he left the Palace all smiles he was met by a file of soldiers, who conveyed him there and then to Damascus, where he has since remained, happier at any rate than those who were sent to Aleppo and other worse places.

December 15th. We dined with Dr. Martin of the Swedish Legation, the great authority on Turkish carpets and a collector of all sorts of works of art, including some charming miniatures of Swedish kings.

We heard there had been some excitement over a row among the sailors outside the Admiralty. They, not having got their pay and not having been sent home in due season, made a disturbance and stoned their officers. The Palace spy who watches the Admiralty officials tried to reason with them but fainted twice with fright.

December 18th. To St. Sophia with Dr. Frew. We had to hurry on account of the hour of prayer coming on and the number of pilgrims, who are rather fanatical.

We then went to the Turbeh of Selim II, lined with beautiful Persian faience, and to a small theological college which was interesting. Each student has a small cell with a wooden platform outside on which to sit and read in fine weather. They feed in 'messes' of four, one cooking. . . . Stamboul was full of pilgrims: many Circassians from the Caucasus with big black head-dresses of sheepskin, something like muffs, and sheepskin coats with the wool inside. They are very picturesque, even more so than the pilgrims of Mongol types who have been here lately.

December 19th. Dr. Clemow (and others) dined with us, very full of the iniquity of the German Emperor in having a fountain built in the gap which was made in the old walls of Jerusalem to improve the road for him.

December 20th. Prize-giving at English High School for Girls. Girls of all nations were there: Greek, French, English, Armenian, German.

In January came heavy snow and there was not much riding or walking. The streets of Pera and Stamboul did not lend themselves to walking in anything but the finest weather, as they were seldom cleaned and there was a great deal of rain and much mud; eminently a 'Galosh post,' as a colleague once put it. He was, as a matter of fact, speaking of St. Petersburg, also a galosh post, and complained of having had so many such. Our hall, when we had a party, was full of galoshes, which took much sorting out. Our door was a few yards from the street, and when Lady O'Conor dined with us we borrowed a sedan chair from the Embassy for her use. Sedan chairs were in frequent use: somebody going to the French Embassy in a chair had the floor fall out below him and was obliged to trot some way like a Jack in the Green on May Day. The only sedan chair I ever met in this country was at Bury St. Edmunds, when a small boy; a party was given for me and one little girl came in a sedan chair from the other end of the town.

February 11th. Von Schlotheim (the Attaché at the German Embassy whom I have mentioned two or three times) is engaged to Mlle. Selim Pacha, daughter of the Syrian Minister of Agriculture. This engagement required the sanction of the Sultan, the German Emperor (the bridegroom being an officer) and the Pope (the bridegroom being a Protestant), which seemed more than the importance of the parties warranted.

February 12th. Madame Turkhan Pasha came to call on my wife. I had to go out and our manservant hid himself while a maid showed her in. A duenna sat in a small room off the drawing-room with a door open between.

February 18th. We met at dinner a new colleague, Countess Brandes of the Austrian Embassy, a young wife. She overwhelmed me by saying that, of course, Society in other capitals meant little to her for she had been brought up in Agram.

February 19th. To a dance at the Greek Legation. The dragoman of the Legation asked me what the general outside world really thought of the dispute between the Œcumenical Patriarch and the Koutzo Vlachs.

February 20th. With some of the Austrians to the Persian Mouharrem ceremony. The Persians belonging to the Shiite division of the Moslem world adore the memory of Hassan and Hussein, the grandsons of Mohammed, both of whom were killed by their enemies.

When the big torches were lit the scene began to be impressive. First priests and people chanting dirges: then men in black gowns with bare breasts which they smacked loudly, others in black gowns and bare backs which they flogged with iron scourges. We thought one was drawing blood, but it turned out to be paint. They began each stroke with violence, but checked their arms at the last moment. Behind came a big crowd of the Persian public all shouting "Hassan Hussein" and beating their breasts. The crowd gradually increased as they went round and round in a circle; then horses came, one covered with a blood-stained sheet stuck all over with arrows; this represented Hussein's battle horse.

There were cries of *"Sou vermedi."* "He (the enemy) gave him no water"—a shocking crime in Oriental eyes. Next came horses draped in black, one with two doves fastened to it representing the pure souls of Hassan and Hussein: then a litter with little children representing the murdered children of Hussein. Last of all came a crowd of men with shaven heads, dressed in white sheets. Presently these began to slash their heads with long knives. They just touched their heads with the knives so as to keep the blood running and, we thought, had smeared some animal blood over their heads as well. An American who was of the party would not look at this horrid sight; but a German lady left her own party, forced her chair in front of ours, stood on it all the time and gloated.

The actors in this drama are mostly Persian donkey-boys hired for the occasion by the Persian Ambassador, who is said to find his post an expensive one.

March 4th. Dined at Russian Embassy: most of the staff of our own and the American Embassies were invited, and the Greek and Dutch. Not perhaps the best way of entertaining! Quantities of servants in pale blue uniforms, and one gaunt six-foot Circassian at the door of the dining-room in a black skirted robe, a chain and a big knife in his girdle.

About this time *The Times* published a series of articles on the Near East by Mr. Spencer Wilkinson. At the end of one I find this sentence: 'As far as I have seen I suspect that the best men among the population of Turkey are the Turks.' I cannot help wondering whether his ideas were formed in the same way as those of my friend the Apostolic Delegate *comme ils sont bons.* Turks in their rôle of conquerors may have been more impressive than the conquered races, but whatever they may be in 1942 I do not think that in 1907 they deserved any superlative praise.

Another article deals with the Baghdad railway, but descriptively and not politically. Wilkinson rightly foresees the possibility of a prosperous future for Asia Minor under a good administration, but points out that any Government would have to face the strange mixture of races and creeds, which 'is a fact not to be forgotten and not to be altered.' All the same it has been drastically altered by the Turks since then, Greeks having been driven out and masses of Armenians killed. The Arab countries have been divided from Turkey by outside interference, which reminds me that when I returned to London in 1908 I found many people, including some in the Foreign Office itself, who knew of no distinction between Turks and Arabs and thought I was somewhat absurd in talking of a break-up of the Empire on these lines.

This was not as bad as a naval officer who came to me once for information to help him in writing a state paper for the Cabinet and the Defence Committee. When I got out a map of the Austrian Empire and talked about Magyars and Italians, Croats and Rumanians, he tore his hair and declared he had thought they were all just Austrians.

We have perhaps almost forgotten that in the years of which I am writing our relations with Germany turned largely on the Baghdad Railway and the question of its construction and control by that Power. Negotiations for joint control were long continued, but failed to reach a settlement. What we did hold out for was the control of Tigris navigation, and the Persian Gulf, and a big share in Mesopotamian oil interests, on the importance of which I heard many lectures from the Commercial Secretary to the Embassy. Versailles put an end for the time to German infiltration through Asia Minor, and now we are more or less back at the point where we left off twenty-five or thirty years ago. Although a German colleague once said to me that there could never be peace between us until Germany recovered her colonies, I imagine that penetration into Asia Minor is, or has been, nearer the hearts of German Governments than possessions in Africa.

March 5th. To the 'Debt' mainly to see the wonderful view from the roof over the Bosphorus and the Golden Horn. We saw also the printing press, electric light plant, engines, binding department and even the coal cellar, which was once a Christian church. There are 4,000 employees. ('The Debt' was the Ottoman Public Debt which was managed by a Foreign Commission, our representative being Adam Block. This was one of the most visible signs of foreign control.)

About this time some concerted movement of the Powers seems temporarily to have got rid of Fehim Pasha, the chief spy, but he was back again before long. I also note that "we have settled the 3 per cent question (relating to the Turkish Customs) and the Macedonian Gendarmerie question, so we are pretty free for the moment."

What had been settled about the gendarmerie I cannot remember, but it must have been a very temporary settlement. A European gendarmerie had been working in Macedonia for some few years, Britain, France, Italy, Austria and Russia being represented, but not Germany, who wished to cultivate the friendship of the Sultan. They achieved uncommonly little in the face not only of Turkish misgovernment but internecine warfare between the European races and the difficulty of maintaining a united front themselves.

To impose on an unwilling country accustomed to manage its own affairs any form of foreign control is, to my mind, almost hopeless, unless the controlling power is prepared to use ferocious brutality, and then only possible for a limited time. I trust this will be in the minds of those responsible for making the next peace.

March 21st. A lovely day. We went to Scutari and saw the dancing

Dervishes, sat out the whole service and saw the cures, the Sheik standing on sick children who lie on their faces before him.

March 23rd. To the Museum where Hamdi Bey (the Director) spoke of the *Émotion extraordinaire* of finding near Sidon the so-called Tomb of Alexander; he expected merely a repetition of other tombs, found elsewhere in Asia Minor. It is a marvellous work of art.

April 11th. My wife and I walked in the valley of Sweet Waters and saw a flight of eighty storks arrive and settle in the meadows.

April 13th. Rode with Lambton. Saw three hoopoes on the hills looking very fine. Also saw Reschad Effendi, the Sultan's eldest brother and heir, very dismal looking in a closed carriage going at a foot's pace and surrounded by outriders and guards. That is all the fun he is allowed and he never sees anyone but his own family. They say he drinks, which is not wonderful. If he goes into a shop it is closed by the police next day. (Reschad, afterwards Sultan, lived in a villa in the country near which we often rode. We knew it as Sandringham. The road near his house was even worse than usual, supposedly to make any attempt at escape more difficult.)

April 19th. After the Selamlik, I and the officers of the *Imogene,* our guardship, waited two hours while the German Ambassador and Sir Nicholas had their respective audiences of the Sultan. Here I might explain that the Sultan, as a rule, only received Ambassadors; Ministers had but a poor chance of an audience. The Belgian Minister did once, after waiting a year, succeed in being received. The Sultan greeted him with: "*Mr. le Ministre je regrette de ne pas avoir pu vous recevoir la semaine passée.*"

Our Ambassador's audience being over we were called in and the Ambassador presented us to His Majesty. He muttered something which the Grand Master of the Ceremonies translated into a flowery speech and we shook hands and backed out.

April 21st. My wife and I rode. It was a lovely day. We found scarlet anemones coming out everywhere, purple and white orchises and purple hyacinths and a lovely little dark blue forget-me-not. There were several storks in the Valley.

April 28th. I go to the Armenian Catholic Church to attend the Jubilee of the Patriarch: the robes were gorgeous but not beautiful; one, peacock blue brocaded with gold worn with a high blue mitre; another, red and gold embroidery. The choir wore dark mustard-coloured surplices with crimson velvet capes trimmed with silver fringe. The Pope's representative sat on a throne on the right wearing a long purple robe and train. The Patriarch himself wore first salmon pink, and then crimson and gold with a huge mitre, and, the most interesting thing of all, the pallium such as you see in the Archbishop of Canterbury's arms. The service was something like the Roman Catholic, but the Gospel was read in Armenian, and at intervals a big blue curtain was drawn between the Altar and the people. The sound of the service was hideous and a great deal of it was hummed in a sort of droning way.

Afterwards we went to the Patriarchate and saw His Beatitude presented with a ring by the Armenian Catholic Community, and with a big Cross and long gold chain from the Pope by the Apostolic Delegate. Then we had champagne and sweet wine and cakes handed round and so home.

April 29th. Rode with Lambton and Monson beyond Kiat Hané and through a very pretty valley back to Sweet Waters: in one place we saw a perfect field of anemones. We met a small string of camels, also our first wild tortoise, and an eagle. We were also chased by one of the big savage farm dogs. We finished by finding the Kiat Hané valley in flood up to the pony's withers, but scrambled out up a precipitous bank. I went first, then Monson, then Lambton. His pony, however, to our horror, when standing almost perpendicular, fell back; Lambton came off and both disappeared under water for an appreciable time; fortunately neither was any the worse. (Lambton, I remember, said it was more amusing than riding in Hyde Park.)

As to the tortoises, these were great big creatures. I once, when riding alone down a narrow valley, heard a loud noise among the bushes on one side which sounded as if a cow might be falling down: it turned out to be two tortoises hurtling down, apparently one in pursuit of the other.

About this time we paid a delightful visit to Broussa; apart from the usual sights I recollect chiefly the Jews in long Kaftans.

We also went for a week to Sinaia in Rumania by way of holiday. The season had not begun and the hotel was nearly empty. One couple had come there because the lady, who was a very pretty young woman, had been so pestered by Rumanian officers in Bucharest that she had to escape. They had followed her carriage through the streets and had even tried to make their way into her apartment. We did not see much of Bucharest itself, but I was struck by the huge tracts of corn land, the miserable huts for the farm labourers and the carts in which some of them were living with their families.

There had recently been a great peasant rising: Bucharest had been in serious alarm and several thousands of the peasants had been killed in the fighting. Many, if not most, of the landlords were absentees, some living in Europe (one did not think of the Balkans as Europe). How the great nobles came by their huge estates I do not exactly know, but I believe the families bearing the title of prince were descended from the Greek Hospodars or Governors, appointed by the Sultan when Rumania was still part of the Turkish Empire.

My idea of the country was that it was in a pretty rotten state, and when in the Great War my acquaintances sometimes rubbed their hands over the entry of Rumania into the war on our side, I begged them not to expect too much.

I find in my scrap-book about this time another *Times* article by Mr.

Spencer Wilkinson, written from Ragusa on his way home. In giving his impressions of Turkey he speaks of the Sultan as a strong ruler and says: 'The strong man is not always loved, and Abdul Hamid, though he has devoted servants, does not seem to be popular.' This would be a most remarkable understatement, but he goes on to say that he has been told by people of all races that 'every class would breathe more freely on the news of the end of a reign under which all are more or less afraid.' The end was very near.

It appears from his article that many people in Europe expected the German control of the Baghdad Railway to lead to German colonization of Asia Minor. The writer scouts this idea, as he says do 'the able and broad-minded German Directors of the Baghdad Railway.' He is, no doubt, right about colonization, but some form of control would doubtless have been established and would now be established if the chance occurred.

CHAPTER V

I SEEM TO HAVE KEPT NO DIARY DURING THE SECOND YEAR OF OUR STAY in Constantinople, but our life was much the same as in the first year— riding, many diplomatic entertainments and much sight-seeing, often in company with Fitzmaurice, who had profound knowledge of the place, the people and the language. He had been twenty years in the country and had a most subtle brain. He could carry on a discussion in Turkish perfectly, but he told me that when Turkish officials thought they were getting the worst of an argument they 'retreated' further and further into Arabic. I used to be told that only about twenty per cent of the words used by educated people were actually Turkish; a much larger proportion were Arabic, and some further proportion Persian: there was therefore room for retreating to prepared positions. On one occasion Fitzmaurice wished to take me to the great Aqueduct of Valens. We were, if possible, to obtain admission from the guard and walk in at one end and out at the other. We went first to a small café near the far end of the Aqueduct, where Fitzmaurice fell into conversation with a party of elderly Turks. This talk lasted at least half an hour and appeared to have a wide range. At the end of the half-hour Fitzmaurice told me he had now permission to cross the Aqueduct. As we went he explained that he had begun by talking of other things: at last he had mentioned the Aqueduct. He had been told no one could be allowed there. Further conversation followed in which all joined and some suggested that after all there was no harm in people taking this walk. At last the guard who was one of the party agreed. This was a typical Turkish conversation.

The riding was as pleasant as ever: the country, the flowers and the odd little accidents that we often met with. One recollection that I have not mentioned is of a certain piece of open ground that we used to pass as we were getting out of the town. There the younger Palace eunuchs used to disport themselves on horseback at some kind of ball game. Their loud squeaks rang in our ears.

Nor have I spoken of our innumerable visits to the Bazaars and our many bargains, made sometimes with the help of Miss Adeline Whittall, sometimes with that of Fitzmaurice, who was an expert in many things, or George Lloyd. In company with the latter we made one of our best buys in a sort of Wonderland fashion. We spied a beautiful silver dish on a high shelf well above the head of the old man who kept the stall. Lloyd, who was an old friend of his, asked if we might look at it. Yes, we could if Lloyd could climb up and get it down, which he accomplished more successfully than Alice.

Miss Whittall was constantly in the Bazaars, which resounded with cries of "Mademoiselle, Mademoiselle" from the sellers when she appeared with a party of tourists.

A variation of programme was provided for us in the autumn of 1907 by the arrival of Sir Charles Drury, Commander-in-Chief in the Mediterranean, on a visit to Constantinople. Battleships not being allowed to pass the Dardanelles the visitors came in the hospital ship *Maine* and *Hussar*, a yacht of 1,000 tons.

A variety of entertainments were given in honour of the Admiral and his staff, but the most interesting was a banquet given by the Sultan at Yildiz Kiosk and presided over by His Majesty in person. This was the only Imperial entertainment at which we were present during our two years in Turkey. All or most of the Turkish Ministers and high Palace officials were present, the whole of the Embassy staff and a large number of officers. We sat at a long table with the Sultan at the head, while at intervals down the sides of the banqueting hall stood guards with revolvers pointed at our backs, which gave one a somewhat creepy feeling. The dishes were brought in at a door facing my seat; they were carried aloft by servants, who came in at a run, and taken to a sideboard at the end of the room behind the Sultan.

Lady O'Conor and Lady Drury sat on either side of the Sultan with the Grand Master of the Ceremonies at hand to interpret. Their conversation was on these lines. The Sultan made a sign, the Grand Master came forward: the Sultan muttered something: the Grand Master moved to the side of Lady O'Conor, salaamed and said: "*Sa Majeste Impériale dit qu'il a fait tres beau temps aujourd'hui.*" Lady O'Conor said: "*Voulez-vous dire a Sa Majesté combien nous sommes heureux de nous trouver ici?*" Salaam. Grand Master goes to Sultan, salaams, and repeats presumably what Lady O'Conor has said. I did not hear that there was any conversation of interest. After dinner we all adjourned to some smallish rooms in the

Palace. The Ambassador and Commander-in-Chief with Lady O'Conor and Lady Drury followed the Sultan into an inner room. Presently attendants appeared with large baskets full of insignia of various minor orders which they handed out to the officers. Then we came away.

In conversation with the Editor of the *Levant Herald* the Admiral appears to have 'dwelt at length on His Majesty's charming manner and affable nature.'

Here is the menu, which has some interest in view of the rarity of Imperial banquets.

DINER
du 25 Redjeb, 1325
et de 21–3 September, 1907.

Consommé à la Royale
Petits pâtés et Boeureks
Bar sauce mayonnaise
Cuissot de Veau
à le Maraichère
Suprêmes de Volaille
à la Clamart
Aspic de homard
Punch
Asperges sauce Hollandaise
Dindonneaux rôtis
Pilaff
Pouding de York
Pain de Pommes
à la Chantilly
Glaces

On the Friday the Admiral and his staff attended the Selamlik, and this visit led to a somewhat ludicrous incident.

We were all early on the Quay at Therapia when it was suddenly discovered that the Embassy launch which was to take us down the Bosphorus was out of action.

What was to be done? Could another ship of any sort be found? Yes: a large coal barge was seen approaching from the Black Sea. The kavasses and Chancery servants brought out chairs, on which they stood wildly waving towels till the barge, attracted by this unusual sight, came alongside. The Captain agreed to take us down, and our brilliant company, with blazing uniforms, went on board and the situation was saved. In the long run the only sufferer was the Captain of H.M.S. *Imogene*, the Embassy guardship, which was moored some way down the Bosphorus. *Imogene* never noticed us in spite of the Ambassador's flag flying, and gave no salute, with the result that her Captain received a rebuke from the C.-in-C., which I thought a little hard.

During the summer of 1907, my wife being at home, I lived in the Secretaries' house at Therapia, close to the water's edge. I believe in former days it had been used by the Ambassador himself, and was a comfortable house but with no heating apparatus of any sort. As Sir Nicholas chose to stay on the Bosphorus till the beginning of November we suffered much from cold, and I can still see Lambton in an armchair in our sitting-room wrapped in the blankets from his bed. During the summer it was very pleasant and we breakfasted on our balconies most luxuriously. On one occasion while sitting at breakfast I heard a tremendous splash and assumed that a horse or cow had fallen into the sea, which would not have been very unusual. A second splash was, however, something quite out of the way. I looked round, could see nothing at first, but suddenly beheld a swordfish leap out of the water and fall back with just such a splash as I had heard before.

During the years 1906-1908 I kept a list of the birds that I came across round about Constantinople. They included eagle, buzzard, raven, stork, heron, shearwater (the lost souls of the Bosphorus), nightjar, hoopoe, golden oriole, wheatear, goldfinch, roller (in Rumania), redstart and many common species.

Towards the end of the year I was sent to inspect our Consular establishments in Bulgaria, and visited Philippopolis, Bourgas, Varna, Rustchuk and Sofia.

I was greatly impressed with the beauty of the country, but some of the towns on my list were still primitive.

At Bourgas, on the Black Sea, we had an unpaid Consular Agent, an Italian with a considerable sense of humour. He wrote to warn me that as I was to arrive late in the evening I must take a cab to the hotel, although it was quite close to the station: to attempt the journey on foot would be *une véritable Odyssée*. Varna, also on the Black Sea, was a most attractive place, with an excellent local white wine. The streets struck me as somewhat imposing, but a foreign engineer whom I met there remarked: "*Ici il ne faut faire que des façades*," so that imposing was perhaps the right word after all.

In the hall of the hotel at Rustchuk was this notice in French (though, or perhaps because, few people were likely to be able to read that language): '*Il est défendu de se battre dans cet hôtel. Si l'on se bat le propriétaire sera obligé, et cà à son grand regret, d'appeler la police.*' There was no fighting while I was there, but I was rather taken aback when shown my room by the sight of some half-dozen beds with a pair of slippers beside each. I asked if all those beds were taken, and was comforted to learn that they were not and that the slippers were part of the normal furniture of the room.

At Sofia I found George Buchanan as Chargé d'Affaires and greatly enjoyed my visit. One entertainment that was a little unusual was the weekly hockey match in which the greater part of the diplomatic body, men, women and children, not to mention the Foreign Minister and his wife, took part. It was uncommonly like the croquet match in Wonderland. Some of the players stood about and chatted, some charged furiously up and down the field, some stood apart and surveyed the scene. It was snowing most of the time, but we all appeared to think it most enjoyable. The Buchanans had a dinner party one night, which included a lady described to me as 'the only lady in Bulgaria.' I suppose this was snobbish, but snobbery on such a scale as that is surely permissible. Afterwards we played bridge. My partner was 'the only lady', and against us were the Russian Minister and a female of high rank who certainly behaved like a lady. When the Minister was dummy he tried to play his own hand by pushing a card forward and murmuring: "*Çà serait une bonne carte à jouer,*" on which his partner resolutely played a worse card, so that they lost heavily.

Bulgaria, I think, was generally popular with travellers, especially the peasants; and they were usually supposed to be more worthy of admiration than the Greeks. I am inclined to think that this was mainly on the *comme ils sont bons* theory, but no doubt they were more solid and less excitable than the Greeks. At any rate, there was a very strong case for their complete independence of the Turkish Government, although they had reached a considerable degree of prosperity under its ægis. At the time of my visit they had Prince Ferdinand for their immediate ruler, but he was under the suzerainty of the Sultan.

I liked Bulgaria and what little I saw of the Bulgarians, although I should be rather put to it to give any real reason for my liking. Bulgaria was uncommonly unlucky in its Prince, and possibly if they had chosen their ruler better they would have been our allies instead of our enemies.

One point about them was new to me. I had a general idea that there was some feeling of kinship with Russia, and gratitude for help in procuring them as much independence as they then had. I was told that this was not so and that, on the contrary, they were jealous of any possible interference by Russia. They have racial affinities with Turks as well as Slavs, and though of the Orthodox Church the Bulgarian Exarchate has been a thorn in the side of the Patriarchate.

From Sofia I went home on leave and returned in the course of the winter by way of Salonica, coming in there for a disagreeable experience of the Vardar wind. I had had a pleasant journey and was struck, as others have been, by the importance which one began to assume on leaving 'Europe' and arriving in the East. At the Turkish frontier, uncertain about future meals, I bought a loaf, of the kind described as 'a yard of bread.' Before I reached my carriage the stationmaster, in his best dress, came to salute me and make conversation. With him I walked up and down the platform in as dignified manner as was compatible with having a yard of bread under my arm. Further along the line I did get an excellent *déjeuner*. Half-way through my meal I noticed that I was alone:

every now and then the stationmaster looked in and smiled, as I thought, glad to see me enjoying myself. At last he came right in and said that if I had nearly finished would I be so very good as to lose no time in returning to my carriage, for though they had been happy to wait for me it was getting very late. This is the only occasion on which I have met with such noble treatment at a railway station.

Salonica, where I stayed with Harry Lamb, the Consul General, was an interesting place, with a considerable mixture of nationalities, Greeks, Turks (it was still, of course, in the Turkish Empire), foreign gendarmerie and other officers, Spanish-speaking Jews and a few other miscellaneous inhabitants. There was at least one good street in which an avenue of trees had been planted at the edge of the pavement. As the trees grew the pavement became congested and the foreign community asked that they should be moved. The Municipal Authorities, anxious to please, cut them level with the ground and stuck the trunks into the roadway further out. They had not flourished.

From Salonica I returned to Constantinople. In March Sir Nicholas O'Conor died.

I felt great affection for him, and admiration also. He may not have been quite in the front rank of able men, but he was a most conscientious public servant, very patient, persuasive, and fully alive to all that was going on around him. His post was one in which anything that could be called 'success' was out of the question, and only an Archangel could have kept the Sultan on the straight path of virtue, brought Greeks and Bulgarians, Rumanians and Pomaks, Koutzo Vlachs, Arabs and Armenians, Syrians and Kurds into harmonious and brotherly relations, or ever convinced the Porte that they could be the losers in the long run by making friends with Germany, while public opinion in England was for ever condemning them and talking hopefully of the banishment of the Turks from Europe.

As I have earlier in this book mentioned the constant exchange of private letters between Ambassadors and the Secretary of State in former days, I may say that O'Conor was much addicted to the habit of writing private letters, which I generally copied for him. He would often say: "Of course I should not think of saying this in a despatch." Seldom, if ever, could I understand why; but human nature tends to prevent people from committing themselves, and it is as well to remember that if they are restricted to official despatches they may, foolishly or not, keep valuable information to themselves. Farmers in Suffolk will hardly write letters at all, fearing, I believe, to commit themselves.

On the other hand, Frank Villiers, when Assistant Under-Secretary in the Foreign Office, used to write regularly to Ministers at out-of-the-way posts, saying with great truth that he knew they liked it. This to some people would not be a sufficient reason, but it is a very good one.

The Ambassador's funeral was a great ceremony. As I had the task of arranging it I was glad to find some writer in the *Levant Herald* commenting on the 'suavity and good nature' of those who directed the arrangements. In a place where order and regularity were practically unknown the work was not too easy; but, fortunately, until the actual service was over and people struggled to get away early, things went pretty well.

After the Ambassador's death, Barclay was made Minister as a temporary arrangement, but I myself left about two months later to return to the Foreign Office.

George Barclay was a man of ability and a hard worker and suffered only from an inclination to tell the Foreign Office what they would like to hear rather than what they ought to hear.

Of Fitzmaurice I have already spoken. He was a man of great intelligence, with a vast knowledge of Turkish ways and Turkish life, and thanks to the nature of his own mind remarkably skilful in following the tortuous train of Turkish thought. In fact his subtlety of thought was such as sometimes to make him nebulous, so that it was difficult to form any exact idea of his real meaning or his real belief. At the same time he was a delightful and witty companion and an excellent friend. When the Young Turks came into power they suspected his attachment to the old régime, in which they were perhaps not altogether wrong. This made his position at Constantinople very difficult. Like Sir Nicholas he was an Irish Catholic. He retired when only fifty-six and, I believe, devoted himself to Catholic philanthropic work in London.

Lamb was another tower of strength in the Near East and a friend of long standing, who has given me leave to quote some of his opinions, as expressed in the letters which I had from him after leaving Constantinople.

One incident in Barclay's régime was somewhat remarkable. Despairing of getting the action he required from the Porte, I forget on which of our usual disputes, he had the brilliant idea of having the *Imogene* cleared for action. She was very old and very small, but it happened that she was thinking of trying to manage a trip to Smyrna. This gave Barclay his chance. The Sultan was known to be terrified of Ships of War of any sort. The *Imogene* was accordingly cleared for action and the Porte gave way. The German Embassy played the same trick, a little later I think, when Fehim Pasha, or some confederate of his, seized and refused to give up a cargo belonging to a German subject. The *Lorelei* was a little bigger than the *Imogene* but not much: she was equally successful.

We said good-bye to Constantinople with infinite regret; it was exceedingly beautiful, the work was full of interest, and life was thoroughly unusual and amusing.

CHAPTER VI

WE WENT FROM CONSTANTINOPLE BY SEA TO ATHENS, WHERE WE STAYED long enough to see most of the best things. Then we went by rail along the Gulf of Corinth to Patras.

This journey was extremely lovely. Here is my description of it written at the time.

The space, a quarter of a mile or so, between the railway and the Gulf was covered in many places with huge patches, fields almost, of pink oleander that made a gorgeous foreground to a picture in which the middle distance was occupied by the deep blue waters of the sea and the background by the grey and blue mountains on its northern shore. This feast of colour lasted for some four or five hours and was so rich that we scarcely looked towards the south, except to give due admiration to the Acro Corinthos, although there, too, there were beautiful hills and villages. Of more material feasts there were less than we could have wished, but bread, the splendid cherries that seem to be peculiar to Greece, and a sort of apricot helped to keep off hunger until we reached Patras.

Whether there are any beauties of Nature or art at Patras I do not know, but it did not look to us particularly interesting. However, we were chiefly intent on the conveyance of our baggage from the train—where it lingered long enough to cause us some concern—to our steamer, whither it eventually accompanied us in a small boat. All I know about the town is that it contains a second-hand book-shop, for an American fellow traveller equipped himself there with a tattered copy of *Fallen Fortunes*, by James Payn, another of *Six Months After*, by a lady whose name I forget, which from the extracts of reviews seems to have made a small sensation in the early 'seventies, and an odd volume of *Gil Blas*, a rather curious assortment for Patras to produce at a moment's notice. Our American friend somewhat unkindly christened *Fallen Fortunes* the Governess's romance and *Six Months After* the young person's romance: nevertheless, we all read them assiduously in the absence of other literature.

I may here explain that the direction of our voyage in the Adriatic was purely accidental. We had intended to take the Austrian Lloyd boat, but being assured at Athens that there was no security of finding berths on that boat, whereas we could be promised a *cabina distinta* on the Italian boat, we chose the latter. Now this incident may be useful to future travellers who suppose, as we did, that a *cabina distinta* implies something rather magnificent: it does not; it merely means that the cabin is apart from the other cabins, and whatever that may be in other cases it turned out in ours to be one that opened out of the second-class saloon, with a small window commanded by everyone who took exercise on the deck. However, we were able at once to exchange it for a large four-berth cabin in the usual place, which as we were only two suited us admirably, except that we shared it with an inordinate number of fleas.

We woke next morning to find ourselves within measurable distance of Corfu, but with time to survey our fellow passengers before reaching the island. The American mentioned already was the only Anglo-Saxon on board, and except for a German with his Greek bride and an old dissatisfied French couple the rest were Italians. Perhaps the most interesting was a young Italian sailor going home on sick leave to Venice from Constantinople, where he had been serving on the Italian Stationnaire. He was exceptionally good looking, but had something odd about his eyes which continually puzzled me so long as I only saw his profile, until I discovered that one eye was brown and the other grey. Our Captain, at whose table we were placed, was the most genial and courteous of men, and another young Italian of thirty or so who had been making a tour of the East and was now going home to his papa, as he said, was also a cheerful companion. The staff consisted of a large and muscular stewardess with a smiling red face and a heavy black moustache, a black-headed steward and a red-headed steward, and a sort of major-domo in a black frock-coat who only appeared once a day to pour us out each a glass of Marsala at the end of dinner. The food, I may say, was liberal and excellent.

But to return to Corfu. The first and only object of most of those on board seemed to be to catch sight of the Achilleion, the German Emperor's visit being of recent date, but I confess that the extraordinary beauty of the scenery affected us more closely. Corfu itself has been so often described that its features are generally familiar and I will merely record my own praise. We stayed long enough to take a beautiful drive and to wander for some time in the gardens of the King's villa, from which there is one particularly lovely view through an opening in the trees over sea and mountain with the great citadel in the middle distance. We were accompanied in our wanderings by an Italian-speaking gardener who pointed out with care not only the beauties of the scene but the wife of the Greek Premier and regaled us with apricots, or rather something like apricots, which he stated to be the fruit of a japonica.

We left Corfu in the afternoon and arrived before long at Santi Quaranta, a small Turkish port which was of interest as having been recently attacked and plundered by brigands or pirates. A more uninviting place for brigands can scarcely be imagined, as the town consists of a string of small houses of the plainest kind, flanked by a ruined castle and all squeezed in between the sea and mountain, the only apparent connection with the interior being by a hill road which, viewed as a daily walk, would make the stoutest heart quail. Nevertheless there seemed to be a good deal of business to be done of some kind and wild men in fez and baggy breeches loaded and unloaded a quantity of something.

The next morning found us at Brindisi, where nearly the whole of our

E

passengers deserted us, not to be replaced, and there we remained all day. I had never thought of Brindisi before except as a junction for India, and it is not usually considered a place for tourists; but we managed to amuse ourselves fairly well by dint of hiring a sailing-boat in which a very stout boatman carried us about the harbour for the greater part of the afternoon. He informed us that he had a great many English friends, had served on magnificent yachts, and received all manner of testimonials which he kept in a large box: I have since heard that he is not unknown to travellers and that the testimonials consist chiefly of virulent abuse. However, he served our turn. He began by taking us to see the Castle of Frederick Barbarossa, on an island at the entrance of the harbour, a building which I do not find mentioned in Murray but which is of some interest, the water-court being most picturesque; a quadrangle of ancient buildings surrounding a court-yard formed by the sea itself, and accessible only to boats which have to shoot the entrance. From the Castle we went back across the harbour to the modern villa of our Consul and were shown his beautiful garden full of lilies and other flowers growing beneath a canopy of orange trees, from which the gardener presented us with two delicious blood oranges. Opposite this villa is another ancient castle, now used as a prison, and scattered about the town a quantity of churches which our boatman assured us was greatly in excess of the quantity of religion.

We sailed from Brindisi in the evening and on the following morning reached Bari. Before breakfast we drove into the town, bargaining with a cabman to take us to the Church of St. Nicholas and back. We passed through a maze of extraordinarily narrow streets to arrive at the church, which is Romanesque and of great interest; unfortunately we did not see the fine crypt, not because we were unaware of its existence but because we wished to annoy a guide who hung round us and refused to be parted from us. Having left the church and returned to our carriage we wished and expected to be taken back to the boat, the more so as it was beginning to be scorchingly hot and as also the hour of *déjeuner* was at hand. The driver, however, had other views and insisted, in spite of all our efforts, in driving us round the modern and totally uninteresting town, zealously pointing out such objects as the post office and the theatre, although our only reply to his remarks was "Take us back." When we did at last regain the steamer our driver added insult to injury by following us on board and into the saloon to demand extra pay. Then, however, our command both of Italian and of change was so slight that silent contempt was for us almost an enforced weapon. We spent a hot afternoon on deck and sailed in the evening across an oily sea, which according to the Italian sailor was *troppo buono,* a condition probably incredible to indifferent sailors, while such oiliness is really not beautiful. The following day found us at Ancona, where we landed somewhat foolishly in the heat of the day and started for the Cathedral, which stands high above the town. So long as we wandered through the narrow streets between houses, among them some fine old palaces, our foolishness was not apparent, but the last lap, so to speak, lay along an open terrace, where even white umbrellas were almost useless. The Cathedral, of the tenth and thirteenth centuries, is not extraordinarily interesting, but being very reluctant to face the sun again we gladly spent some time there before creeping down to the ship again. This was our last day at sea, for early next morning we were approaching Venice, in the way in which it ought to be approached, and by nine o'clock had transferred ourselves from steamer to gondola and were already in the Grand Canal.

Thus ended a voyage which although it offered no startling adventures and showed us no very remarkable 'sights' was full from beginning to end of leisurely charm.

From Venice we went to Milan and so home. When in Northern Italy I have often thought of a tale of my father's of his travels there in the early fifties of the nineteenth century when Austria was all-powerful. Among other places he visited Lucca, then a place of fashion, and went to the theatre. While he was waiting for the curtain to go up an Austrian officer came in and trod heavily, and with intent, on his toes. My father was very angry, whereupon the officer apologized, saying: "I really thought you were an Italian, sir." His compatriot, Hitler, would doubtless have done likewise.

On my return to London I found a Foreign Office very different from that which I used to know. The reforms had actually come into force before my departure for Constantinople, but I had scarcely become familiar with them. Their origin and nature are described in the book on the Foreign Office produced some years ago by Sir Stephen Gaselee and myself. Here I will only insist on one particular feature, that, namely, of minute writing.

In old days despatches and letters when received were folded up and a docket written on the outside fold: below this, space being much restricted, short minutes were sometimes written, but extensive minute writing was rare. The Secretary of State when he received these papers did his own work in his head, so to speak.

Sir Thomas Sanderson, universally known as 'Lamps,' who was Permanent Under-Secretary from 1894 to the beginning of 1906, was a man of vast knowledge and complete competence, but he belonged emphatically to the old school. I will not say that, like the Librarian, Sir Edward Hertslet, he put on a frock-coat when he had occasion to speak to the Secretary of State on the telephone, but he treated him and expected others to treat him as a being of a different order for whose convenience we were so lucky as to exist.

Eyre Crowe, who inspired, or helped to inspire, the reforms, rather looked down on Secretaries of State than up to them and regarded Foreign Office clerks as the really important people; all politicians were for him outside the pale, and even diplomats and the staff of other Government offices were not much better. Himself a man of great ability and untiring industry he was not strong in knowledge of human nature, particularly of English human nature, for he had been educated in Germany and France, and he admitted to not being a good judge of men.

The result, then, of the reforms was a method of conducting business which may have had many good points but was not necessarily to the taste of Secretaries of State: not always, I think, to the taste of Sir Edward Grey, and certainly not to that of Lord Curzon, whom I knew best. For a man with a great volume of business to get through his task was not lightened by having to read not only the despatches from abroad but a mass of comments as well. I do not suppose that Secretaries of State did read all of these comments, but I believe they often found them hampering rather than helpful.

Another change from old days was that we were more businesslike: we came punctually at eleven and hoped to leave at six, though we did often stay late if necessary. Second division clerks, of whom there were now many, had regular hours also to which they adhered, and as they were in charge of the files their absence contributed to our early departure. For anything over their fixed hours they were entitled to overtime pay, but until the war changed our habits I doubt whether they ever earned any. Also visitors, except for members of the diplomatic service on leave, were unknown, and even diplomats were not much encouraged. Crowe certainly did not approve of their dropping in. This I think myself was a pity. Although the general public might take pleasure in thinking that Foreign Office clerks and Diplomatic Secretaries who formerly led such a butterfly existence were now chained to their desks, I doubt whether in our particular profession this chaining was altogether advisable. In the case of the diplomatic service, which underwent reforms similar to ours, I am sure there was great loss.

The sort of life which I have described in the case of George Buchanan at Darmstadt became almost impossible.

Lest I be accused of admiring idleness for idleness sake, or of an undue fondness for irregular hours of work, I may say that I think my father was clearly right when, in the middle of the nineteenth century, he told a Post Office clerk that he must really choose between his work at St. Martin's le Grand and his greengrocer's shop: and when he told another clerk that there was no real necessity for him to leave at four, a doctrine which would be abhorrent no doubt to the strict trade unionist.

There is, however, a mean, and I should like to think that in the future some way may be found by which diplomats can combine a fair share of work with a large share of social engagements of all sorts and so really come to know what is being thought and said in the places where they reside.

Taking up work again, I found myself once more in the Eastern Department and only just in time for the revolution which broke out in Turkey in July.

The British Government was anxious to show the Young Turks good will, but I thought myself that we credited them with more virtue than they really possessed. A writer in the Italian *Corriere della Sera* well said: 'In England they seem to think that a new nation has come down from heaven: that is not the case.' The leaders of the movement were not worthy of their position and Turkey had to wait some years before she found a real man in Mustapha Kemal.

Matters were greatly complicated by the Austrian annexation of Bosnia and Herzegovina and the declaration of Bulgarian independence, undoing the work of the Treaty of Berlin. In condemning Bulgaria's declaration as a breach of Treaty Obligations we were, in my opinion, straining at a gnat, for Bulgaria was not herself a party to the Treaty of Berlin; it was impossible to maintain that Bulgaria owed perpetual allegiance to the Turks, and that she had not shown herself worthy of complete independence. A greater degree of generosity towards her claims might possibly have served us in good stead a few years later.

Glad as I was to see the Sultan's régime brought to an end, I ventured to express some views about the Young Turks that were not very pleasing to Sir Edward Grey; but he admitted afterwards, both in conversation with friends of mine and in his *Twenty-five Years*, that he had rated the Young Turks too high, and that others who knew the country were perhaps right about them.

Abdul Hamid did not at once lose his throne and, according to Fitzmaurice, appeared to accept the new position calmly and presided over his Parliament as if he had been at it all his life. Fitzmaurice indeed had a soft spot for the Sultan and thought better of him than most people; he had also a more justifiable affection for the Turkish people. Abdul Hamid, however, did not avoid deposition very long, and had to end his days in a villa at Salonica.

One friend writing from Constantinople speaks with enthusiasm of the behaviour of the people after the revolution and of the marvellous change in the life of Constantinople: 'No spies, everyone laughing and talking.'

This last phrase may one day, I hope, be quotable as an 'old and true' remark about the countries of contemporary Europe.

My connection with Turkey, however, soon came to an end, for I came up for promotion in the early part of 1909 and was made Head of the African Department.

This was a new line altogether for me, but one of great interest. A considerable part of my work was now administrative, for the Protectorate of Zanzibar was still managed by the Foreign Office, and in practice by the head of the African Department. All the African Protectorates, being technically foreign countries, had originally come under our office, and as they developed into colonies been handed over to the Colonial Office.

Zanzibar followed in 1913. One source of delight in dealing with that small island was that we were not subject to Treasury control or to the Committee of Public Accounts and so had a free hand to do what we thought was desirable. It was like running an English county on auto-cratic lines.

I believe that we were successful, and the island, which had a monopoly in cloves and derived a handsome revenue from the export, was prosperous.

Besides managing the affairs of Zanzibar we dealt with a number of administrative questions affecting tropical Africa generally, such as the traffic in arms and in liquor, as well as the measures for combating sleeping sickness and other diseases. I was once taken to see a horrible film illustrating the symptoms of sleeping sickness and showing fierce fights in a man's blood between red and white corpuscles.

As regards Zanzibar the most difficult matter with which I had to deal was the deposition of the young Sultan, Seyyid Ali, in 1911. He had been educated at Harrow, spoke English perfectly and had intelligence, but he had unfortunately acquired a taste for the wrong aspects of civilization. He was in this country during the negotiations, living in a flat off St. James's Street, and was, we heard, in a very despondent state, sitting with a revolver by his side. It was at this juncture thought proper that I should pay him a visit in the hope of making things go more smoothly. As I climbed the stairs to his apartment I thought of that revolver with considerable trepidation; actually the meeting was as amiable as that with my Kurdish friend at Therapia.

We provided the Sultan with a modest pension with which he was not seriously dissatisfied, although he did speak of a lady friend who 'really was a lady' and whom he would wish to treat with appropriate generosity.

At the end of 1909 I went to Brussels as one of the British Pleni-potentiaries at the International Arms Traffic Conference, and early in 1910 was appointed British delegate at another International Conference on the frontiers between Uganda, German East Africa and the Belgian Congo, so that I was at Brussels altogether for some months.

Before going to Brussels I had a brief holiday of ten days or so in which I took a King's Messenger's duty and went with the Foreign Office bags to St. Petersburg.

I delivered them safely, but had a rather nervous time at the Russian frontier, where there was a huge crowd in the station and much confusion. The stationmaster was very apologetic, explaining that "*Aujourd'hui nous avons deux Grandducs.*" After leaving the German frontier I felt quite as clearly that I had left Europe behind as I did on crossing the Serbian frontier.

St. Petersburg itself was grandiose: everything on a big scale: the principal streets, the palaces and the churches. I had always heard that it was a terribly expensive post, but the hotel was cheap and so were the restaurants; however, one of the Embassy staff explained that what was expensive was the way of living in Russian Society, the subscriptions to clubs, the consumption of champagne and general extravagance. The

Secretaries, some of them on small incomes, found it difficult to compete with this sort of thing and yet were expected to go everywhere.

The Ambassador at this time was Sir Arthur Nicolson, afterwards Lord Carnock. He was very fond of St. Petersburg and the Russians, but he was an incurable optimist. I went to lunch one day at the Embassy, finding my way there through a dense fog. During lunch the Ambassador was descanting on the delightful climate of the place, adding "and to-day would be a fine day too if it were not just for this fog." This remark was received with shouts from his family.

Sir Arthur's affection for Russia was evident when the Great War began and he was Under-Secretary at the Foreign Office. He used to say: "Wait till my old steam-roller gets going," though it is difficult to believe that he really imagined the army to be in a state of efficiency.

In the few days that I was at St. Petersburg I had no opportunity of forming an opinion worth anything about the country. One of the obvious things that struck me was the linguistic ability of the educated Russians; English, French and German seemed to come all alike to them, and I have heard family parties passing accidentally as it were from one language to another and not talking Russian at all.

My journey home with the bags was uneventful and soon afterwards I set out for Brussels with my wife.

We had been there a very short time when the death of King Leopold put an end to all social activities. I had by then met very few Belgian ladies, and when I went for a walk on the day after the King's death was astonished to find several widows bowing to me whom I could not at all remember to have seen before. Presently I realized that there were widows in all directions and, finally, that all the Belgian ladies had put on something like widow's weeds to mourn for their king.

I cannot say that King Leopold deserved many tears, least of all for any domestic virtues, though his management of the Congo no doubt was not thought so shocking by Belgians as by English public opinion.

The administration of the Congo obviously left much to be desired, but I was never quite satisfied that we had not exaggerated its defects after I heard that some philanthropic English body was starting a rubber enterprise of its own and that in a district where we had been led to suppose that all the time of all the natives was taken up by the State.

I daresay it was difficult to persuade Belgians of satisfactory character to go out to the Congo, for they were not, I fancy, very fond of precarious adventures. I remember hearing some Belgian friends discussing the sad fate of a young officer who was being sent to a distant post where he would assuredly be lonely and unhappy. I took for granted that he, at any rate, was bound for the Congo, but discovered eventually that his place of exile was Namur.

The Uganda frontier question which occupied us for some months was a terribly intricate one. I do not think my memory is at fault when I say that the lines of latitude had shifted so as to make things more difficult; or was it the lines of longitude? Whichever it was, our Minister, Arthur Hardinge, took it all in his stride. When the time came to open our case he spoke for two hours in French, hardly ever stopping for breath and without a note. When afterwards I expressed special astonishment at the absence of notes he said that it gave the adversary less opportunity of coming back at him.

The first German delegate, Herr Ebermaier, was more long-winded. Not only that, but he was dissatisfied with the performance of the young German diplomat who interpreted his speech into French. As soon as the interpretation was done, Ebermaier, just to make sure, began again. "*Ich darf wiederholen*" (I should like to repeat), words which we came to hate. We hated it all the more as we all, or most of us, understood German as well as French, and therefore heard the same argument four times over. Ebermaier was a civil servant of bourgeois origin. I once went for a walk with him in the course of which we passed beside an alley reserved for riders on one of the boulevards. By came an officer, cantering and splattering everybody with mud. "*Ach,*" said Ebermaier, "*Herren Offizier,*" and his tone made perfectly clear his opinion of the officer class.

When the Great War came he was Governor of the Cameroons and was chased from place to place in a way which his habits and his figure must have made exceedingly disagreeable to him.

The agreement at which we succeeded in arriving 'appeared very satisfactory to His Majesty's Government,' and they considered it as the result of very difficult and delicate negotiations carried out in a particularly able manner, and they felt that their cordial thanks were due to Sir A. Hardinge, Col. Close and Mr. J. A. C. Tilley for the eminently gratifying result of the Conference.

This 'approval' was also very satisfactory to us. It looks to me now as if the composer's enthusiasm grew as he wrote.

Sir Arthur Hardinge was a man of remarkable brilliance; having started his career as a Fellow of All Souls he ended it as Ambassador at Madrid. If he did not reach quite the highest positions it was perhaps impressiveness that he lacked. Also, he had an oddish laugh. I heard these two criticisms of our representatives at Brussels from two different Belgian friends. The first said of Hardinge: "*Je n'aime pas trop votre Ministre: à cause de son rire.*" The other said of Hardinge's successor, Frank Villiers: "*J'aime beaucoup votre Ministre: il a un si bon rire.*"

Hardinge, as may be supposed from what I have said, was a most fluent talker: sometimes a little difficult to stop and sometimes apt to begin before the flag went down. Once I was sitting with him in his study on the first floor of the Legation when the telephone bell rang downstairs in the hall. Exclaiming that it must be Van der Elst of the Foreign Office, he rushed off, and I heard him as he went down the stairs shouting: "*C'est vous,*"

M. le Chevalier, n'est ce pas; je viens tout de suite, M. le Chevalier; je vais vous expliquer."

We got on very well together and he could be a most entertaining person.

Close, now Sir Charles Close, afterwards Director General of the Ordnance Survey, President of the Royal Geographical Society and so forth, was a tower of strength on such a job as ours. He and his assistant, Captain Behrens, and I made a very happy family party.

Our Belgian collaborators were also great friends of ours; the Under-Secretary for Foreign Affairs, Van der Elst, M. Pierre Orts of the Colonial Office and Albert de Bassompierre of the Foreign Office. Van der Elst, I remember, told me that the Belgians were monarchists by conviction, while the Dutch were monarchists *de cœur*. He used often to spend his holidays in England and afterwards, on my advice, spent one of them at Minehead, where he went out with the staghounds. He told me in a letter: *"Je suis resté douze heures en selle,"* though on reflection that seems, even for the staghounds, a very long day.

Orts was enthusiastic about the Congo: *"Si quelqu'un touche à mon Congo aussitôt je m'emporte,"* he said; I feel sure that he must have done his very best by it, and my knowledge of him made me more reluctant to take abuse of the Congo administration for granted.

Bassompierre was afterwards my colleague in Tokyo and has been a lifelong friend.

One of the ceremonies which we attended in Brussels was the opening of the Colonial Museum and Exhibition at Laeken on April 30th by the young King Albert.

I quote from my diary. Close, Behrens and I went in the train to Laeken with M. Arendt, Directeur Politique at the Foreign Office, and Bassompierre. M. Arendt told me that the old Palace of Brussels, which was burned in 1720, was where the Pavilion of the Princess Clementine now is, with a terrace towards the park. This park was part of the great forest which extended from the Ardennes across Brabant, and was the natural barrier that prevents Flemings and Walloons from mingling.

At the time when the Château was burned the Austrians were in possession of the Netherlands, and the Archduchess who was living there was only with difficulty saved by a soldier, who picked her up in his arms and carried her to safety. This soldier was afterwards punished for laying hands on Her Imperial Highness. Tervueren, where the Museum is, has had a château for some nine hundred years. Charles V and all sorts of Governors of the Netherlands lived there. The Museum is fine. It is more or less a replica of the Petit Palais in the Paris Exhibition of 1900, which King Leopold much admired and asked the architect (M. Giraud) to reproduce for him. The scene under the dome was picturesque enough; Corps Diplomatique to right of the Throne, Chamber to left, functionaries further forward to right and left, with a good sprinkling of monks representing the Catholic Mission.

The king did not make a dignified entry, walking stiffly and rather awkwardly. Renkin (Colonial Secretary) made a good speech and the king read a reply with a bad accent, a bad delivery and worse gestures, as if he were digging someone in the ribs; but he read with some enthusiasm: declaring particularly that the Congo officials were "*à la hauteur de leur tâche.*" Close and I were presented to him and he said a few ordinary words.

We followed H.M. round the Museum for about two hours before escaping, but he went on till six-thirty, when there was only Hardinge and one or two others left in the entourage.

There was a map in relief which Davignon (the Foreign Minister) urged me to look at, as he had been much struck by the magnificence of the mountains round Kivu. According to the scale of the map the height of the mountains would indeed be 75,000 feet.

I renewed my acquaintance with Mgr Pacci, now Nuncio here and formerly Apostolic Delegate at Constantinople. Like me, he does not believe in any very deep change in Turkey since our day.

Sunday, May 1st. Van der Elst came to take us and the Germans to see the Serres de Laeken; very fine: a wonderful collection of cinerarias, also gloxinias, and a beautiful glass gallery some hundreds of yards long lined with magnificent geraniums, a blaze of colour, with a roof hung with fuchsias and heliotrope; a wonderful coup d'œil. Then to the Colonial Garden to see rubber plants and other Congo things. Van der Elst told me of King Leopold's love for small rooms and plain living; he used to come and work with the king in such a small room, and when time came for *déjeuner* it was served on the table at which they worked. He said it was impossible to discuss things with the king: he would listen to no argument, however just. This king is quite prepared to discuss. He sees everything, all the 'pieces' of our discussions for instance, but apparently goes only by impressions, which makes negotiations difficult for his Ministers. Ebermaier told me the (German) Crown Prince was considered intelligent and original and his popularity was increasing and his manners becoming less rough.

On our off days, which were many, we visited most of the Belgian towns: Louvain, Antwerp, Liège, Ghent and Bruges, also Waterloo.

Bruges is, of course, impressively old, but I did not quite reach the state of mind of Mlle Rossignon, a well-known schoolmistress of Brussels. She told me she had been on an excursion to Bruges, but when she found herself in one of the older streets: "*J'ai eu tellement peur que j'ai dû rentrer tout de suite à la gare.*"

We went a good deal to the theatre, so pleasantly cheap, and among the plays I saw several times one which amused me exceedingly: *Le Mariage de Mlle Beulemans.* Beulemans is a rich Brussels brewer, with a charming daughter and a well-bred and intellectual young Parisian as a kind of apprentice; and the play is a satire on middle-class Belgian manners and customs, which was very instructive. The play was afterwards given in London.

I cannot leave Brussels without speaking of the charm and hospitality of Lord and Lady Granville. He was First Secretary at the Legation and endowed with a delightfully sunny disposition.

My next visit to Brussels was in the early part of 1912 when I went with Charles Strachey to attend the African Liquor Conference. This was less eventful than my previous visit. It is, however, perhaps worth mentioning that we found our German colleagues on this occasion sensible and helpful, especially Count Zech, a former Governor of Togoland.

Our Minister, Sir Francis Villiers, had spent nearly all his life in the Foreign Office until, at the age of fifty-four, he had been made Minister at Lisbon. In 1911 he changed places with Arthur Hardinge. He was extraordinarily conscientious and spent unnecessarily long hours in his study, from which Lady Villiers used to beg me to extract him, but he was, I feel sure, universally liked.

In the interval between these two visits the Coronation of King George V had taken place, on which occasion I acted as one of the Gold Staff Officers in the Abbey. We had to be there by six and were entertained at breakfast before and at luncheon after the ceremony by the Duke of Norfolk, the Earl Marshal.

Here is the invitation:

> The Earl Marshal requests the honour of the company of the Gold Staff Officers at breakfast at the State Officers' Court, House of Lords, at five o'clock on Thursday, June 22nd, and at luncheon after the ceremony of the Coronation.

Five o'clock is an earlyish hour for a breakfast party, but we all managed it. Hubert Montgomery, who happened to sit next the Earl Marshal, had a bad egg; if we may believe reports then current the chicken which put its head out of the shell caught sight of a Peer passing by and exclaimed: "Why, there's old Wemyss!" If we may assume that they were contemporaries, they were ninety-three.

The only excitement that came my way was the occupation of seats in my section of the nave by the Abyssinian Mission, who were dressed in lions' skins. It was with some hesitation that I ushered ladies in satin court gowns into the adjoining seats.

Abyssinia, by the way, came within my province as Head of the African Department, and while Menelek was Conquering Lion of the Tribe of Judah, the country was comparatively flourishing.

Another state with which my department was in relations was the negro republic of Liberia. The Republic was represented in London by M. Crommelin, a Dutchman, who was very popular in this country, particularly at the St. James's Club, the haunt of diplomats, and served his employers admirably. A Liberian Mission came over about this time, including the

Foreign Minister, and I met them at dinner at Mr. Crommelin's house. I sat next the Foreign Minister, who was of course jet black, had lost an eye and told me he was very wild in his youth, which conjured up rather a grim vision. Liberia is a sort of social experiment, but in my day, at any rate, the administration left a good deal to be desired.

One of our great preoccupations was the conduct of negotiations with Germany in regard to the possible future of the Portuguese colonies: the policy of H.M. Government met with a good deal of criticism at the time, but owing to the war the proposed arrangements came to nothing.

Of the Congo I have already spoken. This country had always severely criticized the Belgian administration and had not spared King Leopold himself. Possibly, as I have indicated, we were sometimes too severe: philanthropists, however conscientious, may be, let us say, a little inclined to produce the best budget of horrors they can compose. The Congo, originally a free state, had been declared a Belgian colony in 1908, but in view of the state of things which existed then we deferred recognition of the change till 1913. This recognition, when it did come, gave great satisfaction in Brussels and a Belgian friend wrote to me of the graceful way in which H.M. Government expressed themselves and of his satisfaction at the renewed cordiality between our two countries.

Meanwhile, although I had no official connection with things Turkish, I followed the fortunes of that country with profound interest. Nearly all our letters from friends there have something bad to say of the Young Turks. Sir Harry Lamb, then Consul General at Salonica, had welcomed the revolution and hoped for the best from the new Government, though he had his doubts. As time went on he saw that things were going all wrong and in July, 1910, he writes that the Young Turks have entirely gone off the rails: "*perdu leurs boussoles*" (compasses) is his expression, alluding to the reference mark on documents emanating from the Sublime Porte which was called a boussola. 'When one thinks of the smug Jeunes Turcs who have brought the country to this pass one's talons simply itch to get a grip on them.' That was written after the Balkan War had brought all its horrors upon the people of the peninsula.

In June, 1912, he had said: "The Turks now are talking about 1855 and 1878 and protesting their friendship for England, the surest sign that they feel themselves in serious peril. From 1909 to 1912 they did nothing but revile us and brag of the friendship of Germany. Now one hears very little of German friendship, though they still trust to Rumania to stab the Bulgars in the back in case of need."

He also mentions the absolute determination of the Bulgars to accept no frontier which did not include both Salonica and Monastir, a determination which was frustrated in 1913 and will doubtless be frustrated again.

The Bulgars, though they generally had a fair case to start with, spoiled their record by their cruelty, and emulated the Turks in the art of massacre.

According to Lamb they deserved no consideration from us, and certainly they got none.

Of the Mussulmans in the Salonica district he writes: 'Those that have escaped massacre are literally stripped of everything they possessed and will die by the thousand during the winter. We have 30,000 at least on our hands here, and those in the towns, homeless and breadless as they may be, are happy compared with those who remain up country with no means of subsistence beyond what they may earn by picking the vermin off each other's backs."

When the second Balkan War broke out I happened to find myself leaving the office at the same moment as Sir Edward Grey and we walked together for some way. He expressed his horror at this renewal of warfare and said: "Of course all those countries will be completely ruined financially." We did not realize then that countries carry on war somehow, money or no money, and when the Great War began experts hastened to say that it could not last six months as the money would not hold out.

Nevertheless, when the China-Japan war began in 1937 a Cabinet Minister was astonished when I said it would certainly not (as he hoped) be over in six months for lack of money.

To go back a year or two, my wife and I made another Italian tour in 1911. We spent a week or more in Florence and a week in Siena, also a few days in Bologna. Florence is big enough to absorb tourists, Siena is not, consequently it comes within my category of unreal places. Everyone has showered so much praise on Italy as a paradise for travellers that I may perhaps be forgiven for looking at the black side of things. One cause of cavilling to me was the high walls which so often shut out all view of the much lauded scenery of Florence and its neighbourhood. Writers do let themselves go. We had with us a charming book about Siena by Mr. Hutton, but when he told us of the road to il Monistero winding down through the olive gardens and vineyards, and we found that actually it led us through a somewhat dreary market garden, we were not pleased. Bologna we liked very much; it was itself, and it provided excellent white wine of which some was sent after us to England.

In October, 1913, I left the African Department on being made Chief Clerk of the Foreign Office.

CHAPTER VII

CHIEF CLERK OF THE FOREIGN OFFICE IS AN ANCIENT TITLE DATING FROM the eighteenth century and I was proud to bear it. The duties cover all the financial business of the Foreign Office, Diplomatic and Consular Services, and, roughly speaking, all the house-keeping questions. The Chief Clerk is, or is not, according to his nature, a bugbear to all three branches of the Service: at any rate, to all those members of it who consider that their pay is inadequate or fear that their accounts may be examined with too scrupulous accuracy. By this I do not mean to suggest that such accounts are in any way open to suspicion, but merely that officials not trained in book-keeping are fallible.

As to inadequacy of pay my predecessor kept a list of the posts in different parts of the world whose incumbents had proved to their own satisfaction, or at any rate asserted as a well-known fact, that their particular post was notoriously the most expensive in the world. When I saw the list the number was over forty.

As to account keeping, I always have in mind an *obiter dictum* of one of my staff who, having dealt with the accounts of Diplomats and Consuls all his official life, knew the service pretty well. He said: "People sometimes assure me that men who make the most foolish mistakes over their accounts really possess great ability. I never believe it." Allowing something for pardonable exaggeration I think this a truth to be remembered. Really competent people do not make stupid mistakes at any time.

The worst part of a Chief Clerk's duties was his annual appearance before the Committee of Public Accounts of the House of Commons. Some of their probable questions could be foreseen and the answers looked up: some could not: and I have more than once been stumped by questions to which I had to devise an answer at a moment's notice, hoping it was more or less accurate. The Committee were kind to me, especially as the Foreign Office is not a great spending department, and I remember a whimsical smile from the present Lord Rhayader when he caught me inventing an explanation of some supposed horror; he said nothing.

My staff were not members of what is called the Diplomatic Establishment of the Foreign Office. My assistant had been recruited by some old method of special examination and the rest were second division clerks who had taken book-keeping in their examination and were a remarkably capable and loyal set.

I am glad to think that I soon made one change of principle in our work. The practice was for accounts from officials all over the world to be carefully examined and all doubts and queries cleared up before they were settled. This might mean that a man on the other side of the world had to wait months for payment, even though in an account of a hundred pounds or more there was only an item of a pound or two in doubt. I arranged that in such cases the bulk of the account should be settled at once.

A more serious problem was my relation to the Treasury and my responsibility for the guardianship of the purse. Some of my predecessors had, I thought, leaned too much to the Treasury side: that is, they tried to avoid any expenditure which could be avoided rather than consider what expenditure was really wise. I leaned a little to the latter view of my duty. Before long, however, the war broke out and all precedents were apt to go by the board. The war problems as they affected me were the necessity of an enormous additional staff for service either at home or abroad; the finding of space in the office to house all these people; the demands for extra pay or allowances to meet the increased cost of living in all parts of the world; the question of foreign exchange.

The first special duty which came my way was to return to the office on the night when war was declared and join with a number of my colleagues in writing out a thousand times the words: 'His Majesty mindful that a state of war exists between this country and Germany' which had been omitted from some proclamation.

We were there at eleven o'clock when the state of war began, and soon afterwards Lord Drogheda, who had been over to the Admiralty, came in and cheered us, fallaciously, with the news that we had got the *Breslau* and *Goeben* all right.

Two minor problems which beset me early in the war were the necessity of sending messengers to France with bags of gold to discharge various accounts for which French people refused to accept cheques, and the necessity of providing ten thousand goats a week (which sounds fantastic) for the Indian troops in France. To my surprise it turned out that there was no difficulty about this.

When the war started the return of the Diplomatic and Consular staff from Germany and Austria and later from Turkey gave us a considerable nucleus of extra staff for the Foreign Office. The Western Department, dealing with Western Europe, of which Eyre Crowe as Assistant Under-Secretary was in charge, became automatically the War Department.

I believe that his views did not always suit the Secretary of State. Anyhow, having been obliged to take a rest of a week or so, he came back to find himself transferred to a new department for dealing with matters of trade out of which gradually grew the great Ministry of Blockade under Lord Robert Cecil.

Many other big new departments also grew up for whose finance we were responsible; the Foreign Trade department, Prisoners of War department, Passport department, which grew from one man as it was before the war to some two hundred, the War Trade Intelligence department and one or two others, not to mention departments within the Foreign Office itself such as the department of Political Intelligence and the News department.

The duty of recruiting for these departments fell largely to me. There was no lack of applicants for posts, but we restricted ourselves severely to those who were over age or unfit. We had in fact a list of diseases which would have done credit to a hospital. Moreover, we had a flat rate of pay for the men: £200 a year. I assumed, not always with their complete concurrence, that they had other means and came to us in order to do some patriotic work. To a few who reached responsible positions we eventually gave rather more, but whatever crimes we committed I do not think extravagance was one.

At a later period of the war our establishments were inspected by a committee of which the Chief was Mr. Bernard Mallet. Another member was a civil servant rejoicing in the name of Jabstrebwski; I was able to help my colleagues by circulating a minute to the effect that this name was pronounced in the ordinary way, i.e. Jamsky.

They only found fault with one branch of the Foreign Office, namely the Foreign Trade Department which was established in Stafford House, and over which our control was more theoretical than practical. There they did find a rather excessive number of clerks in the registries. I was somewhat concerned about this, but Leverton Harris, who was one of our Parliamentary Under-Secretaries, comforted me with the remark that every committee must justify itself by some criticism.

One fear, naturally, was that I might unawares let in an enemy alien or a quisling, but I never heard any suggestion that this happened.

Up till that time no woman had been seen in the office on duty except a few typists. I had to engage large numbers. I cannot refrain from repeating one favourite story about them which I have told before. In the earlier days a very large number of them were concentrated in one of the vast reception rooms of the Foreign Office, under the supervision of an extremely capable and energetic lady. One evening about eight o'clock a man who wanted some information from these ladies went to see if by chance they were still at work. He opened the door and to his amazement saw that the place was empty except for the Superintendent, who was standing on a chair in the middle. "What *are* you doing?" he asked. "Oh, Mr. X, there is a mouse in the room."

Among the best men whom we recruited in various capacities were a number of University Lecturers and Fellows of Colleges. I believe that during the war, in other offices besides ours, the universities came into their own. The public has, or had, always been prone to regard 'Professors' as people who in the ordinary business of life were incompetent and futile beyond measure. It was now discovered that this was the reverse of the truth; they were not only clever but able. On the other hand, whereas the Public had often expressed a wish to see Government offices run by business men, and on business lines, it was discovered that business men were, taking it by and large, not more businesslike than other people. Another discovery made by business men themselves was that civil servants, like University Dons, were often very intelligent people, and a number of Foreign Office men were offered places in business houses.

I think of two business men in particular, one, a member of Parliament, who presided over one of the innumerable committees that looked into our affairs. I happened to mention the fact that most of us had to take work home in the evening. He seemed quite unable to realize that this was simply because we could not keep the office open half the night; he thought it was

LADY TILLEY
Mushroom Picking at Nara

COURT MOURNING
Author, Lady Tilley, R. M. Tilley

because men played about during the day and expressed himself as much shocked. The other was a gentleman who sat on a committee over which I presided. He was shocked at my saying that some procedure which was suggested would be difficult to carry out. He told us that he never admitted the use of the word difficult. I tried to visualize a state of mind which ignored all difficulties, but I believe he was merely improving on the theory which some people profess that for them impossibilities do not exist. He afterwards became a bankrupt.

The staffing of posts abroad was somewhat more difficult than the staffing of the office, for in an Embassy or Legation men have to, or ought to, fit themselves into what may be called its family life. In former days, indeed, an Ambassador spoke officially of his staff as his 'family.' The same idea prevailed in my day.

I always regarded as one of my best choices that of Ralph Wigram. He had been attached to our Military Attaché at Petrograd, but had been invalided home. I sent him to Washington, where he was, I believe, a little lost at first, but as time went on he showed that he had character and brains as well as charm. After the war he came into the regular diplomatic service and made a distinguished position for himself in Paris before he, alas, died at an early age. He wrote to me from Washington that he was 'really rather terrified' when the Chancery told him that they worked from 9 a.m. to 1.30, 3 p.m. to 7.30 and again after dinner till the early hours of the morning. In another letter he speaks of the terrific energy of Robert Hudson, who was head of the Chancery, and who to-day as Minister of Agriculture is as terrifically energetic as he was five-and-twenty years ago.

What, in spite of my business friend, was difficult, but not, as it proved, impossible, was to find room for all our immense staff in the Foreign Office building. I turned out almost all the solitary occupants of large rooms, used the reception rooms and the resident clerk's rather noble apartments for office work and generally played havoc with our internal arrangements. For this purpose I sought the help of the Office of Works, which was given freely but not always brilliantly. When I asked them to turn a huge room in the Tower, too much out of the way for an office, into an apartment for the Head Office Keeper, they proposed to do so simply by dividing it into two. The poor man, who had a wife and two children, would have found himself living in two rooms each some twenty-five feet by twenty. I insisted on making four rooms and a passage and they graciously gave way.

The difficulty of enabling our staff abroad to meet the increased cost of living and the immense vagaries of exchange was one for discussion with the Treasury. At first they were inclined to say that the matter must be treated on some general system applicable all over the world. This would have meant that a wretched man in Sweden, where the exchange went violently against us, must be left to struggle against adversity until we had devised some remedy which would be equally applicable to a different set of circum-

F

stances in, say, Costa Rica. Eventually the Treasury was reasonable and agreed to treat hard cases at short notice.

As Chief Clerk I had little if anything to do with diplomatic negotiations or with the policy of the Ministry of Blockade, but in the present war I am frequently reminded of the abuse which was showered on the Foreign Office between 1914 and 1918 even when almost the whole world had come in on our side. Critics were astounded that those responsible for the blockade treated the United States or Sweden, for instance, so tenderly. That it might be bad policy to exasperate feeling in either of those two countries did not occur to many writers.

Once during the 'slump' years, travelling on the L.N.E.R., we passed a place where the company were carrying on some improvement on a considerable scale. A man in my compartment said to his friend: "Is it not extraordinary that just at this time when we are all urged to be as economical as possible the company should be spending all this money?" His friend heartily agreed. Five minutes later the first speaker looked up again from his paper and said: "I wonder whether the company perhaps have some reason for spending so much money."

This observation showed, I thought, a wisdom which is unusual among the critical public.

In 1916 a committee was appointed under the Chairmanship of Lord Selborne to consider the reform of the Diplomatic Service. As Chief Clerk I was a member.

The two great changes which the committee made were the amalgamation of the Diplomatic and Foreign Office Services and the payment of allowances to men serving abroad, designed to enable them to live in the manner expected of them without private means. Some people, not I think any of those on the committee, wanted similar allowances to be given to men serving in the Foreign Office so that they might have the same social opportunities as their colleagues abroad. Critics holding an entirely opposite view said that everyone in London had the social opportunities they wanted. The latter theory is quite erroneous, but it would have been impossible to put clerks in the Foreign Office on an entirely different footing from men in other Government offices.

Since then it has often been asserted that men still cannot live abroad on the allowances assigned to them. From what I have seen I disagree. I believe the allowances are sufficient, but I was not Chief Clerk for five years without discovering that no salary from £50 to £5,000 is beyond cavil.

The amalgamation of the two branches of the Service also met with some criticism. Eyre Crowe, for instance, said that from the rank of First Secretary on, that is from about the age of forty, men should be assigned permanently to one branch or the other. His general opinions being what they were I have no doubt that he would have kept all the best men in the Foreign Office: this would have meant that they would have seen less able colleagues promoted to desirable posts abroad which they would have liked, while they had, willy nilly, to remain at home. Such a rule could not have been maintained.

This brings up the constantly recurring question whether men are made for the service or the service for the men. The first sounds right, but we must have bait with which to catch good men. Personally I feel sure that interchange throughout the service is the right plan. When Sir Thomas Sanderson retired and was succeeded by Sir Charles Hardinge, as he then was, *The Times,* after praising Sanderson's many great qualities, said: 'It is hard to acquire a realistic grasp of world politics by a life-long study of despatches at home.' This is true. There is one small danger on the other side of the account. A man who has served for two or three years in Ruritania is apt to consider himself, or to be considered, an expert on that country, but when he has left Ruritania and spent a couple of years at home he may no longer be in fact an expert on current politics in that country; yet his word may be weighed against and outweigh that of the man on the spot. Men abroad have sometimes felt this to be so and been unhappy about it. Lord Curzon, though he had never lived abroad, had visited many Eastern countries long before he became Secretary of State and did not always remember how long.

Lately I have seen it stated in the Press that in future there will be no room for incompetents in the Diplomatic Service, and that no post can be considered unimportant since they are all potential sources of widespread trouble.

This assumes that the Foreign Office has been in the habit of sending incompetent men to certain posts and that a star cast is possible. It also assumes that we can find someone with an unerring instinct for the right men in the right post and a heart hard enough to let him eject generally competent men who have not come up to expectations. As to this last requisite things are less easy than they were. In my day diplomatic pensions were governed by an Act which enabled men to retire on a pension after ten years. The pension was small, but the rule was a very valuable one for those who had to manage the service. I always clung to the Act, but eventually someone in the Treasury with a passion for uniformity assimilated the diplomatic service to the Home Civil Service, which meant that a man could only receive a pension when he was sixty, except in cases of ill health.

It is all very well to say that you must send your brilliant men to small posts as well as great; the United States do in fact do something of that sort, but then they often send men from outside the diplomatic service who are not brilliant at all to very important posts, so they are not a safe guide. Actually, if you send Jones who has greatly distinguished himself as second in command at a big European Embassy to a small post in Central America, he will not like it; you will not persuade him that it may be the starting point of a world war, and he will be wasted and disgruntled. I do not believe that any Secretary of State wilfully sends incompetent men anywhere, but he doubtless says to himself, or his advisers do, that Brown has never had a chance of distinguishing himself, is quite a sensible man, and ought to do very well in a quiet post, and in most cases he does.

Soon after Lord Curzon became Secretary of State there were, owing to the conclusion of peace and the resumption of diplomatic relations which had been broken off, a great number of Embassies and Legations to be filled. He had a small meeting in his room to discuss the best way of doing this and listened patiently to all that had to be said. About one or two men he had had opportunities of forming his own opinion, but he certainly did his best to make a satisfactory selection.

Yet another committee sat while I was Chief Clerk to consider the formation of what is now called the Commercial Diplomatic Service. We had for many years had Commercial Attachés at a few important posts, but it was now proposed to form a regular branch of the service with men of various grades at all, or nearly all, the Capitals. I was myself in favour of being rather modest about our proposals. Some people, on the other hand, thought that every Commercial Secretary must have a proper office and a proper staff under him, meaning that things should be done on a big scale. I was rather afraid that in that case an undue proportion of the Commercial Secretary's time would be taken up in administration and I thought a man might get on better in this class of work with a room in the Embassy and a clerk to himself. The result has been, I believe, sufficiently modest to avoid what I feared.

One of the questions raised was the advisability of appointing as Commercial Secretaries not members of the Consular Service, but men from outside with a business training and business experience. This may sound very wise, but in fact we should be likely to get only men who had not been very successful in business. It is most unlikely that a man who saw his way to a fair career in business at home, not to mention a handsome income, would abandon it in order to take a humbler post as third grade Secretary in a small Capital or even something higher. As it turned out there were at the outset very few suitable candidates from the business world, and although the door was by no means closed against them I believe that of those now serving who have not graduated from the Consular Service few have actually been in business.

At the end of the war we made what I may call a sudden and temporary innovation by promoting several of the most promising second division clerks to the Consular Service. I believed, and believe, that this was a good precedent because the men were caught young. They have certainly answered expectations. If you wait till a man has been doing competent routine work for twenty years or so, however deserving he may be, it is usually too late to change him. There were occasional transfers from the Foreign Office to the Consular Service of men fairly high up, who were doing really responsible work, and that has certainly justified itself in some cases, but I believe the best plan is to take the young ones.

Some interest was taken in the schemes for the reform of the Commercial Attaché and Consular Service by Lord Brabourne, who though several years senior to me had been with me both at Eton and King's. He made some rather startling proposals, upon which I wrote to him that my first recollection of him at Eton was of being told with awe by a fellow lower boy: "Hugessen is breaking White Thomson's teapot with a hammer in lower passage" (White Thomson with whom he messed being the late Bishop of Ely). Brabourne wrote back: 'Perhaps you are right in supposing that the former teapot breaker is a bit of an iconoclast, but teapots and other things which fail to serve their proper purpose may just as well be broken and replaced by a samovar or other more effective instrument." I believe he was in favour of business Consuls. Traders generally used to be rather afraid of them and thought the enterprising man could do his own work better than others could do it for him.

Quite a different task from any I have mentioned was that of giving formal evidence in the trial of Roger Casement. I had merely to make some statements about his Consular career, but I was particularly interested in view of his well-known work in the Congo. During the trial someone gave me a copy of the petition in his favour which was being circulated at the time. The language used was full of eloquence, based, not so much on Casement's own merits, but on the terrible results which his execution would bring about in Ireland. His execution would turn the scale against reconciliation to such an extent that recovery could not take place in our generation.

Similar language, by the way, was used about the fearful danger to our position in India if we were hard on the Sultan of Turkey. The maintenance of the Caliphate in all its glory was said to be indispensable. Unfortunately for the Sultan the Turks themselves thought otherwise.

Holidays, naturally, during the war were few and far between. In the spring of 1917, however, I had not exactly a holiday, but a brief change of atmosphere.

The Government had organized a system for enabling distinguished foreigners to see what was going on at the front. They had acquired a house somewhere behind the front line which was known as the Château des Visiteurs. There was a Colonel in charge of the château and a few officers who acted as cicerones to the visitors. Each party was accompanied by someone from the Foreign Office who saw that their stay in France and their journey to and fro went without incident.

With one such party I went to France. My charges were a Russian Socialist who had been exiled or had fled from Russia, and an American Pacifist. I cannot recall the name of the latter gentleman, but I believe he was a well-known journalist. I suppose, and I hope, that some valuable propaganda was achieved, and I believe that the American did to some extent modify some of his opinions, particularly about German behaviour. The revolution in Russia took place just about this time and the Russian assured me, not very accurately, that it would make no difference to Russian participation in the war. Our particular cicerone was I believe a musician of distinction in private life and he took great care of us and showed us a great deal.

My recollections are somewhat heterogeneous but none the less vivid.

On one occasion we came to what had been a trench in the front line where there were still a handful of men knocking about. The Germans were at that moment retiring and we saw the flames of a burning town which marked their passage. A boy of eighteen or nineteen who was one of the party in the trench told us, waving his arm in the direction of the German Army, that that morning he had been 'all round that bit of country' and could not find the Germans anywhere. I liked the idea of the boy taking a morning stroll to find the German Army.

Another incident was the saddest which I met with. We were walking along a road below which on one side there had been severe fighting the day before. Again there was a young boy wandering over the ground. Presently he joined us and we asked what he had been doing. "My pal was killed there yesterday and I cannot find where they buried him." He, if anyone, had tears in his voice.

We went to Albert and Ypres and Kemmel Hill, from which we looked down on the German lines, and we drove along roads with a sort of curtain of camouflage stuff along the side which looked as if it were a very inadequate attempt at protecting the road from the fire of the enemy. We saw a number of German prisoners, who looked to me to be miserably clad, and one day I saw a German soldier, kneeling dead by the side of the road. His tunic, too, looked wretchedly thin. I pointed out the dead man to our American friend, who said: "Dear me: you are much more observant than I am." I thought that in fact he was hardly an observer at all.

One place which impressed itself particularly on my mind was the site of the village of Pozières. There was nothing but a little board stuck in the ground, inscribed Pozières, to show what had been there. In another village there were ruined walls and an arm-chair or two. While we were there a company of our men arrived with a young officer who was delighted to find such fine quarters.

We intended to have a flight in one of the comparatively rare aeroplanes, but for some reason this could not be arranged. We saw a few aeroplanes about and one German aeroplane being fired on from our lines: a young officer who happened to be with us at the moment observed that "they had apparently run out an Archie." Warfare in the air was in a very embryo state.

What interested the American most of all was a hospital where wonderful things had been done to repair the most fearful injuries to the head. We were shown ghastly photographs of patients taken when they arrived and then the patients themselves were brought in to show how effective the restoration had been. This greatly impressed our visitors.

We had rather a rough passage on the way home and it was only too obvious that the British soldier was not always a good sailor. On the way over we had found General Haig on board. I say we 'found' him because there seemed to be no sort of parade or fuss made over him. On both journeys we had a destroyer somewhere near and I reflected on the apparently extreme discomfort of travelling in such vessels in anything but the finest weather.

Finally, through everything from the moment of leaving London to the moment of return the Russian and the American talked incessantly about everything but the war.

Another but briefer war expedition which I made in January of 1917 was with a party from the Foreign Office arranged by Guy Locock to go to Birmingham at the invitation of Mr. Dudley Docker to see some of the first tanks. I had a drive in a tank round the ground where they were kept in much secrecy, and was taken over various ditches and other obstacles without mishap. Not long before a General had had a similar drive and had fallen out through the open door when the tank bumped over a bank. What pleased us most was Mr. Docker's lamentation that having actually built the tanks he was not allowed to go to his own ground to see them except with a permit from the officer commanding the guard. That officer was George Grossmith. He (and we) thought that savoured of musical comedy.

Ordinarily my work was concerned with civilian matters.

One of the branches of the service in which I had always taken much interest, both before, during and after my Constantinople years, was the Levant Consular Service.

This service, to which Lamb and Fitzmaurice belonged, included and had always included many able men, but it was particularly distinguished in the matter of linguistic talent. The competitive examination for entry into the service entailed such talent. The obligatory subjects included French and Latin and the optional Ancient Greek, Italian and Spanish, German, Russian and Arabic. Ordinarily all candidates took Latin, Greek, French, German and Italian or Spanish. Those who were successful were sent to the university for two years, and then, as I used to say, learned seven other languages worse than the first. Actually they had to take Turkish, Persian, Arabic, French and Russian. Originally they were sent alternatively to Oxford and Cambridge, but as this meant that neither university could make satisfactory arrangements I succeeded in giving Cambridge a monopoly, as the authorities there were very keen about the students. This was due largely to Professor E. J. Browne, the great Persian scholar, but Mr. Roberts of Caius, the Secretary of the University Appointments Board, also took a great deal of trouble over them.

After their two years at Cambridge they were distributed, as required, over the Turkish Empire, which then included the Arabic-speaking countries of Asia, Persia, Egypt and Morocco. Later on, when the Turkish Empire broke up, I arranged to include Russia in the service.

The work done by these men was invaluable and their thorough knowledge of the languages of the Middle East enabled them to deal as effectively as possible with the situation in their respective spheres. Owing to our treaty engagements and our general policy in regard to Turkish affairs our Consular officers in the Ottoman Empire dealt not only with trade matters as Consuls do elsewhere but with political affairs. They had to do what little they could to mitigate the hardships so often endured by the Sultan's Christian subjects.

That state of things has come to an end now, when conditions in North Africa and the Middle East are assumed to wear, and to some extent do wear, a more roseate hue.

All this is really preliminary to an expression of my satisfaction in thinking that the students were grateful for the interest which I took in their doings. Towards the end of December I had a letter from one of them which rather took my breath away as coming from the latest recruit to a more or less high-up official, but nevertheless gave me much pleasure. The writer says:

'I am sure the other students would wish to join me in thanking you for the interest you always so kindly show in our small lives. You have a character for being "human" to a degree which bids fair to bring us all swarming round you in the busy days of August.'

This sort of tribute is surely worth while.

Another institution connected with the East in which I took a private as well as official interest was the School of Oriental Studies, on the Governing Body of which I had been appointed Foreign Office representative in November, 1913.

It had long been a matter of reproach that this country was behind others, especially Germany, in the provision made for the study of Oriental languages, whereas our Imperial interests demanded that we should be ahead of all European countries. The establishment of the school by charter on June 5th, 1916, removed this reproach.

An Act of Parliament passed in 1912 had conveyed to the school the premises of the moribund London Institution in Finsbury Circus. The transfer included not only the fine building but a noble library including many books on Oriental subjects.

The school was opened by the King on February 23rd, 1917.

Under the direction of Sir Denison Ross, the school made an excellent start and has now been incorporated in London University, having meanwhile left its first splendid home.

When the war came to an end and the representatives of all nations assembled at Versailles to discuss the Peace, Lord Hardinge and a large staff from the Foreign Office went to Paris to establish a sort of second Foreign Office there.

I had nothing to do with that business and was never in Paris during the course of the negotiations, but I have always suspected that the prodigious number of experts of all kinds who were there must have been somewhat in the way of progress. The Congress, or whatever it might be called, could not go on for years and years, and to me it has been sometimes a source of wonder that in some six months any sort of Peace Treaty was achieved. As to the terms of the various Treaties much has been said, but it is sufficiently obvious, among other things, that it was impossible to upset completely the work done by history, or by natural and national developments, during hundreds of years and expect Europe to settle down quietly in its new shape. Nationalities were suddenly revealed to the astonished delegates, so I imagine, of which they had never heard, and if these nationalities were to be disentangled it could only have been done satisfactorily, though that is not a very good word, on the plan adopted by the Turks of ejecting all alien races from their midst.

Meanwhile at the Foreign Office the fort was held by Lord Curzon as Acting Secretary of State, with Sir Ronald Graham as Acting Under-Secretary and myself as Acting Assistant Under-Secretary. I was only too delighted to be associated with Graham, who was a very old friend. I laugh when I look at the Foreign Office list of 1919 and note the departments which professed to be under my supervision: the American, the Far Eastern, the Treaty, the Library, the department of Political Intelligence, the News department, the Prize Court department. There were others not ascribed to me with which I also had a connection, such as the War Trade Intelligence department and the War Trade Statistical department and the Historical Section under Dr. Prothero, formerly of King's. About most of these I knew very little, but they were full of men of great ability, many of whose names are now familiar to readers of all sorts of serious literature: Edwyn Bevan, A. J. Toynbee, Stephen Gaselee, Eric Maclagan, John Bailey, Geoffrey Butler were in the Political Intelligence and News departments. John Buchan was in some independent position and was described as Director of Information; all the same he was highly pleased when I told him that his books were favourite reading at my son's preparatory school: that he said was the kind of popularity he liked best.

Lord Curzon, who became Secretary of State, *de jure*, later in the year, had the reputation of being a difficult man to serve. To me he was very kind and I enjoyed working under him. He was occasionally querulous, though not I think often in a really bad temper, and he said things which to his surprise annoyed people a good deal. Although he sometimes thought proper to be severe I do not believe that he was out to hurt.

When he was supposed to be angry it sometimes fell to me to appease him. "The Marquess," said the Private Secretaries one day, "is in such a temper: do go in and put things right." I did, though I have no recollection of the cause of his excitement. I believe, however, that it was on this occasion that another little breeze sprang up for a few minutes. He was busy with some file of papers and I meanwhile was looking out of the window. Suddenly he exclaimed: "This is really too bad; this is intolerable; such things cannot be allowed." I asked what had happened. "Why here is a letter from the Foreign Office full of insufferable nonsense and the man has the audacity to say that he is directed by the Marquess Curzon of Kedleston to say such things." I explained to him, what he of course knew perfectly well, that, unfortunately for him, he was responsible for every letter that issued from the Foreign Office, and I saw no way of mending matters.

He sometimes exaggerated a little his own trouble and difficulties in getting through his work. On one occasion he was to attend a dinner given to celebrate the conclusion of his agreement with Persia, and deliver an epoch-making speech. When I left him about seven-thirty he said he must go home at once as he had not yet thought about that speech; I could not quite swallow that. Unfortunately, when the speech was delivered it turned out that no shorthand reporter was present, whereupon he insisted that the newspapers, or news agency, should send one to his house the following morning when he would make the speech (an affair of three-quarters of an hour or more) over again.

On another occasion he took the chair at a Government dinner in honour of a Chilian Special Mission for which I had collected the guests. The day before he had a sudden idea that no suitably important people had been invited, whereas if he had been consulted it would have been very different. Ultimately I was able to assure him that all was well as it was.

When the time came for his speech he told us that though he had travelled much, Chile was one of the few countries which he had never visited, greatly as he had always wished to do so. He had thought so much of the beauties of Santiago, and the long road winding up into the mountains from which one could look back over glorious views, and so on and so on. Personally I very soon realized that all this was taken out of a detective story which I too had just read, and in which the murderer had escaped by the road so eloquently described by the Marquess; I hoped no one else had read it, least of all the Chileans.

One of the guests I had collected for this dinner was Dr. Ryle, then Dean of Westminster, and a former fellow of King's. Next day the Chileans were to lay a wreath on the tomb of the Unknown Soldier in the Abbey, and Dr. Ryle promised that if I would produce the music of the Chilean National Anthem he would have it played on the organ. I succeeded somehow in obtaining the music and the effect was admirable.

The Chilean Mission was invited to a private luncheon at Buckingham Palace, to which I had the honour of being bidden, and there was also a dinner about the same time to Senhor Epitacio Pessoa, the President-elect of Brazil, who was in Europe at the time of his election, as representative of Brazil at Versailles.

As he was not actually President there was some doubt as to how he should be treated, but we followed the example of Italy and Belgium in giving him full honours. The only person who was not entirely satisfied was Mlle Pessoa, a very young girl, who found herself taken in to dinner at Rome by a Royalty of over eighty, at Brussels by a dignitary of much the same age and at a banquet in London (not the Palace banquet) by the Lord Mayor.

When I was presented to Senhor Epitacio Pessoa (Sr. Epitacio, as he would be called in Brazil), I little thought that I was shortly to have the honour of his much closer acquaintance, and I think I may say friendship, when I became Ambassador at Rio.

Another potentate who came to London and was entertained at a State dinner about the same time was the young Shah, a youth with what is I think spoken of in the case of important people as a full habit of body. His reign was short, and I find it difficult to believe that this was a disaster for his people.

While the Versailles Conference was in progress Ronald Graham took a month's leave, and I temporarily acted as Head of the office. Lord Curzon insisted on my occupying the enormous room below his in which the Permanent Under-Secretary sits in state; this was an unusual arrangement but made me feel more important than I was. However, the Marquess was very considerate and said pleasant things when the month was over. I told him that as a matter of fact, after numerous interviews, and giving attention to one or two special subjects, I had no time to do anything but sort out the papers which ought to go before him and put them into the appropriate boxes, otherwise work would have been held up indefinitely. He was not at all surprised. He himself worked at night and until the early hours of the morning, which meant among other things that he often had to write letters with his own hand, and he began his work again in bed later in the morning. One way or another he got through a tremendous amount of work. I once told a friend that Lord Curzon was very human, and he said: "Nonsense, everyone is human," which was far from being true.

When Ronald Lindsay was made Permanent Under-Secretary I wrote to congratulate him. In his reply he said: 'Surely you have sat near enough to the fire to know how disagreeable a seat on the hob can be.' Lord Curzon did not make it too disagreeable.

Two or three other jobs came my way during these years.

While Versailles was still in progress Mr. Sigismund Goetze offered to decorate the walls of the corridor at the top of our Grand Staircase. Victor Wellesley, himself an artist, and I were sent to his studio to inspect the sketches, but, fortunately perhaps for us, I do not think anyone paid much heed to what we said, for the question was made a Cabinet one and the Cabinet decided in their favour. All I achieved was the dropping of a brick. In a note to some higher authority I mentioned the 'naked figure of Belgium' which appears in one of the pictures. This note was passed on by my unreflecting correspondent to Mr. Goetze, who was exceedingly angry. He said he had never painted a naked figure in his life: the figure was a nude.

Then came the foundation of the Institute of Historical Research. I somewhat vaguely represented the views or interests of the Foreign Office, but what I chiefly recollect was the dinner party arranged at the Athenæum to give the scheme a good start. There were a dozen or more history experts, or like myself quasi-experts, and a dozen millionaires. As two or three of them came into the room I heard one say to the other: "I really cannot think why I should be invited to a dinner of historians." "I," said the other, "appreciate the reason only too well."

The historians and millionaires alternated round the table, and I am glad to say that the guest next me contributed a very large sum indeed to the Institution. Whatever I may sometimes have said I have never pretended to myself that this munificence was inspired by the brilliance of my conversation.

Since then I have followed the fortunes of the Institute, which was bound to prosper under the guidance of Professor Pollard, and have sometimes attended meetings and lectures.

At intervals there have been meetings at which English and American professors and students of history have been brought together. On the last occasion the programme included various expeditions into the country: and the party which I joined visited Knole and Penshurst. An American lady with whom I made acquaintance was particularly interested in the trees in the park at Knole, because she had often read about the glory of the trees in English parks and wondered whether what she had read was true. She now declared that they had nothing like it at home.

She was of a different turn of mind from an American gentleman whom I met at an Archæological meeting in Suffolk. He had come to the meeting by accident, having taken the wrong train from London, but he stayed on to see what was to be seen. He told me that he had already been for some weeks in Europe and had seen Germany, Denmark, Belgium, Holland, and France, and now England: nowhere was there anything to beat his home town of Minneapolis.

Then most important of all came the Institute of International Affairs. I believe the embryo state of the Institute was in the shape of a group formed in Paris during the conference, with Mr. J. W. Headlam, the historian, as one of the authors of its existence. After Versailles a committee, with Lord Robert Cecil as its chairman, was formed to set the Institute going. Lord Curzon regarded the idea with abhorrence, but he allowed me to join the committee, primarily, I fancy, to curse rather than to bless.

Our chief work, as far as I remember, was the collection of members. We each drew up lists of people who in our opinion took a serious interest in foreign affairs. The lists were vetted by the committee and we then invited our nominees to join. They nearly all did, but I was able to drop one brick here. I asked a friend in a Government office, who was, I believed, very much what we wanted, if he would join and he agreed; but next day came an indignant letter from one of his colleagues asking how it was that he too had not been invited. I said we should be only too glad to include him, but we could not deal with everybody at once.

Then came the great question whether the Staff of the Foreign Office should be allowed to join. Lord Curzon's immediate reaction was to say "Certainly not," and I believe Crowe had the same idea. My task, once more, was to appease the Marquess, which I succeeded in doing to the extent that we were allowed to join but not to make speeches. Since then the Foreign Office and the Institute have to the best of my knowledge worked in complete harmony, and at the Annual Dinner the Secretary of State has often been a speaker.

It is quite unnecessary here to dilate on the rapid and prodigious growth of the Institute and the work it has done and is doing. I have never addressed a meeting, but was asked to do so when I came home from Japan in 1931. I consulted the proper authority at the Foreign Office, who replied that there was no objection whatever to my giving an address provided that I did not touch on politics. I offered to talk about the scenery of Japan, but this did not seem to appeal to the Institute.

In January, 1921, when I was just starting for Brazil, I received a charming letter from the Secretary of the Institute expressing a wish that I should take the Chair at a meeting at which Mr. Fisher was to speak on the League of Nations. The invitation was somewhat in the nature of an honorary degree from a university, but unfortunately I was unable to accept.

During all this time I had, of course, any amount of ordinary political work. After the Versailles Conference, when the Foreign Office resumed its normal shape, Lord Hardinge returned to his post as Permanent Under-Secretary, to be succeeded in 1920 by Crowe. I became Assistant Secretary in charge of Middle Eastern affairs.

This was a very active sphere of movement. War between a really new Turkey and Greece was in progress. Irak was in process of settlement and everywhere there was excitement. Lord Curzon was deeply interested in the Middle East and we had the advice of all sorts of experts. The Emir Feisal, as well as Colonel Lawrence, were among those who attended various meetings. Irak was being administered with the help of officials from India who did their work extraordinarily well, but the policy of His Majesty's Government, as I sometimes reminded my friends, was not "as much independence as was compatible with efficiency, but as much efficiency as was compatible with independence."

Palestine was another thorny question. Lord Curzon by no means forgot the rights of the Arabs and wished to make them fit in with the Jewish policy which had been already declared by His Majesty's Government.

I saw one day a scheme drafted by a junior and was filled with horror at the prospect of what it meant for the Arab population. I said so and passed it on to Lord Curzon. He said: "I entirely agree with Sir John Tilley," and I returned it for amendment to the junior. The latter, however, had the best of it, for he said: "I suppose you realize that both you and Lord Curzon had already seen that draft and had made no observation." We may, of course, have had it in our hands without any special attention being called to it, but I felt rather crushed.

The story, I hope, suggests that Arab interests were not overlooked although the Arabs themselves were obviously not satisfied.

Among my most frequent diplomatic visitors were the Ministers respectively of Georgia, Armenia and Azerbaijan, three republics carved out of the southern part of the old Russian dominions. Less frequent were the Ministers of Estonia, Latvia and Lithuania, similarly taken out of the north-west of those dominions. It was not always too easy to remember what their respective fears and aspirations were, but we all got on very well. What astonishes me is that after my departure from the Foreign Office, though not, I suppose, in consequence of it, Georgia, Armenia and Azerbaijan suddenly faded away. The Soviet Union swallowed them up, as lately Latvia, Estonia and Lithuania have been swallowed up. Yet I cannot recall any uproar in this country over this destruction of the independence of Georgia, Armenia and Azerbaijan. It may be that the uproar was there but not loud enough to reach me either in Brazil or even in this country when I was preparing to go there. Georgia, Armenia and Azerbaijan, of course, still exist as members of the Soviet Union, and I may be wrong in thinking that they do not make their voices heard in the direction of Soviet policy.

I had a characteristic letter in April, 1920, from Lord Bryce, who was then eighty-two. He had just learned from Arthur Hardinge that Fez was accessible to travellers. He was taking Lady Bryce for a tour in the south of Spain, which she had never seen, and wished to extend his journey into the interior of Morocco. He wanted me to put him in touch with local authorities. He made the journey, and I was glad to think that at that age his enthusiasm for fresh knowledge was unabated.

Towards the end of 1920 I was working in my room at the Foreign Office when about eight o'clock Lord Curzon's Private Secretary put his head in and said: "If you have any ideas about dinner you had better be off, for the Marquess is on his way back from the House of Lords." I hurriedly made up my boxes for despatch to higher authorities and was reaching for my hat when a messenger came in and announced that His Lordship wished to speak to me. My heart sank, but I went to his room at once, hoping for the best and fearing the worst.

Instead of starting to discuss Middle East affairs he said: "I want you to go as Ambassador to Brazil." This was a thunderbolt, but, as I quickly made up my mind, of a pleasant nature. I told him that I must ask my wife before giving a definite answer and he agreed, with an admonition that he greatly hoped that I should accept. I did so next day.

Our Embassy in Brazil was of new creation. It resulted from a tour of South America made by a special Mission, headed by Sir Maurice de Bunsen, in 1918. Their report urged that we should be represented by an Ambassador in South America, and that Brazil being by far the largest of the South American countries the choice should fall on Rio de Janeiro. The first Ambassador was Sir Ralph Paget. As quite a young man he had done remarkably well when more or less accidentally left in charge in Tokyo. Later he had spent seven years in Siam, not everyone's choice but I believe his favourite post. He loved heat. After leaving Bangkok he succeeded Sir Fairfax Cartwright at Munich. Munich was one of those places where diplomats were supposed to lead an idle life, but during Cartwright's tenure of the post it was a source of most valuable information about what was going on in Germany. Paget did not care much for Munich and was soon moved to Belgrade, then to the Foreign Office and then to Copenhagen. He had scarcely received his appointment as Ambassador at Rio when he came to see me and said that he proposed to resign. I said: "You can't do that now, before even taking up your post; besides, you have told me more than once that you hoped some day to be an Ambassador." "Well," he said, "I am an Ambassador." I told him this was all nonsense and go he must, and he went but only stayed about a year.

During the nineteenth century, diplomatic missions were carefully graded. Ambassadors were exchanged between the Great Powers only; they sent Ministers to represent them in the smaller countries, which themselves exchanged Ministers. Gradually changes came. For many years we sent Ambassadors only to Paris, Berlin, Vienna, Constantinople and St. Petersburg. Rome became an Embassy in 1876, Madrid in 1887, Washington in 1893. After the war Brussels was, so to speak, rewarded for her sufferings with an Embassy and Rio was elevated about the same time. Meanwhile the countries of both North and South America had sent Ambassadors to each other in all directions. The Papal Nuncio ranked as Ambassador and in Catholic countries was regarded as the 'doyen' of the diplomatic body.

However, so far as Great Britain was concerned, Ambassadors in 1920 were still rare and the position was a proud one. In the countries where Ambassadors resided they alone had a right to audiences of the Head of the State and in some countries this was very valuable. Here they were always made Privy Councillors on appointment. Since then the number has grown very much and they are now divided into first and second class.

I have always thought we were rather weak in the matter of Embassies and too prone to follow the example of other Governments, or to listen to the cries of those interested in the trade of particular countries, on the same sort of principle that we should risk the loss of India if we were not civil to the Caliph.

By January, 1921, I was ready to start for what was a new world in more senses than one. As I started this book by speaking of background I should say that I had meanwhile acquired a new one, by inheriting in 1914 a house and fifty acres at Felsham in Suffolk, a place which I had known and been fond-of all my life. This solved a problem which distracts many families returning on leave or retirement from distant countries: whether to settle in London or the country, and if the country shall it be Cornwall or Northumberland. If you have a fixed home you make the best of it; at least it is wise to do so.

CHAPTER VIII

WHEN I FOUND MYSELF BOUND FOR RIO DE JANEIRO I REMEMBERED THAT I was not the first of my family to undertake such an adventure.

In 1829 an uncle of mine, a young man of twenty-four, having failed to make good in this country, was sent out to Brazil with various letters of introduction in the hope, apparently, that he would do better there.

I think some of his letters may be of interest, especially to anyone concerned about the history of South America; and that, not although, but because, they are simply the letters of a feckless young man to his mother and sister, intended to give them some idea of his doings. The introductions came from a Mr. Lane who had been in partnership with the young man's maternal grandfather, Mr. Thomas Fraser. The firm of Lane, Son and Fraser, previously Lane and Booth, had been in existence, it appears, for some hundred and fifty years, but I have never discovered that they had any connection with Brazil.

Here are some extracts from the letters:

Rio de Janeiro,
11th July, 1829.

Dear Mother,

I have before me yours of the 24 April and am glad to find you are all well; the Hector *did not leave London till the 1st of May and arrived here last Saturday. We have London papers to the 27th May. When I last wrote you by the* Ganges *I was in bed, altogether I was confined to my bed 10 days and three days afterwards to the house and can hardly yet call myself out of the Doctor's hands. During the time I was in bed I took an immense quantity of physic, a quart bottle every day besides pills and powders without the least effect on me. For two days I was in the most excruciating pain in my stomach and the Doctor then told me that if the pain increased immediately to send for a barber to put on 20 leeches. As the pain greatly increased I did so and had to*

*pay the barber 2s. for each leech, say £2; they took a great quantity of blood
and relieved me and the physic soon after took effect. All the time I was in bed
I was not allowed anything to eat, not even a morsel of bread; my diet was
2 cups of weak tea and 2 cups of broth very weak indeed with a little barley water
at night and a hot bath every evening. I was not at all aware that I was in any
danger but Mrs. Otten told me afterwards that the Doctor had nearly given
me up; he came twice every day and sometimes 3 times; he is an Englishman
and is decidedly of the opinion that all the passengers and crew were poisoned
by the Steward. All have been taken in the same way; the Captain was very
bad and has since had a relapse owing to using too much exertion after his
recovery, the Mate was taken ill the day we landed and is not quite well yet.
During our illness while all were in bed on shore the Steward robbed the vessel,
he took the Captain's watch and several other things and it has since been
discovered by an accomplice of his that it was their intention to have robbed
the vessel in the night about 1000 dollars worth of property but the watch was
missed in the morning. The Steward is now in prison and will be tried for the
theft as well as for poisoning as it is supposed it was only the Captain and
Mate that he wished to poison in order to get them out of the way; a bottle
of sugar of lead is missing from the medicine chest and the Dr. says it would
produce exactly the effect it had on us. Several of the men are still at the
Hospital. I am now quite recovered though of course very weak and almost a
skeleton. I am not allowed to eat much and to keep very quiet, and walk out a
little; the least thing I am told may bring on a relapse. Just as I was getting
well a scorpion bit me on the fore finger of my right hand which swelled the
whole hand up to my wrist; it is at last reduced by poultices; the immense discharge showed the bad state of my blood; the skin is off the greater part of the
hand and I can only write with my middle finger. I am not yet able to write
up the books but think I shall be able to start next week.*

*I have dined with Mr. Dutton twice, he is a very pleasant friendly man,
there was a grand procession yesterday which I saw from his house; the
Emperor was expected but was not there; he passed me however in his carriage
this morning and made me a low bow in return to my taking off my hat. I
was alone but had seen his carriage before and had a description of his person;
he is a very fine looking man, rather dark, black hair and eyes and large
mustachios and whiskers; he has no guard with him, it was his private carriage;
it is an old dark green chariot something like a poor English Doctor's drawn
by four mules, 2 postillions and one outrider on a mule, the livery is dark grey with
silver round the wrist and collar and a silver hatband, altogether very mean
looking but he has some very superb carriages (English) and some fine horses.
He rides about alone some times; he seems to be much liked, is quite at his ease,
he keeps company with the English more than any other nation. The whole
of the Brazilian Navy is commanded by English Captains. The soldiers
cut a very poor figure here. Murders are frequent and never taken any notice
of by the police unless it is urged.*

G

Rio de Janeiro,
11th July, 1829.

Dear Susan,

I am afraid I shall not be able to send you a very amusing letter as from my illness I have been about a very few miles; out of the town seems pretty enough and I am told some parts rather farther are delightful; when I have been here long enough to see if my Brazilian history is correct I will send them to you as soon as I get an opportunity. I can give you no account of the ladies as I never see any; they do not walk about except on grand holidays and then are dressed most superbly. I saw yesterday a few in carriages, they were dressed in Satin gowns covered with gold and silver spangles with a profusion of diamonds and other stones in their heads besides roses etc. I do not think you would much like this place at least I am sure you would not like Rio whatever you might do a few miles out of it. The houses in the Country even, as often have no gardens as not. The public Gardens are rather pretty but very small; they are full of oranges and limes and a variety of other trees and on one side is the bay by the side of which there is a long seat commanding a beautiful view of the Mountains round the bay covered with Palm Cocoa Trees and all the shipping in the harbour besides vessels sometimes coming in from sea. There is also a pretty walk to the skittle ground and the ground is very pretty, it is a sort of Tea Garden kept by a German at the top of rather a steep hill. I went there with two gentlemen yesterday evening; we played at I do not know what the game is called but it is something like skittles, which you know is only a plebeian game in England; here it is only gentlemen that play; we had some coffee and for my coffee and paying for playing I had to pay 2d.; we had some oranges but he did not charge any thing for them, in fact just outside the Garden we might have picked as many as we liked off the hedge in the public road, this you can do almost everywhere. I am told there are some very beautiful flowers and birds in the Brazils but have not seen any with the exception of Parrots; there is a regular Parrot and Monkey market in the town and either may be bought very cheaply.

You would no doubt be at first disgusted at the sight of the black men. Every now and then I meet a dozen chained together and some with large iron collars round their necks but these are only the prisoners who have committed some crime or other; the generality of the blacks are treated very well, they are all clothed; sometimes I see a few with only trousers but very seldom; they make a most tremendous noise as they carry goods through the streets 30 or more together calling as they run along with the things on their heads (which is the way they carry everything) Yanga Yanga as loud as they can bawl—Rio itself is a shocking dirty hole, the bottoms of all the houses are either stores or shops but you cannot tell what they are without looking into them as nothing is hung outside the door and there are no windows to hang things in; they have only shutters which are closed at night the upper parts of most of the houses have windows but not all.

The Emperor's Palace is a very insignificant building; it was formerly a merchant's house but he has four other Palaces at a short distance; he never lives in Rio though he comes here frequently; he holds a levée every Saturday.

Minas Geraes,
Gongo Seco,
24th November, 1829.

My dear Mother,
   I wrote you a few lines on my road from Rio to this place which I suppose you will receive before this. I have been here now six weeks and like the place and my situation very much. I was engaged in Rio to come here at a salary of about £50 a year in English money beside my living, but on my arrival here it was increased to £60 as they thought 50 too little.
   The Partners are two Cornish Miners whose term of agreement with the Company has expired; their names are William Jeffree and James Cornelius each about 35 years of age; Cornelius is a married man and intends going home to Cornwall in about a twelvemonth to settle his children (boys) to some business and then return; they have both been here about five years but have only been in business on their own account since last May. There are only two stores here, one kept by a Portuguese and one by us; the Portuguese only sells dry goods, that is clothing etc. and grocery wholesale but Capt. Lyon will not allow him to retail so that we supply the whole of Gongo with all the necessaries of life which we get from Rio, we are butchers and bakers also, there are about 180 English miners here and about a hundred more coming; there are 2 Surgeons and 1 assistant one Engineer and one assistant. The principle Engineer is Mr. Baird, husband of the lady I came out with a very pleasant and kind man and much liked here. I am very often at his house and also at Capt. Lyon's indeed I go to every body's house here and we are all quite at home just like one family.
   The Commissioner and his private Secretary, 8 clerks employed by the Company and 5 mining Captains beside a few Portuguese, I believe about five, there are about 400 blacks belonging to the Company (who are very well treated and seem very happy), and nearly 150 Brazilians about half of these are cooks and washer-women and the rest Mechanics or rather labourers, we have now and then a travelling tailor who stops a month or two and one black shoemaker but the principle wearing apparel comes from Rio. I forgot to mention the two Surgeons and Engineer have their wives and families here and also 6 miners' wives. When the first party of English miners came out there were only six houses in the place now there are above 100 and buildings going on fast as they are very much crowded for want of houses, but there are so few Brazilian carpenters that they get on very slowly besides which they are very lazy and the English carpenters are employed in the mine. The Gongo estate is about one square mile or rather more; any Englishman may build a house and have as much land as he likes by asking Capt. Lyon; they can also get as much wood as they like to build with from the woods; no Portuguese or Brazilians are allowed to live here with the exception of those that were here before the Company was established unless by leave of Capt. Lyon but he is very shy in letting them even sleep on the estate, as he is afraid of their buying gold which would be an inducement to the blacks to steal it, which even now happens. The Mine is paying very well and likely to last for some years; the gold is sent down to Rio about

every six weeks on Mules guarded by one clerk and two miners besides a troupeiro or guide and 2 blacks; they go in about 20 days the distance is about 360 miles all up and down hill over mountains and through rivers several of which in the rainy season the horses and mules are obliged to swim over. The rainy season is just now commencing and lasts till the end of February; it generally rains about half the day and the sun is often out the other half.

This place lies quite in a valley with high mountains covered with wood all round, altogether very picturesque rugged and beautiful but like most part of the Brazils very barren, the ground being of an irony substance mixed with clay and a great deal of rock, there are very few vegetables in fact they are quite a treat, the only fruit worth eating are oranges and Iacadacubas something like a goose-berry. Beef is almost the only meat here; it is pretty good but nothing like English meat owing to the want of pasture for the animals which are all very thin; fowls and poultry are plentiful no fish, horses are very cheap about from £5 to £8 each, everybody keeps a horse here the roads being very bad. I sold the one I came up the country on to pay what I owed in Rio, but shall buy another soon; keeping them costs very little about £6 a year; at present I have the use of anybody's horse as many keep two but have not been many long rides owing to a sore toe occasioned by little insects getting under the nails called Bichoux; at first they are scarcely perceptible but eat their way into the flesh and grow nearly as big as a pea; we generally apply to the blacks to get them out with a pin, my foot is now getting well and I hope I shall not have any more as I have now adopted the only plan to keep them away viz by wearing boots and putting them on before I get out of bed as they are on the floors in the house.

There are not many birds here; plenty of monkeys in the woods; what birds there are very pretty I now and then go out on a shooting excursion in the woods and yesterday shot two Paraquets, I mean to get them stuffed when I have time, I intend to make a collection of birds, insects (which are very numerous) and snakes which are very beautiful and easily preserved in a bottle with spirits; there are a great many snakes here some rattle snakes which are the only poisonous ones, I saw one last week which a black had caught alive. In March I am going to Rio to make arrangements there for a regular supply of goods as they have hitherto been buying their goods much dearer than they need, they are all brought from Rio on mules, the roads not allowing carts and there being no navigation. The road from Rio here is in some parts beautiful for leagues and leagues through woods crowded with all sorts of trees in some parts they have clumsy cars drawn by ten oxen but they can seldom go more than 2 or 3 miles so that they only go from the different farms to supply the neighbouring villages with Indian corn and beans. Mandioc, a dry root ground up into a sort of saw-dust which the blacks and natives eat instead of bread (we have English and American flour) and Fonçinha which is the fat cut out of the large pigs dried and salted; these with a little coffee which is not very good constitute the living of a Brazilian with which they seem very well contented; their only drink is Ristil and Cashas two strong spirits distilled from the Mandioc and Sugar Cane; the Ristil is very good and the dearest that is from the Sugar Cane. Milk is very rarely to be met with all over the Brazils a few cheeses are made but not very good. I must now leave off writing for a little while as I am very cold; it is the mornings which are sometimes very cold as well as the evenings; in the middle of the day if the sun is out it is very hot but not at all oppressive as we have always a fine breeze.

Morro de Saint Vicente,
1st November, 1831.

My dear Mother,

By-the-by perhaps you might like to hear a little of the Politics of this country. I am no great Politician and know very little. There has been a great hubbub in Rio hundreds of murders and a great many families have left Rio for Portugal, Madeira, etc. 400 left in one day last month and so anxious are the Regency for them to remain in Rio that they caused them all the delay they could in giving them passports saying they were afraid if so many Portuguese left the city would be taken by the blacks; but of this there is no fear as there is a large Naval force in Rio of English, French and American now all in the Harbour ready at a moment's notice, indeed were it not for the British force the French would have taken Rio before this. Don Pedro is by some expected to return shortly, others say not. I believe nothing but his return to the Throne will make this country quiet again at least not for some time. The mines are very quiet though an English miner was stabbed in Gongo a few weeks past and died but this was nothing political and might have happened in any other part of the world. I do not hear that any English, French, German or other strangers have left the country on account of disturbances; it certainly is not very pleasant living in Rio as it is impossible for any one to leave his house after dark; Some insult was lately offered to an officer in the British service, upon which the Admiral immediately brought his whole force in their boats to the landing place before the Palace and unless he had received instant satisfaction would have taken Rio without delay; upon sight of the British Sailors and Marines of course armed and ready to land all the houses and streets in the neighbourhood were instantly evacuated, but an apology was given in less than 10 minutes by the Brazilian Captain at Arms. Our Consul has told the Regency very plainly that in case of any insult being offered to an Englishman and they not taking any notice of it they must take the consequences. They are terribly afraid of the English force; it certainly is a very formidable one. I think I have now told you all I know about it.

During the hundred years which passed between my uncle's arrival in Rio and mine Brazil had made rapid progress, but not so rapid, surely, as her progress during the last twenty years.

Rio itself was very different from the shabby city described by William Tilley, but many people in this country were, I found, unaware of the changes which had taken place. Poor William Tilley died of yellow fever very few years after those letters were written: in my time yellow fever had been practically wiped out largely through the brilliant work of Dr. Oswaldo Cruz, early in the present century, but people persisted in telling me that it was dangerous to go to a country where yellow fever was so prevalent. Others had heard that the Brazilian ladies still drive about in the fashion described by my uncle in satin gowns and diamonds, whereas, as a matter of fact, Brazilian ladies to-day are particularly well dressed. On the other hand, although nowadays they mostly go everywhere, this is, I believe, a comparatively modern innovation. It is not so very long since husbands expected their wives to stay at home during their absence. Indeed, I do remember a lady explaining that she could not come and call at the Embassy because her husband was so much occupied that she was seldom able to go out. I also remember seeing, when on my way to call on some English friends, an English lady standing at the door of her villa. I told these friends that I had noticed her, and that though I had met most of the English Colony, I did not think I had ever seen her before. They explained that her Brazilian husband liked her only to go out on Wednesdays.

As a city Rio de Janeiro when we arrived there was magnificent. It is even more magnificent now. The most splendid feature is the Avenida Beira Mar and the other Avenidas stretching along the sea-front. No city in the world, of which I have ever heard, can compare in beauty with Rio, because no city has such a marvellous setting, between the open Atlantic, the bay and the mountains, with all the added beauty of trees and flowers, and the constant efforts of man to make his share in the landscape still more splendid.

I must descend a little from the sublime to describe the origins of the great Avenida Central which runs through the heart of the city from sea to sea. Not many years before our time this district was a network of small streets. The Government decided to sweep them away. They accordingly let it be known, or rather believed, that they were going to institute a new property tax; they then invited the owners to send in their own assessments of their property: this was done, the figures being as low as compatible with the barest probability; the Government then bought up the whole of the property at the owners' assessment.

There is much that is handsome among the buildings of Rio, but practically nothing that is old. The sunshine of which the city has so large a share contributes a great deal to the impression of gorgeousness.

William Tilley speaks of the slaves as being well treated. I believe this was generally the case, although masters must have been somewhat nervous about the *Escravidâo* (slave population) in their houses. We once inspected a large house which we thought might be suitable for an Embassy: the owner showed us with a wave of the hand a great basement in which in her youth *a Escravidâo* were shut in at night behind iron bars. This reminds me of another house which we inspected and which had been occupied by a former Prime Minister with a good many enemies. The place was like a fortress. The windows on the first floor were slits through which no murderer could have climbed, and at the top of the stairs were high iron railings and gates to be locked at night. Slavery was abolished in 1888.

William Tilley settled, as has been seen, in the province of Minas Geraes, near the famous goldmines of Gongo Soco, which were English property: he speaks too of the 'irony' nature of the soil. Most of the gold digging in his day was surface work and the hills are scarred in all directions; now, of course, the gold is taken from deep mines. The iron of the Itabira district is still a potential source of enormous wealth; when I rode from Bello Horizonte, the modern capital of Minas Geraes, to Morro Velho, now the great gold mine, my horse's shoes at one point rang on the iron just below the surface.

When the letters were written Brazil had enjoyed her independence of Portugal for only seven years (since 1822), and it was still evidently somewhat precarious. I was there for the celebration of the centenary of that independence.

The great wealth of the country when I went there in 1921, as for thirty or forty years before that, was derived from the coffee trade. As I not infrequently reminded the Foreign Office, speaking broadly, Brazil lived by selling coffee to the United States. Coffee represented half of her export trade, in 1920 fifty-two out of a hundred and seven million pounds; of that about two-thirds went to the United States, a fact which placed the latter in a powerful position when it came to making any sort of trade agreement. We imported by comparison practically no coffee. For the period January to September, 1941, 87 per cent of the coffee export went to the U.S.A.

As it happened my term of service in Brazil roughly coincided with the supremacy of coffee. There had been during the previous century a variety of other notable exports: gold, diamonds, rubber, sugar, dyewood, which had had their ups and downs; since my time other great industries have grown up; others again remain almost untapped. Never was a country with such potential wealth. I once ventured in an after-dinner speech in London to say that what Brazil wanted most was genius if it were true that genius meant 'an infinite capacity for taking pains.'

The taking of pains is more common than it was in Brazil, but in hot climates it is not a very popular duty to impress upon the population. Workmen and labourers of all sorts in our own country are naturally and properly ambitious of good houses, good food, good clothes, and good coal. Where the climate looks after the heating question, where a little food is easy to come by and goes a long way, where clothes are hardly wanted for protection against the weather, people are not terribly anxious to work long hours even for good wages. After all, even in Ayrshire in my youth I used to be told that the miners worked four days a week and hunted two.

Of course, I am not suggesting that the climate of Brazil is much the same everywhere. Even Rio and S. Paulo, a night's journey by train apart, are very different, S. Paulo being very high with sometimes a drop of twenty degrees in the temperature towards evening, while further south the climate naturally becomes milder. Broadly speaking, however, labourers can live a fairly easy life on a small wage. In Rio itself the young children of the poor houses near our gate went about naked for the most part, and so far as we could see through the windows the furniture of those houses was conspicuous by its absence.

There is still a large negro population in the country, but I believe it is diminishing; I have been told that the climate does not suit them very well. Not only that, but the traces of black blood among people of Portuguese race are also diminishing.

Apart from the negroes there is now a large alien population of Germans, Italians and, in smaller numbers, Japanese and Spaniards; Portuguese can hardly be considered aliens. The Italians are mainly in S. Paulo, to the number of a million or more (between 1886 and 1941 approximately 1,373,000 immigrants arrived from Italy). Germans are also in the south; Japanese in the south, and in at least one colony in the north, to the number of several hundred thousand. The Italians mix pretty well with the Brazilians: the first German colonists who came, more or less by accident, to Petropolis in the hills above Rio are Brazilianized, but the colonists of recent years have made great efforts to maintain themselves as an independent community with their own schools. After or during the last war, when trouble was feared from these German colonists, the German schools were closed and teaching in Portuguese wisely insisted on everywhere. Now there are rumours of fresh efforts on the part of the Germans to obtain some kind of autonomy, and undoubtedly the German Government have their eye on Southern Brazil as a field for German expansion. The Japanese are also likely to be troublesome in proportion as they are unlikely to mix and inter-marry with the people of the country, and many wise Brazilians are strongly opposed to allowing any further Japanese immigration. To my mind it is quite impossible to believe that a satisfactory result can be produced by inter-marrying between the two races or that any Japanese authority would encourage such a thing, and equally impossible to believe that it is desirable for any country to have a large permanently alien community in its midst.

Syrians I have not mentioned, but there are a certain number of Syrian pedlars going about generally known as Turks.

One other preliminary observation seems to be required which is that anyone reading about Brazil has to remember the size of the country. It extends much over two thousand miles from north to south, the same sort of distance as from Paris to Moscow, and has a coast line of three thousand five hundred miles. Before going to Brazil we read about some town in Rio Grande that we thought sounded a pleasant place to go to in the summer: when we got to Rio we found that by the only possible means of transport it would take a week to reach this spot.

I say all this partly because people in this country often asked whether

I had been to this or that place, obviously thinking in terms of England; nor did their ignorance always end there. A relation of mine had a letter from a lady saying that her son was acting as tutor to a family in the Argentine; this lady had heard that my relation had a cousin who was 'Governor of Rio' and she ventured to hope that the Governor would be kind to her son when he came to the capital. It seemed to me odd that the lady should be· so completely ignorant about the conditions in South America when her beloved son was living there. That people should assume that Spanish is spoken in Brazil is not so odd. I once met an old friend who was very high in the Education Department of the L.C.C., if not actually in command; he asked me about a mutual acquaintance and I told him the man was in Mexico. "Ah," said the L.C.C. man, "that is the capital of the Argentine, is it not?"

I attribute this sort of ignorance not to the failure of public and other schools to teach my generation, or even the next, much about geography, but simply to the fact that so many people close their minds against knowledge of that sort. I say 'people' and not 'English people' because I fancy that most other races, by no means excluding the people of the United States, do the same.

Such was the country in which we arrived at the beginning of 1921, not far from midsummer. The summer Embassy, the only house owned by our Government, was at Petropolis, up in the hills at a height of some three thousand feet, fifty miles from the capital. Until yellow fever was defeated the Ambassador lived permanently at Petropolis, which was also the home of the Emperor, and only paid occasional visits to Rio.

We spent our first night or two in a comfortable modern hotel, but it was the only one of its kind, whereas before we left there were at least two other fine modern hotels and others that were quite good.

A member of the English community, which numbered several thousand, lamented my departure for Petropolis because I should be 'no good to them' up there. That was a fallacy. I used to go down to Rio for the day at least twice a week, which was quite often enough to do any business which required my presence, and the President of the Republic himself spent most of the summer at Petropolis, Ministers coming up regularly. The French Ambassador lived almost entirely at Petropolis and the American Ambassador and most of the European representatives spent at least a great part of the summer there.

The Consulates remained open in Rio.

The British community lived mostly at Nictheroy, on the other side of the Bay, where they had their own club and their own church; they came across for business in the morning by steamer and went back in the evening, many of them seeing regrettably little of their Brazilian neighbours.

One member of the community, unusually unobservant, remarked to me one day with pride that one gradually in the course of years picked up knowledge of the country; for instance, he had just discovered why it was that so many Brazilians were christened Joseph or Mary! (He might have said both!)

In due course I presented my credentials to the President, Dr. Epitacio Pessoa, at his Petropolis Palace. Dr. Epitacio, as he would normally be spoken of in Brazil, filled that office with great dignity. He was a lawyer of wide attainments and, after his term of office, became one of the Judges of the International Court at The Hague. I have already mentioned his visit to Europe and his reception at the Courts of London, Rome and Brussels. He had returned meanwhile to Brazil with a wider outlook on international affairs than some of his predecessors and some even of his successors.

Although Brazil was preparing to celebrate the centenary of her independence the Republic had only existed since 1889. In that year the Emperor Dom Pedro II was compelled to abdicate after a reign of fifty-eight years, during which he had done a great deal to promote the ideas embodied in Brazil's motto, Order and Progress. The monarchy came to an end not so much from any serious dissatisfaction with the rule of the Emperor, although the abolition of slavery had caused disaffection among the landed proprietors, as from the fact that it seemed unfashionable in America, where Republics covered the greater part of the two continents.

The President is, or was in the days of which I write, elected for four years and his Ministers were responsible to him and not to Congress. I once asked a Brazilian Minister what he would do if his policy were fiercely attacked in Congress. In substance his reply was that it would make no odds to him. Nevertheless Presidents used to take some pains to arrange as far as possible to have a majority in Congress, little as it seemed to me to matter. They also made great efforts to arrange for a successor who would carry on their policy, but in this they seldom were able to effect their purpose. Presidents came, in practice, from different States in succession.

Brazil was then a strictly Federal Republic, the constituent States having a large measure of autonomy, financial and other; if, for instance, one of the States failed in its obligations, it availed nothing to complain to the federal Government.

It must be remembered, however, by anyone who reads these remarks that the Constitution has been changed altogether in recent years; Congress has disappeared and the powers of the States have been much modified.

When I was in Brazil any serious disaffection with the policy of the Government could only show itself in the form of an attempted revolution. This sounds worse than it really was, for revolts in South American Republics are not usually of a very bloody character; even the downfall of the Emperor having been effected quietly and quickly. The people of Brazil are not, I should say, war-minded, and if they were told so would probably reply, and not without justice, that they were considerably more civilized than some of their European relations. The alternative of Parliamentary Government on our system might not really suit them.

A Chilean friend with whom I was once discussing the question said that if the Government of his or other South American countries depended on a Parliamentary majority it would have to be changed every week, which would be tiresome.

Although the Brazilians are not war-minded they are certainly apt to be hot-tempered; and as men of all classes and characters carry, or did in my time carry, arms in the shape of revolvers or knives, sudden affrays and blood-letting and even sudden deaths were not uncommon. Nor have I forgotten that last century they took part in the fierce war against Paraguay when the male population of that country was almost exterminated.

Of Brazilian society I will only say that it is very unlike the picture many people in this country had of it in 1920. It was often supposed that there were numbers of very rich people in Rio and ultra-smart ladies. Actually, rich people are comparatively few and the ladies, as I said before, very well dressed. The wealth of the old families was considerably reduced by the abolition of slavery: and new fortunes were rare in 1920 when manufactures were few and far between and trade not very highly organized. As to education, I found that nearly all educated Brazilians of Rio spoke perfect French; indeed, a French Ambassador once told me he thought it was the best out of France. For the theatre they depended entirely on annual visits from French companies, and their reading was mainly of French literature. All the same I made two complete failures with attempts at French jokes.

On one occasion I went to a big luncheon party where we waited an interminable time for lunch to be announced. I asked a lady near me, the wife of a foreign Minister as it happens, and not a Brazilian, if she knew why we were waiting. She told me that our hosts had discovered that there was no bread in the house. I replied, remembering Marie Antoinette: "*Alors, mangeons des gâteaux.*" My friend merely explained that the confectioner lived even farther off than the baker.

Felix Pacheco, when Minister for Foreign Affairs, received the Ambassadors every Monday. We used dutifully to go and if we had no business to transact we made a little conversation. Remembering this time Ste Beuve, I christened these interviews 'Causeries du Lundi!' One day I saw in a Brazilian newspaper a reference to the Minister's receptions which the British Ambassador so wittily described as Causeries de Ste Beuve. That must have puzzled the readers.

Ministers coming from other parts of Brazil sometimes could not speak French at all, or could not speak it well. Many children in Rio are educated by French priests, for instance in the Benedictine monastery. They are not usually great travellers even in their own country. A young Brazilian friend, himself a writer, once told me that he had hardly ever slept out of Rio; many certainly had never been any further than Petropolis.

Having made a start on our day-to-day life in Petropolis I seem to have fallen back on generalization; I will now return to my diary, a somewhat scanty one.

I find that our first guest was Dr. José Carlos Rodrigues, proprietor or part proprietor of the famous newspaper *Jornal do Commercio*, which claims, probably with right, to be the best newspaper in South America; and author later of two stout volumes of commentary on the Old Testament.

Dr. José Carlos had been often in London and had many English acquaintances, among them Lord Bryce, who had been a friend of his for forty years. When Lord Bryce died José Carlos wrote to me expressing his sorrow, and saying among other things that Bryce was the best conversationalist he had ever met.

I speak of my friend as José Carlos, as that is the usual way in Brazil. One seldom speaks of Mr. Jones; it may be Mr. John Jones, but oftener Mr. John, oftener still Mr. John George Jones or Mr. John George. This practice of dropping the surname altogether is very common and makes it uncommonly difficult to know who people are. A prominent instance is Dr. Washington Luīs, President of Saô Paulo in my time and later of the Republic, whose surname I cannot remember ever to have heard. Sons bear the same name as the father, and you meet Mr. John George and Mr. John George Filho (son), neither with a surname.

Our next guest was a Canadian; then came the Minister for Foreign Affairs, who had come up to Petropolis for a Cabinet meeting. He was Dr. Azevedo Marques, a Paulista and not a politician. He was always most friendly and courteous in our frequent conversations. Dr. Epitacio, by the way, came from the north of Brazil.

A few days later came the officers of H.M.S. *Weymouth* and *Petersfield*. This is a reminder that up till then we had had a South American squadron, but this was their final appearance before dispersal. A little later came *Gloucester* and *Southampton*, and the Commander-in-Chief, Admiral Hunt, came to stay with us. Admiral Hunt had more energy than any man I have ever met: he brought the best lawn tennis player of the squadron with him, and during every moment of the day that was available he played lawn tennis, rode with me, took long walks, or, if there was no other exercise to be had for half an hour, helped my daughter to catch butterflies. He had done, I heard, a tremendous lot of shooting in South America, and someone who had happened to follow in his footsteps found great piles of birds that had to be left behind. Before the Admiral, however, we had two or three other guests whose names suggest a variety of memories.

At the end of March came Lady Elizabeth Cochrane, who was visiting the scenes of her ancestor's triumphs. The name of the 10th Earl of Dundonald, better known as Lord Cochrane, is one to conjure with in many parts of South America: as an Admiral in the service of Chili and Peru and later of Brazil he had played a great part in securing the independence of those countries between 1818 and 1822. His name is constantly quoted in Anglo-Brazilian celebrations and he deserves his fame: talk of Admiral Cochrane is not a mere cliché; I believe he gained real gratitude.

Here I might mention two phrases which are often to be heard when

Anglo-Brazilian relations are spoken of, but from different points of view. One is 'Palavra de Ingles,' the word of an Englishman being as good as his bond and good enough for other people to swear by; the other is 'Para Ingles ver,' just for the Englishman to see, which compares well with what my friend in Varna said: "Ici il ne faut faire que des façades."

Since writing this I have come across a record of a speech at S. Paulo by one of my hosts there in which he made out that the phrase 'para Ingles ver' implied a compliment to our race, but I rather doubt this.

On April 3rd, I find Mr. Arno Pearse lunching. This modest entry in my Visitors' Book is really of monumental importance. Mr. Pearse was the General Secretary of the International Federation of Master Cotton Spinners and Manufacturers Associations of Manchester. He had come out to report on the possibilities of growing cotton, or rather extending the cultivation of cotton, in Brazil. He went home full of enthusiasm, and the cotton trade during the twenty years between his visit and the present time has made huge progress. This trade has not only brought fresh wealth to Brazil, but has stood the country in good stead by producing an alternative to coffee. Agricultural friends at home have sometimes told me that one ought to have a farm of five hundred acres at least, so that one may have a variety of crops of which some at least ought to be profitable. The Brazilians have a farm of two thousand million acres in which an incredible number of crops and every kind of wealth can be cultivated, if not with simultaneous at least with alternating success.

Mr. Pearse on his return to England published a book about his mission on the title page of which he quotes a statement made by me, rather more magniloquently than is usual with me, at an International Cotton Conference held at Rio in October, 1922.

I seem to have said: "The enormous possibilities of Brazil as supplier of cotton to the world have already come to the knowledge of consumers of this raw material in all parts of the globe, through the Report of the International Cotton Federation published early this year. In fact, I doubt whether any other trade Mission to a country has performed its work with such great care or attained results of greater educative value."

In Mr. Pearse's book he gives the value of the cotton exports for Brazil for 1916 as £119,000, in 1920 as £5,502,000. In 1940 the value for January–September was between £7,000,000 and £8,000,000, although the milreis had less than a third of its 1920 value, and whereas an enormous proportion of the coffee went to the U.S.A. and very little to Britain, a large quantity of the cotton came to us. I have already quoted myself as having said that Brazil required more genius; genius was a little lacking in the cotton trade for some time, inasmuch as it was not carefully enough graded to suit importers, but I believe that matters have much improved in this respect.

On April 10th Mr. G. Miller lunched. He was the Superintendent of the Leopoldina Railway, one of the great British undertakings which has done so much for the development of Brazil.

The most flourishing of all and the best known is the S. Paulo Railway, linking S. Paulo and the port of Santos, with which railway I now have the pleasure of being connected; but the Leopoldina Railway serves the capital, linking it up with various surrounding districts by a remarkable network of lines, and also, by its ferry service, with the big suburb of Nictheroy. The Leopoldina has to struggle with a great number of contracts originally made by the Government with various small companies and has also to contend against the extreme unwillingness of the Rio public to pay a reasonable price for their tickets. I once made a two days' tour on the Leopoldina, up hill and down dale all the way. The suddenness with which the train dashed round hairpin bends while I was trying to have a bath made me more nearly 'seasick' than I have ever been. The railway serves an area of 200,000 square miles.

On April 17th came Sir Edward Goulding and Sir Henry (and Lady) Harris. They came from the great gold mine at Morro Velho of which they were directors; another undertaking of immense value to Brazil. Of that I will speak at more length when I describe my own visit to the mine.

At the end of April we left Petropolis and went down to the Embassy at Rio.

The house at Petropolis was a very pleasant one to live in; a bungalow in the so-called colonial style, that is early nineteenth century, with a good garden running indefinitely up the side of a hill. We looked down on our neighbours on one side and up to them on the other. From the latter we were separated by a big hedge abounding in snakes, and as our daughter played with a neighbour's child we were a little nervous about it. There were plenty of snakes too in our garden. An English lady who came to stay with us was surprised, I don't know why, to hear this. "Do you mean to say," she asked, "that there are actually snakes in this garden?" "Yes," I answered, "there is one!" pointing to an English visitor who at that moment leapt about two foot from the ground as a snake glided past him. Our English governess, whose home was in Petropolis, told us that people "were complaining very much this year about the snakes," evidently thinking that the authorities ought to do something about it. The preparation of antidotes to snake bite is very important in Brazil and there is a famous snake farm at S. Paulo and others of less importance elsewhere. I, too, leaped very high from the ground when I found myself once about to tread on a sleeping coral snake, and we saw many whilst riding in the *Matto* (forest or uncultivated land), but they usually were only too anxious to get away. Once, too, at a picnic by a river ten or twenty miles from Petropolis we laboriously killed a snake with our sticks: it was a very tough snake and when we reported our victory to Brazilian friends they recognized it at once as a snake which was not only quite harmless to human beings but exceedingly useful as a devourer of poisonous snakes.

The gentleman who performed the standing jump in our garden was, by the way, Archdeacon Hancock, the British Chaplain at Rio, who had come up to lunch. I am not sure if it was he or his predecessor whom I had met at a Government luncheon in London given in honour of Dr. Epitacio Pessoa. When we had taken our places we were all, at any rate I was, thunderstruck by a call from the toastmaster: "Pray silence for the Archdeacon of Brazil." When I reflect upon the Archdeaconry in which I now live covering perhaps 200,000 acres I sigh at the thought of that of 2,000 million acres in which I once dwelt.

Here comes the Archdeacon again. On June 2nd, in honour of the King's birthday we gave a children's party. We heard that one small child was much interested in the great people he was to see. "What is an Ambassador?" "He is the representative of the King." "Will he be dressed like the King?" "Perhaps he will be in a beautiful uniform" (which he was not). "Will the Archdeacon be there?" "Yes, I expect he will." "And does he represent God?" "In a way, dear, he does." "Will he be dressed like God?" I should have felt rather small, even in uniform, if the Archdeacon had come dressed like the gentleman in Isadora Duncan's party at Marseilles.

The house where this party took place had been rented as an Embassy House by my predecessor, Ralph Paget. It had great merits and great drawbacks. The greatest merit of all was the glorious view from the roof over the bay in one direction and towards the hills in the other: a view worthy of ranking with that from our house at Pera. It contained three very big rooms, dining-room, drawing-room and study, and a sort of glazed-in verandah which made an extra sitting-room, but accommodation for servants was scanty, the house having presumably been built in the days of slavery. There was also a garden big enough to give a party in. The chief drawback was its inaccessibility. It stood on the hill of Sta. Thereza, perhaps five hundred feet or more above the town and approached by baddish roads. Some people, such as the French Ambassador, refused to bring their cars up the hill. Those who did not know the right road and took the most direct, which was terribly steep and cobbled, were apt to arrive at our parties, as the wife of a Brazilian Minister put it, *suffoquée de peur.*

The garden somehow was of little use for flowers, and even the Petropolis garden was not what we hoped. Everything came out all the year round instead of by seasons: and there was never a very great show at any time. There was too much sun one day and too violent rainstorms the next and too high winds the third. At Petropolis among other things we tried rhododendrons brought from a similar altitude in China and given to me by Mr. Lionel de Rothschild; they were planted in a sheltered position, but the wind was too much for them in the long run.

Birds, however, we had in plenty, including humming birds which were, to me, unexpectedly fearless, coming quite close to us as we sat in the garden. Our chief bird friend in our Rio garden was the 'Bem-te-vi' (I see you distinctly), a name which is supposed to represent its cry. It was mainly bright yellow and was I believe in the nature of an Oriole. There was a great collection of stuffed birds in the Rio Museum and while we were in Brazil a German lady sent a collection of 1,500 skins of birds shot by her in the *Matto* near Para. I was told that there are about that number of species in Brazil, being more than three times the number of the European species, but I have never verified the figures. The first officials made their collection from the windows of the museum, formerly the Emperor's Palace, from birds in the surrounding park.

Towards the end of June my wife and I paid our first visit to S. Paulo. This was a ceremonious occasion; S. Paulo being accustomed to receive Ambassadors on their first visit in a manner worthy of a semi-independent State. The first result of this was that having left the train we had to stand for what seemed an interminable time while a band played not only the Brazilian National Anthem and God Save the King but the Paulista Hymn as well. We left the station in a State carriage, with a cavalry escort, that is, with much the same ceremony as was used on the occasion of my presentation of credentials. Most of the high officials of the State were present on the platform and there was a Guard of Honour outside the station.

A member of the British community had most kindly lent us an excellent house for our stay of several days. We were told that some such arrangement was felt to be necessary because there was no hotel at which it would be suitable for my wife to stay. Before we left Brazil there was more than one fine modern hotel in that city, and the population, which was about half a million at the time of this visit, is now about a million and a half.

The *Times of Brazil* describes our visit as 'Sir John Tilley's Tour of Triumph to San Paulo.' Certainly everyone, Brazilian and British alike, was very kind to us. The President of the State, Dr. Washington Luiz, gave us a State banquet, the British community organized a big reception, and there was a Chamber of Commerce dinner at which I made a speech. We also visited the famous snake farm at Butantan; saw the virus being extracted, and admired the snakes, which were allowed out in a sort of garden, as well as a newly discovered and extremely poisonous snake which frequents the tree tops.

From S. Paulo we went with a large party to stay at the 'Fazenda' Tres Barras, managed by Mr. Charles McNeill, a day's journey by rail followed by a long drive over very elementary roads. One of our party was Sir David Hunter Blair (Father Oswald in religion), and the energetic Consul at S. Paulo, Mr. Abbott, and Mrs. Abbott went too. At a station well up-country we found that there was a party of British subjects to receive us, representing a small British colony. They had hired a band to play the National Anthem and made a great occasion of it. Talking to the leader of the party I happened to ask him where his home was. He said he came from Scotland, but his home was in a small place of which we should never have heard. I said we knew Scotland pretty well and he then told us he came from Ayrshire. I persisted in asking where in Ayrshire. From

DUCK-HUNTING

LADY TILLEY

Maybole. "Well," I said, "my wife is a daughter of Sir William Cuninghame of Kirkbride, on one side of Maybole, and this is Sir David Hunter Blair of Blairquhan on the other side." It was certainly remarkable that three representatives of Maybole should meet on the platform at a small country station in Brazil.

The 'Fazenda' was a cattle ranch of considerable size and we had a delightful ride over the estate. From Tres Barras we went on by a still more elementary road than the last to the 'Fazenda' Dumont, a famous coffee estate and the home of Santos Dumont, the aviator of early days. Father Oswald sat beside the driver and particularly enjoyed the excitement of avoiding the enormous potholes in the roads.

We were not, unfortunately, there at the right moment, a very brief one, for seeing the coffee in flower, which is described by everyone as a sight of wonderful beauty. At the time of our visit harvesting had begun and beans were spread out on the ground near the Fazenda house. Although we did not see the flowers the great sea of green on the red earth was a fine sight.

The coffee industry, for which Brazil and especially S. Paulo is famous, is not by any means indigenous, the first plants having been brought there in 1727 and export on any scale having only begun between 1835 and 1840.

From Dumont we returned to S. Paulo and so on to Santos by the S. Paulo Railway. This famous railway was first opened to traffic in 1867, and in 1901 a new route was completed known as the 'new Serra' (or hill side). The difference of level between the top and bottom of the Serra is eight hundred metres, the distance only ten kilometres, and the gradient round about 8 per cent. The trains are run by a system of rope haulage, and the route is divided into five inclines.

As I am now myself connected with the railway I do not wish to advertise its wonders too loudly, but I think I may say that the Brazilians themselves take great pride in the railway (*a Inglesa*), both in its construction and its running. At the time of my visit in 1921 money was extremely plentiful and people declared that the whole line was scrubbed by housemaids every morning.

At Santos we had a fresh round of ceremonies, the unveiling of a war memorial in the English church, and a reception, banquet and ball.

Santos, the port of S. Paulo, from which the greater part of the coffee is exported, is like the capital of the State, a rapidly growing city. Its climate, however, is extremely hot and many British families who do business there have their homes in S. Paulo, where the climate is much more temperate and there is a regular winter. There is a tremendous rainfall on the Serra, and some years ago we had a fall of twenty inches during the week-end (three days).

Returning to S. Paulo we had tea at the 'Alto da Serra,' the top of the inclines, where there is a small British colony of railway employees, and that night we returned to Rio.

H

When I look at the immense amount of space devoted to our San Paulo tour, by the Press both of Rio and S. Paulo itself, and the comments made, I think it must have been considered as a success.

Some time this autumn (or spring) I paid a visit to Bello Horizonte, the capital of the State of Minas Geraes and Morro Velho, where is the great gold mine.

Bello Horizonte had been planned as a splendid city and there were broad streets and avenues in all directions. Up to that time the buildings had not followed suit and the appearance of the city was consequently a little odd; magnificent roads bordered by insignificant houses. From Bello Horizonte I rode over to Morro Velho, a mounted policeman carrying my suitcase in front of him. It was a ride of some hours across country and the most striking moment was when my horse's feet clanked on the iron in the soil.

I reached Morro Velho about ten and my hosts told me that breakfast would be ready as soon as I had changed. About ten-thirty we sat down to fish and eggs and cutlets and sweets and tea and coffee and wine. I was to go down the mine at two, and I was asked whether I should like a cup of tea first. I rejected this offer, not being fond of tea at odd moments and not realizing that two o'clock was tea-time; the meal at ten-thirty had really been luncheon, the mine officials having breakfasted at six-thirty. Dinner was at six, and we went early to bed. These hours are all right if they do not take one by surprise.

The mine itself was extremely interesting, but the expedition was somewhat arduous. The whole depth was over six thousand feet, the deepest in the world I was told; but this descent was made in five stages, there being a longish walk, or rather crawl, between the foot of one and the head of another. At the bottom was a still longer crawl. The mine was well ventilated except the section where the men were actually working, which was extremely hot. Those who know anything about gold mines will realize that the gold does not glitter all round one, but a speck or two is pointed out here and there. The mine is an enterprise of which the English company, and particularly the General Manager, Mr. Chalmers, who had rescued it from a somewhat precarious position, had every reason to be proud. Mr. Chalmers only once appeared at a meal, being remarkably shy, but he lent me a delightful mule on which I went for a long ride in company with another member of the staff. At one point we had to climb out of a deep lane into a field above us: the place looked impossible, but the mule stood up more or less perpendicularly and made nothing of it. She also cantered well, which I believe is not common with mules.

There was a small and happy British community at Morro Velho, all connected with the mine, and the visit was altogether a very pleasant one.

The company continues to flourish and pays a handsome dividend.

We had many guests during the winter (or summer according to our ideas), including a dinner on the King's birthday, but I only pick out a few guests as texts. One of these came to an Eton dinner for which I collected eight old Etonians besides myself: this was Sir David Hunter Blair, otherwise Father Oswald, or Abbot Oswald when he became Abbot of Dunfermline, who had accompanied us to Tres Barras and was at the time living in the Benedictine monastery at S. Paulo. He had an excellent sense of humour and was always a welcome guest. Talking about the fondness of Brazilians for giving their children classical names, he told us of a child brought to him once by poor Brazilian parents in Pernambuco to be baptized. At the proper moment he asked what the child was to be named. "Alcibiades." "Nonsense, Alcibiades is probably in Hell," he declared. "I shall christen him Joseph." Another Etonian was Mr. Tarver, of the Western Telegraph Company, son of Harry Tarver, for many years a well-known figure at Eton as a French master. What the connection of the Tarvers with France was I don't know, but Harry Tarver's brother, Frank Tarver, also taught French at Eton for many years. Once when he was going to France for the holidays some other Eton masters were on the boat crossing to Dieppe. As soon as they landed they bribed a small French boy to run after Frank Tarver crying: "Rosbif. Goddam." He was not amused.

In September Lord Bessborough, the Chairman of the S. Paulo Railway, with Mr. Vernon Hinde, the Secretary, came to Brazil on a visit of inspection; they came to dinner at the Embassy and we asked the Minister of Viaçâo (transport) and a number of railway magnates to meet them. The Board of the S. Paulo Railway have always made a point of keeping in close touch with their staff in Brazil through personal visits by the directors; and during my years in Brazil the company was extraordinarily flourishing.

On October 21st we had a big dinner party of a different type altogether, for the guests included General Mangin, the hero of Verdun, and General Gamelin, at that time head of a French Military Mission which was helping to organize the Brazilian Army. General Mangin was on a complimentary mission to Brazil and a day or two later gave a great dinner and ball on the French cruiser *Jules Michelet*, which had brought him. Incidentally he was a good deal disturbed because so many of his Brazilian guests failed him, leaving great gaps in prominent places at table. I believe they were nervous about the possible movement in the Bay. Perhaps owing to their default we saw more of the General than we should otherwise have done, and we spent a good deal of the evening with him in his private cabin and made great friends. He certainly had all the appearance of a dashing soldier, and a caricature by Madame Hermes da Fonseca, wife of a former President, properly represents him with dark hair *en brosse* and a most aggressive nose and chin.

Exactly why the French were so anxious to cultivate the Brazilian Army I do not know, but Brazil had been one of our Allies during the War and French soldiers at any rate were a good alternative to Germans. Still, if General Gamelin was one of their coming men they kept him a longish time in a place where he had nothing to learn.

The Americans had a Naval Mission in Rio and consequently secured the contract for bringing up to date some of the Brazilian warships in American ports. I believe we might have had a Naval Mission during the war, but the Admiralty had said they had no officers to spare. I thought this a pity, for it is difficult to believe that officers from the reserve list could not have been found for such a purpose, at any rate as the nucleus of a mission.

On November 1st came Bishop Every, the Anglican Bishop of Argentina and Eastern South America, in whose diocese we were; a noble title and covering an even larger area than the Archdeaconry of Brazil, but not to my mind so high-sounding. Bishop Every was an admirable Bishop, but embarrassed me once considerably by taking me as the subject of his sermon while I was sitting at his feet.

On November 9th we had another large dinner at which the principal guests were Marshal Hermes da Fonseca and Madame Hermes, his young wife already mentioned.

It must have been on this occasion that the Marshal and Madame Hermes surprised us by staying till a very late hour after the guests had gone. At the moment we ascribed this to the charm of our conversation; actually, as it turned out, they hoped to slip home at midnight and escape arrest for complicity in a revolutionary movement. They succeeded, but very shortly afterwards the Marshal was arrested and lodged on board a warship in the bay. He was an old man and I do not think he long survived his imprisonment. We were at least fortunate that they did not ask for sanctuary. There would have been nothing very unusual in this, and during a later revolutionary movement one of my colleagues was put to extreme inconvenience by one of the opposition leaders who took refuge in his house, remained there for some time and made a practice of conversing with his supporters through his host's window.

Another guest at this dinner was Leopoldo Gotuzzo, a young painter of Italian origin who had studied in Paris and Rome and several of whose pictures we possess. The kingdom of Art in Brazil had exceedingly restricted limits; exhibitions were few and far between, and I think it is true to say that there was no Brazilian School of Painting. For that matter the parent country, Portugal, has never been rich in painters. One difficulty about landscape painting in Rio is, I believe, the too brilliant light.

November 22nd. Our chief guest was Sir Ernest Shackleton on his way to the South Pole. He stayed some time in Rio for repairs to his little ship *The Quest*, of one hundred and twenty tons. She was originally intended for a North Polar exhibition and was by no means well suited for the South Pole, where the difficulties of navigation are more severe. I liked Sir Ernest very much, but I could never discover what were the precise objects of his expedition; it seemed to be a sort of bow drawn at a venture, though he did not tell me that. He said he hoped to obtain an explanation of the 'Resaca,' a kind of tidal wave which bursts suddenly on

Rio from time to time and does immense damage by the destruction of embankments and roads on the sea front. Looked at purely as an entertainment the Resaca is a magnificent sight: huge waves fifty feet high breaking over the embankment walls of the Avenida Beira Mar.

Shackleton was not in very good health and he died aboard *The Quest* shortly afterwards in the South Atlantic.

Lest I may appear to suggest that our entertainments constituted a continuous series of successes I will mention one small party which owing to my bad handwriting was not a success. I invited a very clever young lady, of partly English extraction, who was employed in the museum, to come to dinner and bring her brother, also a very promising young man whose acquaintance we wished to make. Unfortunately she took my 'br' for 'm' and brought her aged mother, who was hardly able to move and still less able to speak.

Another visitor about this time was a young naval officer who was attached to the Embassy for a short time and had qualified as a Portuguese interpreter. I took him to see the Minister of Marine, with whom I usually spoke French, and explained that the young man could happily speak excellent Portuguese. The Minister began in that language, and the officer stared and stammered. I translated the Minister's remark and answered it myself. Then we tried again with the same result. Finally I carried on the conversation again myself in French. When we left I asked my friend what all this meant.

He told me that in order to pass his examination he had with the help of a friend translated some of his war experiences into Portuguese and learned it by heart. When the viva voce examiner started a conversation by some remark about the weather the young man exclaimed: "That reminds me," and reeled off his saying lesson with obvious success.

I nearly always spoke French myself on such occasions, but was capable of speaking Portuguese. The ordinary rule for Ambassadors is to do all their business with the Foreign Ministers, but I once arranged to see another Minister on some rather technical matter, in regard to which I thought we had reason to complain rather seriously of our treatment. This particular Minister not speaking French I spoke Portuguese and was probably a little blunter and less graceful than I should otherwise have been. Very soon the Minister stopped me and said: "If you wish to say disagreeable things you must say them to the President of the Republic." I thought, and still think, this an odd view and felt quite sorry for the President, but I managed to calm the Minister down before I left.

Before Christmas we returned to Petropolis and stayed there till the end of April. Nothing much out of the way happened during this summer, but we did a good deal of riding in wildish country, much of which has by now become suburban and populous. I went down to Rio twice a week at least and one of the joys of that journey was the sequence of colours provided by the flowering shrubs: white, red, yellow, purple.

The journey by the Leopoldina Railway was very comfortable and provided no incidents, except that once the train stopped unexpectedly between two stations and a Brazilian woman, fearing the worst, at once leaped out through the window, cutting herself badly in the process.

Of animal life I recollect seeing very little from the train, though most of the country through which the train passes was practically uninhabited. There were monkeys about Petropolis, but I seldom saw one, though a big monkey was killed one day in our secretary's garden. Monkeys when available are, I believe, a popular article of food with the poorer classes.

The winter of 1922 was much like the previous winter until the Centenary celebrations began in September.

Riding was practically out of the question in Rio and our best amusements were concerned with the water: picnics on one or other of the islands in the bay were often a feature of the Sundays, a bathe and then lunch and after siesta a little voyage to some other point. Once we passed a school of porpoises apparently playing a ball game. I believe that what looked like a ball was really a crab, but one porpoise tossed it up and another caught it and passed it on to a third; then the first porpoise got it again and so on. On one island where we sometimes picnicked orchids grew on a tree near the water, which reminds me that a guest once came from England to stay with us armed with a trowel for digging orchids out of the ground. Sometimes we had our picnic and bathed on the shores of the open Atlantic. On one of these occasions I had an extremely disagreeable experience. Thinking the plans of the younger members of the party (probably Kathleen McNeill, now Mrs. John Dewar, who was the life of many parties) too adventurous, I selected for my bathe a nice little round pool among the rocks, deep but only some ten or twelve feet across. I was much enjoying myself when a huge wave suddenly threw itself upon my pool and the water swirled furiously round and round carrying me with it. I expected at any moment to be carried out to sea and could only try to hold on to the jutting rocks. At last the wave subsided, leaving me in peace but with a good many nasty cuts.

Sometimes we went over to the Rio Sailing Club on the other side of the bay, a British club of which I was honorary president, and took part in the sailing races. I never got beyond acting as crew, but still look with pride at a prize handed over to me by the owner of the winning boat in which I once sailed. It is eminently Brazilian, or perhaps Portuguese, being a small figure of Neptune standing before a large shell which forms a toothpick holder; not an object which often figures among people's plate in this country. Those sailing days were very happy.

A more exciting adventure for us was our first aeroplane flight. An American with the auspicious name of Hoover brought a plane to Rio and took passengers up for short flights of half an hour round the bay at a height of a thousand feet or so. This was not so modest an affair as it would be now.

On June 10th Miss Talbot came to stay. Miss Talbot was a daughter of the fourth Lord Talbot de Malahide, a friend of Dom Pedro II. The Emperor on one of his visits to England had invited Lord Talbot to bring his daughter to Brazil, and these two accordingly set off. Unfortunately Lord Talbot was taken ill on the voyage and died at Madeira in 1883. Miss Talbot always wished to finish the journey, and as her brother, the fifth Lord Talbot, had married a cousin of my wife's, when we went to Brazil she saw and seized her opportunity, nearly forty years after her first essay. This pleased our Brazilian friends greatly.

At our dinner parties this winter, and in fact always, we tried to include as many Brazilians as possible. Many of our colleagues did not do this and at their parties one met only other diplomats, which seems to me a mistake.

So far as hospitality is concerned one's duty is surely first to the people of the country, then to one's colleagues and distinguished visitors, and thirdly the British community, putting first the leaders of its activities. Some people at home do not realize this and I once received an indignant letter from a gentleman in England whose daughter had recently married a young Englishman in some minor position at Rio. My correspondent said that his daughter had not received from us the hospitality which she naturally expected, but I was perhaps not aware that she had been presented to the Queen.

About the middle of July a military revolt broke out. We had made plans to pay a visit to S. Paulo and went off by the night train. When we arrived Mr. Abbott, our Consul, and others came to the train to meet us and told us that a revolt had broken out in Rio, so we decided to go back by the next express, that is the night train, from S. Paulo.

When we arrived we found that shells had been flying over the Embassy and my daughter had gone off to stay with one of the secretaries who lived outside the town. At luncheon time we heard firing in the distance. This turned out to be the end of the insurrection. A company of revolting troops, all in fact that remained, had established themselves at Copacabana, the suburb of Rio on the Atlantic shore, and had fought against a loyal force, greatly superior in number, till their last man was killed or driven into the sea and drowned.

On several occasions there were rumours of revolts, but nothing actually happened. Once we heard firing in the bay: the household came to tell us there was a naval revolt: we all hurried to the windows and watched the smoke of the ships' guns only to learn at last that they were firing a salute in honour of the Minister of Marine, who had gone out to assure the crew of his confidence in their loyalty.

August 28th. Cardinal Gasquet lunched with us. He had come to Brazil to consecrate the Benedictine Abbey Church of São Paulo, which had been ten years in building and which we had seen and admired in the course of our visit to São Paulo. Cardinal Gasquet was not far short of eighty, but was full of energy and was a charming guest.

He brought with him his secretary, Father Langdon, who told me about St. Benet Biscop mentioned earlier in this work. We asked some English Roman Catholics to meet the Cardinal, among them Henry, now Sir Henry, Lynch, and his mother and brother.

Sir Henry Lynch represents in Rio the interest of Rothschilds, for many years English bankers and financial supporters of the Government of Brazil. He has long done yeoman service for British interests in Brazil while always loyal to Brazilian interests.

We met the Cardinal again next day at the Nunciature, when the Cardinal Archbishop of Rio was also there. Cardinal Arcoverde of Rio was very infirm, but we were specially interested in meeting him as being a distinguished Brazilian of Indian blood, which is considered a matter for great pride.

August 9th. We had a dinner and dance for a team of English cricketers from the Argentine who came to play a Rio team, the star turn from the Argentine being C. H. Gibson, a former member of the Eton XI, who had played, I think, for the Gentlemen. The team played also at Santos and S. Paulo, and being chosen from a much larger community were likely to be a stronger team than any Brazilian side.

August 16th. We had a dinner party at which the guest of honour was the Italian General Caviglia, described as 'the hero of Vittoria Veneto,' who had come as special Ambassador from Italy. We had heard somehow that the General was an ardent fisherman, and we therefore asked an equally ardent English fisherman to meet him. This was General Crofton Atkins. After dinner Atkins drew up near General Caviglia and started the subject of fishing by asking whether his favourite form of the sport was dry fly, or whatever it might be, he himself being equally keen about everything. Caviglia replied that what he really liked best was putting down a net overnight and finding it full the next morning; an answer which proved a damper to the conversation.

Another guest was Senator Lauro Müller, a former Foreign Minister and a member of one of the principal committees of the Senate, I think that of Foreign Affairs. He had a grievance against fate. The weekly meeting of the committee was fixed for an hour which made it utterly impossible for the Senator to go to the 'pictures' on that day, thus leaving his week incomplete. I tried to imagine Lord Curzon or Lord Grey boggling at the hour for a committee meeting at the House of Lords because it broke the complete sequence of their visits to the cinema.

During all these months preparations were going ahead for the celebration of the Centenary of Brazilian Independence.

One of the works undertaken was the levelling of the Morro do Castello, an isolated hill sticking up in the heart of Rio, near the exhibition grounds. So far as we could see, this work was begun by two or three men with spades and seemed likely to last till the next Centenary. After a time a new plan was evolved by which the hill, several hundred feet in height was washed away on some American system. Even so the washing was not completed till long after the Centenary was over, but when the work was finished the improvement in the plan of the city was great. At the same time land was being reclaimed from the sea on which to lay out the grounds of the Centenary Exhibition. This also was a notable improvement.

Since then at least one other hill similar to the Morro do Castello has been removed.

CHAPTER IX

THE CENTENARY FESTIVITIES BEGAN ON SEPTEMBER 6TH, WHEN THE President received the special Ambassadors, myself included.

The British Government had done honour to Brazil by sending H.M. ships *Hood* and *Repulse* to take part in the Naval Review. The United States sent the *Maryland*: she arrived before our ships, and her praises as being the 'biggest battleship in the world' were loudly proclaimed by the American colony. Unfortunately for her, after a day or two she was completely dwarfed both by *Hood* and *Repulse*.

On September 7th, the anniversay of the day on which Dom Pedro I cried "*Independencia ou Morte*," there was a great review of troops by the President. We all attended in the Presidential stand. In the course of the morning we saw the wife of the Spanish Minister make a low curtsey to another lady; a strange happening in Brazil. The unknown lady turned out to be the widow of the heir to the monarchy. Her husband had been the eldest son of the late Infanta Isabella, the Emperor's daughter. With her were her children, her son being now the heir, and the Infanta's younger son, Dom Carlos de Braganza, and his wife. They had come from France at the invitation of the President to take part in the celebrations. The Infanta's husband, the Conde d'Eu, had also been of the party but died on the voyage. The body was embalmed and remained on the yacht which had brought them, or it may have been at the port of landing, and was eventually taken back to France for burial. The Imperial family consequently took no part in any of the social gatherings.

That they should be there at all was a testimony to the good feeling of the people of Brazil, for, though there were many of the old families who counted theoretically as Monarchists, the great bulk of the people were undoubtedly Republican.

Dom Carlos a few days later came with me to pay a visit to H.M.S. *Hood*. He and the Princess had a small room at an hotel in Rio and my wife and I were received by them there: the only obstacle to any form of ceremonious behaviour being that the size of the room made it necessary for us to get up from our chairs by turns. Nonetheless they were most kind and friendly hosts. Now, I believe, the Imperial family have their home in Brazil.

A number of the officers from our ships lunched and dined with us, including the Admiral, Sir Walter Cowan, who also gave a ball on board the *Hood*. Though I do not think that social entertainments were his favourite suit, that magnificent ship was duly admired by his Brazilian guests.

Other British guests were Lord Dundonald and his sister, Lady Elizabeth Cochrane; Lord Dundonald had crossed the Atlantic in a very small yacht with a crew of a dozen and himself in command. They had rather a rough and long passage, and as he had forbidden any use of alcohol the crew had not altogether enjoyed it; however, though a little late, they achieved a somewhat remarkable success in arriving at all. Lord Dundonald missed some of the festivities, but I see that he dined with us on September 14th, when we had also some Canadian guests who had come for the celebrations as representing their Government.

A further contribution by the British Government to the splendour of the proceedings was found in the British Pavilion erected in the grounds of the Centenary Exhibition. The exhibits were not very striking and we had had considerable trouble in persuading the Government to have a Pavilion at all. In the end a considerable part of the cost was defrayed from subscriptions raised in London.

Afterwards critics in London expressed some wonder and vexation that I had not, like the American Ambassador, arranged for the conversion of the Pavilion into a permanent Embassy house. The Americans, they said, were always so much cleverer in this way than ourselves.

I ventured to point out (1) that the Pavilion was built largely by subscription, and that the subscribers wished it to be presented to the Brazilian Government as a Museum; (2) that a bungalow consisting of three huge halls with a vast basement, built in the form of a public gallery, would not have been easily convertible into a residence; (3) that the site was extremely unsuitable for an Embassy, being close to a noisy street both before and behind; (4) that the American Pavilion was built as an Embassy house to be temporarily used as a Pavilion in the Exhibition; (5) that the American Ambassador nevertheless practically refused to live in the house. If I had waited a little longer I might have added that the American Embassy was in a very few years removed to the house in another part of the city which I had in vain pressed our Government to buy.

Here is briefly the whole programme of the celebrations, which shows surely that the Brazilians knew how to do things.

September   6th.   Reception of special Ambassadors.
                     Fancy Dress Ball at Jockey Club.
September   7th.   Review of Troops at 8 a.m.
                     Salute of National Flag by Pupils of National Schools.
                     Great Reception at the Presidential Palace at two
                       o'clock.
                     At four o'clock.   Opening of the Exhibition.

At eight o'clock. Torchlight Procession through the city.

At nine o'clock. Gala Performance at the Opera of *Guarany* by a Brazilian Composer.

At ten o'clock. Fireworks.

September 8th. At two o'clock. Opening of Great International Congress of American History.

At four o'clock. School-children's Procession.

At ten o'clock. Private and Popular Performances at the Theatre and Concerts in the Exhibition Grounds.

September 9th. Naval Review. Racing at 'Derby' Club. Reception at American Embassy. Athletic Games. Public Dances in the City Gardens.

September 10th. Opening of Education Conference. Racing at Jockey Club. Banquet by the Government in Honour of Mr. Hughes, the U.S. Secretary of State. Ball at British Embassy.

September 11th. *Déjeuner* at Naval Club in Honour of Foreign Naval Officers. Concert and Ball given by Belgian special Ambassador, M. Max (the Burgomaster of Brussels in the Great War).

September 12th. Dinner at the Palace in Honour of the President of the Portuguese Republic, followed by a Ball.

September 13th. *Fête Venicienne.*

September 14th. Dinner and Ball at the Foreign Office in Honour of the special Ambassadors.

The final fête was given by the Mexicans. Mr. Hughes and M. Max were perhaps the most prominent of the Foreign Representatives who came to Brazil for this occasion. Mr. Hughes, as far as I could make out, spoke no foreign language and appeared to be very reserved. Burgomaster Max was very lively and we found him most friendly.

On the night of the Belgian Ball, our own chauffeur being exhausted, we hired a car of which the driver turned out to be exceedingly drunk; this made the descent of the hill of Sta. Thereza remarkably perilous and we ended our journey on a lamp-post from which we walked the rest of the way. My wife stood for some time beside M. Max while he was receiving, and he confided to her that a considerable number of foreign officers were gate-crashers.

Our own Ball was, I believe, a success. Our three huge reception rooms could be turned practically into one, making a splendid ballroom with room to sit or stand out to one side. The verandah with steps leading into the garden gave easy access to a big supper tent, while a further tent joined the first to the Chancery offices in the garden. The great flat roof was arranged as a sort of lounge, with light refreshments, and many people spent most of the night there enjoying the marvellous view of Rio, always brilliantly lit, and the bay by moonlight. Mr. Hughes was one of them and I believe never came down till he finally left.

The Portuguese President stayed some little time in Rio and was present, among other occasions, at a lecture given in some theatre.

That evening my wife, having been scrupulously punctual for many months, and invariably obliged to wait a long time for the other chief guests, thought she might give herself five minutes' license. Result, when we arrived at the theatre we found that on that particular night everyone else had been scrupulously punctual. The grandees having taken their places in the front row every alley-way had been filled with chairs; as our places were at the front everyone in the theatre, some of necessity and others following their example, rose to receive us, including the two Presidents with their wives and the Cardinal Archbishop.

Hardly were the Centenary celebrations over when a deputation from the Inter-parliamentary Association arrived, including six members of Parliament with several ladies; Sir Douglas and Lady Newton, Sir John and Lady Norton Griffiths and others. On the morning after their arrival the six members came to call on me, and after a little preliminary conversation asked if I had any fresh London news. I said: "Only that there was to be a General Election," at which they bounded in their seats and with difficulty restrained each other from flying back to London forthwith.

They all dined with us and met a number of prominent Brazilians and later were entertained by the Brazilians at a dinner, where there was much speaking, some of our statesmen even venturing on French.

On the 19th Dr. Miguel Calmon among others dined; he became Minister of Agriculture in the next Administration. While occupying that post he took occasion at some public dinner to criticize severely British and Dutch Colonial Administration. His remarks were duly reported in the papers next morning, and as I had not been present and the Dutch Minister had, I went round to see what my colleague had thought of the proceedings.

He told me that like everyone else he had applauded loudly. "Surely not," I said, "considering what the Minister said about your country as well as mine." "Oh, but I don't understand a word of Portuguese; I merely applauded because everyone else did." "But what do you think now you have seen the papers?" "I don't read the papers, not knowing Portuguese."

On the next suitable occasion when I had to speak I quoted with approval an eloquent tribute paid by the Minister of Agriculture on some other occasion to British methods. The then Presidential household were highly amused and delighted at this way out.

In November Senhor Epitacio was succeeded as President by Dr. Arthur Bernardes of the State of Minas Geraes, and we had a new Foreign

Minister in Senhor Felix Pacheco, hitherto Editor of the *Jornal do Commercio*.

Dr. Arthur Bernardes was much less a citizen of the world than Senhor Epitacio, and his reign, as it turned out, was much troubled by insurrections. Early in December we moved to Petropolis, but the President was not so much in evidence there as his predecessor. Most of the other Ambassadors were, however, in residence.

One, M. Fallon, the Belgian Ambassador, dined with us one night in January. I always remember a sad remark of his. He had been talking of the war and Belgium before the war: "*Et nous étions si heureux,*" said Fallon with tears in his eyes.

In February we went home on leave. There were many banquets in our honour and the Press had a good deal to say on the subject.

The *Jornal do Commercio* said that thanks to my efforts a fresh impetus had been given to Brazilian relations with Great Britain; formality had disappeared and a much deeper interest was shown by public men of Britain in things Brazilian; while the *Times* spoke of the striking demonstration at our departure, indicating the cordiality of Anglo-Brazilian relations. The *Times* said there was a general feeling that we were rapidly regaining our pre-war commercial position, and, as a matter of fact, we did about this time regain our place at the head of the imports into Brazil.

Earlier in these memoirs I have spoken of the habit of some Secretaries of State of writing private letters to the Ambassadors and, even if they did not actually do business in that way, keeping in pleasant touch with them. I had every reason to be grateful to Lord Curzon in this respect, for I had a number of quite personal letters from him. In one written in August, 1921, he begins: 'Your very amusing letter (together with more than one despatch) have given me much pleasure.' He was glad to know that I liked the place so much, and that I allowed a spirit of 'gaiety' to pervade my official reports.

We had decided to go home by way of North America, taking a Lamport and Holt boat from Rio to New York, where we hoped to stay a week. On the way we spent a day at Trinidad and a day at Barbados.

At Trinidad the Governor, Sir Samuel Wilson, took us for a long drive, my chief recollection being of the trees bright with the red Immortelle. There was a Ball in the evening, and although I urged that I no longer danced, Lady Wilson insisted that everyone in Trinidad danced, which was, I believe, a fact, and I gave way.

Barbados was also of great interest. When we arrived we were taken up to our vast bedrooms at Government House and I looked out over a charming garden. There I saw several gardeners, one with a large 12 on his back and another with 14. I asked Lady O'Brien, the Governor's wife, whether she had taken the idea from *Alice in Wonderland*, but it appeared that the gardeners were prisoners doing their daily task. In Barbados, too, we had a long drive and saw among other things the little colony founded by the Royalists who fled from England during the Great Rebellion, and still surviving.

Before we left Rio an American friend who came to wish us a pleasant journey had urged us to make allowances for bluff. This was valuable advice. Some people go to the States (and elsewhere for that matter) full of the idea that everything is marvellous, well ahead of anything at home, life far more efficient and far more luxurious than it is in London, much less the English provinces. Having arrived they see precisely what they have been told to see, and even if they have any suspicions that things are not quite all they were led to expect they dare not say so for fear of being thought stupid. Even so, people travel in France and dare not say the food is bad for fear of being supposed to have no taste, although in country hotels the meat is often, or was when I last travelled there, as tough as leather. Similarly people who travel in England dare not say the food in country hotels is good; they mostly say what they have seen in some newspaper, even since motoring has revolutionized these hotels.

However, to get back to New York, we had only three days to spend there, our boat having broken a screw and been two days late. This, and a certain amount of dawdling to please a large party of American tourists, had annoyed me considerably. When we arrived in New York I was a little surprised that Lamport and Holt's agent did not come to see us. I heard afterwards that, realizing what my frame of mind was likely to be, he had studiously kept away.

One of the Consulate staff came to meet us and carried us off in a taxi to our hotel, leaving our luggage to follow by the much vaunted 'express.' The advice of our American friend at once came into play. The taxi to my surprise was a remarkably shabby old vehicle, but when I remarked to the Consul that this must be very exceptional, he said: "Not at all, they are all much the same." We got to the hotel about four, and expected our luggage to be there about the same time. It actually arrived late at night. More allowance for bluff. Our rooms in one of the most famous hotels were small but quite pleasant and very dirty. The Consul told me servants would not clean anything in New York. The heaps of dirty snow at certain street corners were, we were told, waiting to be cleared away in the course of a coming election, when the payment to be made for the work would win someone some votes. Nor were we impressed with the crowded subway or the management of traffic in the streets.

Having worked off these grouses I would go on to say that like the rest of the world we were properly impressed by the wonderful outlines of New York's vast buildings, especially as seen from the sea, and were quite ready with admiration for many other things. We saw, however, nothing that thousands of others have not seen and described, and except for a luncheon with the Consul General at his Club and a luncheon with friends at Sherry's we saw nothing of Society. It did seem to us that sky-scrapers mean an unduly large population in New York per square mile; so long as people stay in their flats it may be all right, but when they emerge they take up too much room.

Arrived in London we had a good many public dinners, including one given by the South American Committee of the House of Commons, a body which I think must have faded away. On that occasion there was a big gathering collected mainly by Sir John Norton Griffiths, and I see that my health was proposed by Sir Philip Lloyd Graeme, afterwards Sir Philip Cunliffe Lister, and now Lord Swinton.

While at home I was elected, thanks to George Duckworth, a member of the Society of Dilettanti, then not very far short of its bicentenary. Its dinners when I was at home on leave, and since my retirement, have been a frequent source of interest and amusement. The initiation ceremonies include a series of profound obeisances to the President chosen for the evening. Lord Inchcape, who was admitted on the same evening as myself, whispered to me that enforced humility was very good for people who were not much accustomed to the exercise of that quality.

In August I returned alone to Rio, my wife continuing her holiday, and at the end of the month paid another visit to S. Paulo.

Soon after my return I met an English friend who said: "This must all look very small to you after London." I said: "On the contrary it looks simply vast." Miss Olivier, in her book, *Country Moods and Tenses*, speaking of the Infinitive mood, quotes the *Oxford English Dictionary* as defining Infinitude as 'the quality of being infinite, boundlessness, immensity, vastness.' These are the sort of words that I should use about Brazil. Rio itself, with the Atlantic on one side and the great bay on the other, stretching for many miles along their shores, with its views of near and distant mountains, always gave me this same idea of vastness.

My first notable visitors this time were Lord and Lady Bessborough, who came on a S. Paulo Railway visit, bringing with them Lord Ridley and his mother, Lady Ridley. They stayed in Brazil some time and saw a great deal. I had a dinner for them, mostly of leading Brazilians.

On November 8th, on behalf of H.M. Government I handed over the British Pavilion to the Brazilian Government, who were represented by the Minister of Justice, Joaô Luiz Alves, a remarkably able man. There was a big gathering and Lord Bessborough, who had been to S. Paulo in the interval since our last meeting, came back for it. I made a longish speech in French which seems to have been a success.

The *Jornal do Commercio* described it as a complete departure from the type of speech usual on such occasions and 'a vigorous and impressive history' of Anglo-Brazilian relations. An old member of the British community writes to me that it is 'remarkable for the Velho Orgão to ventilate such undisguised admiration.' He goes on: 'As one of the "old men of the village" to offer me his very sincere congratulations; a record has been established,' etc., etc., all of which was very comforting.

I had referred in my speech to the decoration of the walls with pictures

of the Seven Seas: and went on to speak of the love of Englishmen for the
sea, of their great voyages of discovery and then of the great voyages of
the Portuguese in the fifteenth and sixteenth centuries which took them
as far as India and China. I quoted a letter addressed to King John II
by Politian and recorded in the first chapter of the *Cambridge Modern
History*. Politian, 'the foremost scholar of the Renaissance tenders to the
Portuguese king the thanks of cultivated Europe. New lands, new seas,
new worlds, even new constellations, have been dragged from sombre
darkness into the light of day.'

I spoke also of the romantic expeditions of the Brazilian *Bandeirantes*
into the interior of their vast country, of Canning, of the fact that the
principal decoration of the Foreign Minister's office was a portrait of
Canning's emissary, Sir Charles Stuart; of the incredible wealth of Brazil,
of our need of her products, notably cotton, and finally of my wish for and
hope of better mutual knowledge between our two countries.

On the evening of that day my wife returned and by the same boat
came Lady Curzon on her way to Buenos Ayres. She spent the night with
us and we gave a dinner for her and afterwards there was a great reception
and Ball at the Palacio Itamaraty—that is, the Foreign Office. There
was much confabulation beforehand as to whether there should be any
dancing; I assured them that Lady Curzon would like it; the Brazilians
feared that she would consider a Ball too frivolous. When I told Lady
Curzon this she was highly amused and I was able to reassure the Ministry
by telephone. When the time came Lady Curzon played her part extremely
well and the Brazilians were much impressed. I had charming letters from
Lord Curzon and Lady Curzon about her visit.

In December we went back to Petropolis. This season was enlivened
by polo, organized by some of the younger Englishmen. I see that I
actually wrote a poem on the subject of the polo for the benefit of Kathleen
McNeill, who replied in a poem of her own; not having ventured to ask
Mrs. John Dewar's permission, I print neither poem.

At the end of 1923 came a financial mission headed by Mr. Edwin
Montagu and including Sir Charles Addis, Lord Lovat, and Sir William
McLintock. There was some doubt in people's minds as to the origin of
the mission, which was a private affair arranged by those interested in
Brazilian trade.

Not being very certain of the attitude of the Brazilian Government
I made no great parade of the occasion, but we saw a good deal of the
various members and Lovat and Addis stayed with us. Before their
departure they made a number of wise recommendations for the benefit
of the Brazilian Government and suggested various economies, but I am
afraid nothing very much came of their advice.

In April I had a farewell letter from Lord Curzon, hoping that some
day we might be again associated, and adding that Lady Curzon still talked
enthusiastically of her visit to us.

We had had quite a pleasant summer at Petropolis, and apart from ordinary business and amusements I must record one experience of my wife's. She had gone to visit some public institution for the aged poor, and while there the Sister in charge pointed out to her an old man walking about with nothing on but a night shirt. This did not seem particularly strange, but the Sister explained that the old man was one hundred and twenty years old. He had been going about in that state for some little time, having announced one morning that he had put on trousers every day for a hundred years and did not mean to go on any longer.

In May the Government gave a great banquet in honour of Cardinal Arcoverde to celebrate the Jubilee of his Priesthood. The Cardinal, as a Prince of the Church, was treated as Royal, almost super-Royal, for he sat on a very high chair (said to be a relic of the Empire) well above the level of his fellow guests. His Eminence, who was not only aged but very infirm, was unable to deliver his speech himself and it was read for him, nor did he enter into any conversation. The occasion, however, was the subject of much comment, as indicating the intention of the Government to reaffirm its Christian and Catholic character.

In September the light cruiser squadron under Admiral Brand spent a week at Rio, and we had another long round of festivities. We gave a dance for the officers, but the midshipmen were a little blasé, for this was nearly the end of a tour during which they had attended, if I remember right, ninety Balls. All the same the midshipmen (Lord Borodale, now Lord Beatty, was one) thought they had a better time than the senior officers, for not being wanted so often for ceremonies they had been able to see rather more of the places which they visited. One of the entertainments was a luncheon on the terrace of a restaurant half-way up Mount Corcovado. There was a fog which gave Admiral Brand the opportunity for some humorous remarks about the efforts of his hosts to make him feel at home. The Admiral made himself very popular.

Another ceremony which was the cause of considerable trepidation to myself was a review in the square before the Presidential Palace, which took place on September 7th, one of the Brazilian Anniversaries. Owing to doubts of the loyalty of the Army only the Municipal Guard and the Cadets were to march past with some Brazilian naval detachments and men from our ships, for whose presence I had arranged.

The President stood on the balcony of the Palace to take the salute, and as our men were taking part he did me the honour of asking me to stand beside him. The first part of the ceremony passed off without incident, but the cadets were for some reason late in arriving and we stood for a very long time in solitary grandeur on the narrow balcony. What was mostly in my mind was that we were within easy range of the houses on the other side of the square, and although there was said to have been a search made I felt no confidence that someone would not presently appear with a rifle or that he would be sure to hit the President. However, except for a

I

sense of general depression, nothing untoward (I believe this is the classical word) happened.

In January, 1925, we gave a big dinner to celebrate the appointment of Raoul Régis d'Oliveira as Ambassador to Great Britain.

In proposing his health I expressed my conviction that he and Madame Régis would earn unbounded popularity in London and that no choice of an Ambassador could possibly have been happier. Fifteen years later, when I went to say good-bye to Régis before his departure from London, he reminded me of that speech and said, very modestly, that he hoped his mission had realized some of my kind prophecies. It had indeed surpassed them, for the position of Régis and Madame Régis in London Society was quite remarkable.

I once ventured to tell Mlle Régis d'Oliveira of a paragraph which I, but not she, had seen in a London paper. It was a complaint that nowadays people liked everything that was foreign better than what was English: things had gone so far that the most popular girl in Society was not English but the daughter of the Brazilian Ambassador.

Régis d'Oliveira and Madame Régis were certainly an ideal pair as the representatives of their country or of any country, having the great gift of charm as well as talent and good looks. They did not actually leave Rio till March.

About that time General Pershing, the American Commander in the Great War, arrived at Rio. Among other celebrations he was entertained by the British Legion at a cocktail party in their Club, at which, as Honorary President, I took some part and proposed his health. He, too, was a popular guest.

The British Legion in Rio had a very numerous and well-organized membership, and though I had no record of military service myself, I saw much of them and received a great deal of kindness at their gatherings, not forgetting a noble cigar box when I left.

In 1924 and 1925 there was serious revolutionary trouble, and a certain amount of fighting in São Paulo, where the anti-Government movement was strong, and there was some Separatist feeling. I managed to make some arrangement for taking away British subjects if necessary, but the need did not arise. A somewhat humorous feature of the troubles was the complaint made in the Press of the wicked behaviour of some German immigrants who had been enlisted by the insurgents and provided with rifles; having got these rifles into their hands the Germans let them off and killed people, which was accounted a serious breach of hospitality.

There was no doubt a feeling in São Paulo that they earned a very large proportion of the country's wealth while, compared with Rio, their share of influence was too small, but I still doubt whether the feeling really went very deep.

The movement unfortunately prevented us from seeing more of Brazil, as we had contemplated an expedition to Parana and other places in the south, but were warned that in existing circumstances it was impossible. My eldest daughter did go in May, 1925, with a party of friends to a remote place in Matto Grosso. They travelled by a special train which the authorities had kindly provided and then drove a hundred miles by car across country to the farm where they were to stay and have some shooting. On arrival at the farm they found it deserted by their hosts, and an old negro who had been left in charge explained that the rebels were quite near and they had better make haste back to the railway, which they did forthwith. Being unwilling, nevertheless, to give up their holiday altogether they stayed a few days at the railway station, which they shared somewhat uncomfortably with a company of Government soldiers.

From the station they rode hither and thither over the country and had great fun pursuing and photographing tapirs and ant-eaters, besides killing some game.

Another result of the insurrection movement was that in 1925 the President, Arthur Bernardes, was from time to time marooned in Petropolis; there being serious fear that he would be attacked on the way to Rio if he attempted the journey. Consequently Madame Bernardes had to do the honours of the Presidential Palace even at official banquets.

Among other visitors early in 1925 Colonel Fawcett came to lunch with us at Petropolis, and I saw him again in Rio in May, not long before his departure for the interior. Colonel Fawcett's theory was that somewhere near the western frontier of Brazil, behind a barrier of mountains, there was the remnant of a white race, entirely cut off from communication with the outside world. I believe his theory was that they had migrated to this area some ten thousand years ago and had there developed a high civilization. His ideas were founded on stories which he had heard from Indians living in the frontier districts; and his intention was to visit and re-open communication with the lost tribe.

He was aware that his journey would be a dangerous one, but he showed me a ring with some inscription on it which he believed would be a talisman when he came to deal with savage Indians. After leaving ordinary civilization in Matto Grosso his first hard trial would be to cut his way through dense *matto* for about a fortnight. He had already tried this once before with a young American companion, but the young man, Fawcett told me, could not do without food, whereas it was only possible to carry a very small quantity and depend otherwise on such snakes as they could kill. That did not satisfy the American and they had to turn back. This time he had with him his son and his son's friend, two fine tall young men, and as he himself was a big strong man he was confident of success.

After cutting their way through the *matto* they would come to a district inhabited by pygmies. These would give no trouble as they were very timid: they had moreover no speech. After the pygmies they would come to the country of the cannibal Indians, where the talisman was to come into

play. The expedition was to be a very long and slow one and I was not to
expect any news of it for at least a year.

I asked if he was to have the help of the Brazilian authorities, especially
of General Rondon, himself of Indian origin, who was a real authority
on everything concerned with the interior of Brazil. Fawcett said no, the
Brazilians might interfere and spoil everything and he would rather play
a lone hand. I pointed out that after all the country belonged to the
Brazilians and they had a perfect right to be consulted, but Fawcett was a
fanatic and would not listen to reason.

My daughter and her friends saw him off at S. Paulo in May. He was
never heard of again.

About the end of June in this year we went off on a visit to the Ouro
Preto gold mines at Passagem in Minas Geraes. This was the district in
which the search for gold had been prosecuted a hundred years earlier and
it was here that the hills had all been scarred in the process. The existing
gold mine was of the usual pattern, though not so deep as that of Morro
Velho.

We were the guests at Passagem of Mr. Bensusan, the manager, and
Mrs. Bensusan, and they took endless trouble to show us everything of interest
in the mine and in the surrounding country. Passagem differed from Morro
Velho in that the mining community was not self-centred, but formed only
part of the population of a small town. The number of employees in 1925
was nine hundred and the inhabitants of Passagem numbered some four
thousand.

One of our expeditions was to the neighbouring town of Marianna,
the seat of an Archbishopric. There we visited the Cathedral and were
astounded to see the whole of the Chancel panelled with Chinese red
lacquer, covered with figures in gold. I gained great 'kudos' among the
party by putting the date at the middle of the eighteenth century because the
figures looked like Frederick the Great's Grenadiers. The wonder was how
this lacquer came there. We were told that it was done by a Chinese work-
man who had been employed on the gold diggings. We were also told that
in the early part of the nineteenth century there was a great deal of money
in Marianna, thanks to the gold, and as the town was three weeks' journey
from Rio most of that money was spent on the spot. Hence the elaborate
churches and some excellent houses.

Afterwards Mr. Bensusan wrote to tell me that he had heard from the
Archbishop that the panels were done in Marianna itself by a Jesuit in 1756.

On our return journey we rode on mules from Passagem to Ouro
Preto, which is also an interesting old town, old, that is, as Brazilian
towns go.

For this year 1925 we had abandoned our house on the hill at Sta.
Thereza as being too inconvenient of approach for those who wished to come
to the Embassy, and we took a house in Botafogo, the residential quarter
near the sea front. This house was not nearly so good as regards the

reception rooms, but it had better bedrooms, and it had an excellent garden with a tennis court. For the King's Birthday we were able to put up marquees in the garden which answered the purpose admirably; otherwise we had to limit our dinner parties to about twenty.

The value of a garden in Rio is immense, and the absence of a garden provided one of my strongest objections to the Exhibition site. When we first saw the house at Sta. Thereza we were disturbed to find that cars had to stop at an appreciable distance from the front door. We asked what we were to do about our guests when it rained. The answer was that it would not rain between April and December, and though this was an exaggeration it was a pardonable one, for only once did it cause any sort of inconvenience. Ordinarily, when you have continual sun and continual, though it may be moderate, heat, plenty of room out of doors is most desirable. Moreover, with all that sunshine, which is one of the glories of Rio, the sun is for some reason, which has a scientific explanation, not dangerous: sunstroke is unknown; sun helmets are unknown, and young people play lawn tennis in the afternoon bareheaded; lawn tennis or football for that matter.

Also this year we had the happiness of welcoming Pat Ramsay, our Constantinople companion, now complete with wife and family, as Counsellor of Embassy, and with Bob Howe, obviously destined for a successful career, as Secretary, we were very happy.

We were now approaching the end of our Brazilian life, and about June and July I was surprised to find friends, Senhor Epitacio Pessoa, for one, congratulating me on my appointment to Tokyo.

When the Japanese Minister joined in these congratulations I was still more astonished and could only repeat that I knew nothing about it. At last a telegram came from the Foreign Office informing me that to save time they had asked the Japanese Government for my *agrément* before communicating with me. The real explanation was that someone had forgotten to send me the usual telegram offering me the post. The position had been a little embarrassing, but I soon got over it and began to look forward to my new and still more strange life.

In due course the series of farewell banquets began and we received immense kindness from both our Brazilian and English friends. I mean friends in the literal sense of the word, for we did feel that there was a delightful air of friendship about.

I had to pay my farewell visit to Madame Bernardes instead of the President, who was still a recluse, and at last in August we sailed in the *Arlanza* for England.

I hope that I have made it plain that we left, for very many reasons, full of regret and *Saudades*; *saudades* being defined as longing for an absent friend.

At the same time I hope that I have also made clear not only my admiration for all the wonders of Nature in Brazil, but my conviction that they will all gradually be brought into employment for the benefit of that great country. Brazil may, like other countries, have troubles, but she is not likely to disbelieve the saying: *Deus é brasileiro.*

CHAPTER X

I STARTED FOR JAPAN ON JANUARY 7TH, 1926, MY SON GOING OUT WITH me as Honorary Attaché.

I had spent most of my leave at home in Suffolk, but in brief visits to London had seen something of representative Japanese and others interested in the country.

There was a dinner at the Japanese Embassy at which we met young Prince Chichibu, the second son of the Emperor, who had been spending some time in England and hoped to stay considerably longer. He was living with General and Mrs. Laurence Drummond, who had taken a house for him at Coombe, and we also met him at dinner there. Later he went to Oxford, but after one term was recalled to Japan on the death of his father when he became heir presumptive. He spoke English very well, seemed to take kindly to English ways and went about quite unpretentiously, making many English friends. What his feelings about this country were I cannot pretend to know, but in any case he exercised no influence in his own country.

I had, of course, more than one talk with the Japanese Ambassador, Baron Matsui, and a scrap of conversation has often recurred to me. There was a great deal of trouble in China about that time, which much disturbed our trade and our general relations with that country. Baron Matsui said that there had often been periods of trouble in China in the past but in the end someone always turned up to put things right. "We may wait fifty years and then we shall find everything going well again." I said: "That may be all very well for you, but my Government likes to hear that things will be going well again next week."

Equally, of course, I had a farewell interview with Sir Austen Chamberlain, who was then Foreign Secretary. It was very brief, and from that time till my retirement my intercourse with British Foreign Secretaries was limited to one other conversation with Sir Austen during my first leave from Japan and a few minutes with Mr. Henderson when I said farewell to the Foreign Office. I did not therefore feel that I had any sort of personal relation with my chiefs. I cannot recollect anything in the nature of a personal letter, and very few private letters of any sort. Sir Austen, however, was reported to be a very tired man by this time, and overworking himself terribly, so that he probably had no time for extras. Indeed, some people say that personal relations are unnecessary, and as long as no fault is found with a man he ought to be satisfied. I still think there is something meagre about this system.

Our journey to Japan was for the most part uneventful. We spent a day at Aden, where we were kindly received by the Resident and saw the wonders of the place. My chief surprise was at hearing that the place was not an unpopular station even with ladies. Our next stop was Colombo: then came the lovely island of Penang and then Singapore, where we stayed two nights with Sir Lawrence and Lady Guillemard at Government House. It was hot, but not too hot, and my bedroom was the biggest I had ever seen; going into the room in the morning I only discerned after a minute or two that there was a servant in a distant part of it. I was taken out to see the new naval base on which work was beginning and decided not to enlarge on the subject at Tokyo.

From Singapore we went on to Hong Kong, where we dined with Sir Cecil and Lady Clementi, always good friends. They were at Mountain Lodge at the top of the Peak, wrapped in damp fog, and the last part of the journey in litters of sorts was somewhat alarming because at times my litter seemed to hang practically in mid-air and over a precipice.

At Hong Kong I took part in a kind of Council of War, at which the Governor, the Admiral, Sir Edwyn Alexander Sinclair, and Jamieson, the Consul General at Canton, were present. They were very indignant at the treatment which British subjects had been receiving and the violation of various Treaty rights. The Admiral seemed to be in a warlike mood. I said: "You must not imagine that our Government will listen to any talk of armed force; certainly not unless British subjects suffer much more seriously than they have hitherto." The Admiral turned to the Consul General and said: "Well, your duty is pretty obvious." "What do you mean?" "Why, you must go into the native quarter of Canton and be murdered."

As I anticipated, our differences with China never led to actual war, but we sent troops to Shanghai in 1927.

Before I left Brazil a friend had sent me a copy of a letter from a brother of his who lived in Hunan. The writer foresaw a rising of all Chinese against foreigners within the next few years, simply because they had imbibed the current ideas of self-determination.

He was not far wrong, but as it turned out the Japanese have directed this anti-foreign feeling against themselves as the chief enemy rather than the Europeans.

From Hong Kong we went on to Shanghai, where I saw Barton, the Consul General, and so to Kobe, where we landed. Two of the Embassy staff had come down from Tokyo to meet me, and while I was greeting them, saying good-bye to our Captain and keeping an eye on the luggage which we wanted at once, and the luggage which was to follow, I was constantly pestered by an American lady reporter asking all sorts of idiotic questions. I only relate this incident because I read afterwards in her newspaper that I looked benevolent, which I was very far from feeling.

We had a night's journey in the train and in the morning passed the station at Yokohama, still more or less in the ruinous state in which it had

been left by the great earthquake of 1923. Then Tokyo, where the rest
of the big staff were waiting to receive me.

We drove off almost at once to the Embassy which, such as it was, was
to be our home for five years. The house stood in a very large compound
close to the outer moat of the Imperial Palace. The old Embassy House and
all the houses for the married members of the staff and all the offices, everything in fact, had been destroyed in 1923. My predecessor, Sir Charles
Eliot, who was a bachelor, had had a bungalow built for him in what I
believe is called Canadian wood pulp. A bungalow such as this, I was told,
had great merits because in case of an earthquake and the collapse of
the roof you could push the ruins off your bed quite easily. Apart from this
the merits were small, but there was a very big dining-room and an equally
big drawing-room, with no other sitting-room except the Ambassador's
study. The bedrooms were very small, and there was a little guest house
close by in which during our stay in Tokyo many illustrious guests found a
very modest shelter. We persuaded the Office of Works to add another little
bungalow for two English servants. The English Clerk of the Works put
into that bungalow a Japanese bath, that is a large barrel in which the
bather sits up to his neck in hot water. He tried to argue that English
servants would be sure to like it. I said that an English lady's-maid would,
I was quite certain, wish to leave at once on sight of it, and he eventually
put in an ordinary one.

Besides our house there was only the Chancery office and a small lodge
occupied by an old Japanese woman, the widow of a former Embassy
servant. The little house was overshadowed by a cherry tree and the old
woman lived in constant anxiety lest in the course of rebuilding operations
the tree should be cut down, for her husband's soul was in it.

Sir Charles Eliot, I believe, liked heat, but had arrived at having neither
heat in winter nor coolness in summer, for large glazed-in verandahs had
been put up in front of the study window, and in front of our bedroom
windows, keeping out such sun as there was in winter and most of the
air in summer.

He and I had different temperaments in another respect also, to the
disgust of the Clerk of the Works. Eliot had strongly objected to having a
cat in the Embassy, which committed, as he said, the social indiscretion of
producing kittens in the study. The cat was got rid of and then I came
and complained bitterly of the smell of dead rat under the study floor.

The Clerk felt that between an Ambassador who objected to cats and
another who objected to rats he had a bad time. I believe the best thing to
have for rats is a snake or two in the roof, but we never arrived at that.
Consequently rats used to gallop round the frieze of the dining-room till
they were swept off by the 'boys' with long brooms and killed by our dog
on the floor.

The Clerk of the Works was an emissary from the Office of Works
branch at Shanghai, which is, or was, maintained there to supervise the

numerous Government buildings in the Far East. The only beautiful thing about the Embassy compound was a double avenue of cherry trees on the road outside, which one of my predecessors, Sir Harry Parkes, I think, had obtained leave to plant.

Before leaving for Japan we had had a meeting with Colin Davidson, the Consul at Tokyo, who was at home on leave. He, as a member of the Japan Consular Service, had spent over twenty years in Japan, mostly attached to the Embassy. We asked him about the climate. Was the winter pleasant? No, horrible. Was the summer hot? Yes, terribly hot. Then probably the spring was the best time: in the spring it rained without ceasing, and the autumn was not much to boast of. Moreover, there is something missing, oxygen or ozone or something, in the atmosphere, which makes it very lowering for Europeans. However, I cannot say that our health suffered from any of these drawbacks.

The Japan Consular Service, to which Davidson belonged, was one of the special branches which the Foreign Office maintained for many years. Their belief was that in Eastern countries, where life was entirely different from European life, and the language extremely difficult to master and the mentality of the people still more so, the best plan was to have a set of officials who would devote their lives to the particular task of acquiring as complete a knowledge as possible of the country. I believe the idea was right, but they eventually came up against the old problem: are the men made for the Service or is the Service made for the men?

I, too, had come up against this problem again not long before I went to Brazil, when forming one of a selection committee for the Consular service. We sometimes asked bright young men whether they would like to be considered for the China or Japan service, which had special attractions in the way of pay and promotion, but they nearly always said they did not want to be so far from home; which was rather a sad falling-off in the spirit of adventure.

However, when I went to Japan we had in Tokyo at least three brilliant examples of what the Service could turn out: Harold Parlett as 'Japanese' Secretary, George Sansom as Commercial Councillor, and Colin Davidson as Consul. They were all great Japanese scholars and very able advisers.

I understand that the Foreign Office are giving up all these special services, which in my opinion is a great mistake. Some men may find it tiresome to spend their whole official lives in one country, or at any rate in one part of the world, but I believe that British interests have in the past benefited and will continue to benefit by having real experts in countries which have not only a very different language but a very different habit of thought to ourselves.

My predecessor, Sir Charles Eliot, under whom Parlett had served for six years, once told me that besides being a man of ability Parlett was the most conscientious and industrious man he had met; and this was not a mere *obiter dictum*, but a serious estimate.

However, I will tell one story against him. Soon after my arrival, while walking with Davidson, I observed that there were not many cars in Tokyo. He assured me that I was mistaken. There were now a very large number. I still said that compared with London, or for that matter with Rio, I was inclined to disagree. A few days later he told me that after this conversation he spent five minutes by his watch looking out of the Consulate window in the busiest part of the town. He had counted eighty cars, which after all was not very many. A few days later I again started the same conversation with Parlett. Like Davidson he said I was mistaken and he could prove it. "Davidson, sir, the other day counted the cars passing the Consulate and in five minutes there were two thousand." "No," I said, "that won't do. Davidson counted them for my benefit and there were eighty." "Well," said Parlett, "two thousand is what Davidson's clerk told my wife."

Whatever there may have been in Tokyo there certainly were not many private cars in the country: when we drove, as we sometimes did, to places fifty to eighty miles away from the capital, we seldom passed one; indeed the roads, except the great trunk road from north to south, were anything but good for cars. In Tokyo itself, by the way, there were practically no taxis. The pace of the ox still to a large extent prevailed. Except in the main business streets people stood about in the middle of the road oblivious of the possibility of being run over; we did in fact run over a man in Yokohama once who was standing at a street corner: fortunately we were going, necessarily, very slow and the man was not much hurt; moreover, when we made inquiries of the police about him we were told that it was a matter of no importance for the man turned out to be a Corean (and therefore according to Japanese ideas deserving of a worse fate). Rickshaws were not very much in evidence, but there were always some about and a few ladies came to the Embassy in them.

Japan, in fact, was by no means so Westernized as many people have believed. This is not a point on which it is possible to speak with exactitude. The Japanese had undoubtedly in the last sixty years learned much, both from the military and the industrial points of view, but their manners and customs had changed very little, and by 1926 were, if anything, beginning to revert to type. Some young men and women made a parade of wearing European clothes and living a more or less free life, but at Court while we were in Japan the ladies who had been wearing European clothes in 1926 were wearing Japanese clothes in 1930. During the last year or two I found the Minister and Vice-Minister for Foreign Affairs much oftener in kimonos than when I first went. Many, probably most, Japanese, even of high degree, if they wore European clothes during the day changed to the kimono when they went home in the evening. At the theatre and at the railway stations where there were always crowds, those crowds, male and female, were mostly in Japanese dress.

Japanese ladies were even in 1926 going much less into European society than they had done some years back. One well-known lady who brought her young daughters to dance at our house, and enjoyed it, had soon to give it up as otherwise the girls would not find husbands. That same lady, a widowed Countess, told us that when she went home with her daughters after an evening party she left the car some way from her house, as her mother-in-law would be annoyed if she knew what they had been about. Englishmen who had lived in Japan many years told me that they used to make Japanese friends fairly easily, but that was no longer the case.

So with the teaching of English. When I first went, there were a considerable number of English professors and teachers in the universities and colleges. While I was there the number was gradually diminishing. The Imperial University pleaded poverty, but I heard that the authorities were saying there were enough Japanese qualified to teach English, and that it was unnecessary to go on importing Englishmen. That there were many Japanese so qualified was quite untrue, for the Japanese are ordinarily poor linguists, and the English that they taught was correspondingly poor.

I have just come across the print of an opening speech made by some high Japanese authority at the Annual Convention of English teachers and addressed to the Minister of Education, who was evidently present. My copy is in English, but was probably a translation, made perhaps for my benefit.

The speaker insists on the absolute necessity of teaching the students 'ordinary plain English—*futsu no Eigo*.' I should not have seen his point so well had I not heard from Englishmen engaged in teaching Japanese that they were expected to adapt their lessons not to the knowledge and capacity of the student but to his general standard in his school. That is to say, they found themselves giving lessons which their pupils were quite unable to understand, because their pupils would have felt themselves dishonoured (a very important point in Japan) if they had been given lessons suited to a lower standard. Their pupils, of course, really assimilated nothing.

It must have been a Japanese student of this sort that I once made acquaintance with on some boat on which I was travelling. He was reading with great assiduity a play of Shakespeare's, but when I asked him about it he admitted that it conveyed nothing whatever to his mind.

I may add here a note about the effect on English classes of the Japanese practice of keeping a watch on what they call 'dangerous thoughts' among the students. Teachers have told me that they have suddenly missed this or that youth from their class and on inquiry have discovered that he had been removed from the university for having these 'dangerous,' i.e. leftist, thoughts.

One of the first addresses which I myself gave in Japan was at a Convention of Japanese Middle School Teachers. It was the first of many which I gave in a variety of universities, colleges and schools of all sorts;

and these provide the best audiences, in my opinion, for an Ambassador who wishes to speak on friendship and mutual understanding. Political addresses are naturally barred: in no case could one be found speaking, for instance, to the Black Dragon Society, the ultra-nationalist body who have much to answer for in helping to mislead their country; while ordinary social gatherings hardly admit of any serious talk.

In looking back at my speech I see that I began by referring to some decoration in the form of a tripod on the walls of the staircase by which I had arrived. I said that Japan, Britain and the United States were the three legs which upheld the tripod of peace, and the support of everyone of them was necessary to ensure that peace. Among other things I urged them, if they wanted to be successful teachers and it was at all possible, to make some stay in England, not only in London but in the English country, because I believed that the English language could not be properly taught without an understanding of the English scene and the English atmosphere. Also I ventured to remind them that England and not America was the birthplace of the English language, and urged them to teach their pupils not merely English but correct English.

As I have already said, the Japanese are now learning English from Japanese teachers whose own knowledge is indifferent, but their answer may be, especially at the present day, that a little bad English is quite enough for a great nation like the Japanese where the relative standing of the two countries is very different from what it was forty years ago or less.

Another educational establishment which I addressed about the same time was the American School in Tokyo on the occasion of the 'Graduation of the High School and the Eighth Grade Classes of 1926.' Graduation in England means something a good deal more advanced than was, I imagine, to be found at the American school. I looked into some of the class rooms; in one a geography lesson was in progress and the lady teacher was explaining that lines of latitude were so called because they were on the sides of the globe.

I have said that the Japanese were poor linguists. At the Foreign Office, of course, there were plenty of men who had been many years abroad and spoke excellent English, none better than Baron Shidehara and Mr. Debuchi, the Minister and Vice-Minister. Nevertheless, even in the diplomatic service there were Japanese who spoke well but apparently did not understand much.

For instance, in the course of some diplomatic conference which had been going on at Peking there had been a misunderstanding on the part of the Japanese Minister. Talking to the Vice-Minister I expressed surprise at this, for I knew their Minister in Peking quite well and he spoke good English. "Yes," said the Vice-Minister, "he would be all right talking alone to you, but he would not be able to follow general conversation, especially if the British and American Ministers were talking to each other."

I asked one of our language experts about this and he said I must remember that the Japanese mind went through a double process during conversation. Hearing an English word he had to translate it into a picture and from the picture into a Japanese word.

In much the same way, the slightest mispronunciation of a Japanese word leads the Japanese to conjure up a wrong picture or no picture at all.

For this reason I very soon gave up the attempt to learn any Japanese beyond a few ordinary expressions. At least two years' devotion to the study of the language is required in order to produce any useful results: and that obviously the Ambassador cannot give. To talk a little and make mistakes would involve him in all sorts of difficulties.

Travelling by a boat on the inland sea I once asked a Japanese hotel-keeper, who spoke English and in whose hotel I was going to stay, about a placed called Toza. I explained that it seemed to me to be about thirty miles from Beppu where he lived and that I wanted to drive to Toza, which I believed was an important railway junction and take the train there. He said definitely that there was no such place: he had lived in that country all his life and could not fail to know of it if it existed. A little later I saw him studying a map: the names were in Japanese characters, but I could see at a glance the place I wanted and pointed it out. "Oh," said my friend, "but that is Tozu, a very well-known place: you said Toza, so, of course, I did not know what you meant."

I had another such conversation with the Japanese who taught me what little I did learn. I asked the meaning of a word used by one of the Japanese Princesses while I was sitting next her at tea. He said there was no such word. I persisted and he said that of course Princesses used many words that ordinary people did not know and that might be the explanation. Some days later, when he had more time to ponder over the matter, it turned out that I had put an 'i' where an 'e' ought to have been or vice versa and thus completely stumped him. The word in question simply meant 'a little bit' and was addressed to a waiter.

The point of all this is to suggest that there is much more difficulty than at first appears about satisfactory intercourse between English and Japanese.

Another difficulty is that foreigners are rarely invited into a Japanese house. There are some great houses in Tokyo in which there are rooms designed for the entertainment of foreigners, at a time, no doubt, when Westernization was more popular, but very few Japanese, in my experience, will ask foreigners into an ordinary Japanese house. They do not know whether their guests, even if they wanted them, would appreciate sitting on the floor, drinking quantities of *sake,* or whether those guests, perhaps, would properly understand the inferior position of the women of the house.

I once went to see a Japanese, the eldest son of a very great family, who was going to show me some possession of his. He met me at the door and led me through long passages to his own room. On the way we passed a

Japanese lady with some children. As he went on he muttered—'my wife'—but he did not stop. She and the children were on their way, I heard later, to spend the day with some of the Imperial-family.

A Japanese lady who had lived in England once told us that she would give ten years of her life to be back there, as even the maids were better off than Japanese ladies of high rank.

At a big dinner in connection with some International Conference I was astonished to hear a delegate from one of the Dominions refer in the course of his speech to their having been privileged to see something of Japanese family life. When, after dinner, I asked what this meant, as I did not know that they had had any such opportunities, the speaker explained that they had seen something through the open shutters as they walked along the street.

In fairness I ought to add that it is just possible that some Japanese might make the same sort of complaint about our country.

Once when we were dining at the Japanese Embassy in London about 1919 my wife asked the Ambassadress if she would like to come to a small dinner at our house. The Ambassadress, Baroness Matsui probably, jumped at the chance: she said they went to many great parties but were so very seldom invited to an ordinary private house. Nor in fact have I, so far as I can remember, ever met Japanese in my friends' houses unless perhaps when there was some special connection with Japan.

Then about the country itself. The four islands which make up Japan cover roughly the same area as Great Britain and Ireland; if you add Corea and Formosa the area is nearly twice as great. There is a greater variety of climate. The northern island, Hokkaido, has a climate something like the north of Scotland, while the southern part of the main island and the two smaller islands of Shikoku and Kyushu have quite a mild climate. The Japanese people mostly like a temperate climate best and will not settle either in Hokkaido or in Corea or Manchuria, though a number of families have lately been persuaded by the Government to transport themselves to the latter country. There is, as everybody knows, a large Japanese population in Brazil, and a still larger population in California. There is also a considerable number in the eastern parts of the United States, Canada and elsewhere. It is important to remember these facts about Japanese emigration, because it is not true to say that the Japanese are confined within such narrow limits at home that they must find outlets for their surplus population.

I should be inclined to say that the people have no religion. 'Shintoism' teaches various traditions and superstitions, respect for ancestors, the propitiation of evil spirits and so forth, but no morality to speak of and no particular convictions. One form which respect for ancestors takes is the custom of reporting to them from time to time on the current affairs of the family, or before engaging on any considerable undertaking. The Emperor and the Imperial Family regularly carry out this obligation. Once when I asked about an ex-Minister whom I had not seen for some time I was told that he had gone to make a report to his ancestors whom he had been obliged to neglect of late owing to pressure of business. There is also an annual festival in honour of the spirits, when their shrines (and they in the shrines) are carried in procession and food is set out for them; though this is not a specially Japanese idea seeing that we did something of the sort on All Souls' Day up to the Middle Ages.

There are innumerable Shinto deities, the number being constantly added to. While I was in Japan a former great statesman, the Marquess Ito, was given a place just below the goddess of the prostitutes.

A large number of the Japanese are, nominally at any rate, Buddhists. Moreover, recently attempts have been made to copy for Buddhists various Christian rites and institutions and one reads about Requiems and other services, as well as Young Men's Buddhist Associations. When I made this comment to Davidson, the expert, he would not admit it and declared that these Buddhist ceremonies were older than their Christian counterparts. Nonetheless I remain convinced that there is such an attempt to offer the sort of attractions which the Roman Catholic Church offers, indeed, some of the hymns might suit a Protestant congregation quite well, and it would doubtless greatly surprise Gautama to hear his followers singing about the joys of Paradise which they hope to share with him.

A missionary who knew the country well did once tell me that among serious Japanese there was a tendency to believe in some definite Deity. There are also some hundreds of thousands of Christians, Roman Catholic, Protestant and Orthodox, the latter congregation owing its origin mostly to the popularity of one Russian missionary.

However, for most Japanese I suppose the focus of their religion may be said to be the Emperor. It is exceedingly difficult to put this theory into words. When I arrived in Japan the reigning Emperor was a lunatic. The present Emperor, who was then Regent, came to the throne while I was in the country, and had not given any evidence of a definite personality. This would suggest that the veneration felt by the people of Japan is for the throne were it not that the Emperor is to be regarded as a Divine Person, descended from a long line of Divinities.

The Imperial Rescript issued at the time of the present Emperor's enthronement begins thus:

'Our Heavenly and Imperial Ancestors, in accordance with the Heavenly Truths, created an Empire based upon foundations immutable for all ages and left behind them a throne destined for all eternity to be occupied by their lineal descendants. By the grace of the Spirits of Our Ancestors this great heritage has devolved upon Us.'

The Prime Minister's reply begins:

'Your Imperial Majesty, having, in fulfilment of the Great Precepts of the Heavenly and Imperial Ancestors succeeded to the throne destined for all eternity to be occupied by one unbroken line of Imperial Descendants, hereby graciously performs the Ceremony of Enthronement.

'When the first Heavenly Ancestor sent her Heavenly Scion down to this land, She presented him with the Sacred Symbols and commanded him to reign over these islands as a realm belonging to him and his descendants for all time to come. The Heavenly benevolence being co-extensive with heaven and earth, the foundations of the Empire were everlastingly fixed.'

There is no reference either in Rescript or reply to any other Deity.

Ever since the Restoration in 1868 this theory of the Divinity of the Emperor and the absolute obligation of loyalty has been sedulously preached, and is taught in all places of education. What it comes to seems to me uncommonly like the Nazi creed. When I went to Japan Hitler was unknown, but I did realize that what Japanese statesmen were anxious to establish quite firmly was undeviating loyalty to the State as a 'religious' duty, one might almost say in the absence of any other religious duty.

Also I may say here that one of the first things that was impressed upon me was that during the war feeling in Japan was mainly pro-German rather than pro-Ally, although it had suited her to come in on our side.

The Prime Minister's reply quoted above makes much of the skill with which the Emperor Meiji, after the Restoration, blended old with new in forming the Constitution. Actually there was a good deal more old than new.

There was certainly a Diet in which the Government of the day was often attacked, but it only sat for two or three months in the year, and in the interval between its sessions the Government was carried on by means of decrees of the Privy Council. There were two changes of Government while I was in Japan, but when I asked my experts what was the reason for one of these changes, I was told that it was probably not brought about by the Diet or by feeling in the country, but by an intimation from the Lord Privy Seal to the Premier that his usefulness was exhausted. The Lord Privy Seal was not a member of the Cabinet, but a high officer of the Court, in fact the Power behind the Throne. The office was held by Count Makino, a man of great ability and wide knowledge of foreign politics, for whom I had a great respect.

I may say that much the same qualities were possessed by Baron Shidehara, who was Minister for Foreign Affairs during the first and third of the Governments with whom I dealt. For him I felt the same regard as for Count Makino, and incidentally he represented one of the great business houses of Japan.

In later years several attempts were made to murder them, as being men

BAIKO ONOYE
Actor of Female Parts

DIPLOMATIC BODY AT KYOTO FOR THE ENTHRONEMENT

of known moderation, and in one attempt Count Makino had a hair's-breadth escape.

One of the differences between the Japanese Constitution and our own was that the Army were not subject to the Cabinet, but took orders only from the Emperor. With a Sovereign of strong and independent will this might involve many dangers, and still greater dangers arise from the practical autonomy of the Army. It is true in theory that the money for the Army has to be voted by the Diet, but in practice this seems to present no inconvenience to the military rulers.

I presented my credentials to the Prince Regent on March 3rd.

There was nothing very imposing about the Palace. We went through a long corridor to a big European-style hall, where we waited, thence by a Japanese corridor with matting on the floor until on our right the shutters which close in the rooms were seen to be drawn back and we had arrived at the Presence. The Audience Chamber was not large, the Emperor standing at the back with two or three officials beside him, one of whom acted as interpreter. The most difficult part was the backing out, as one was apt to lose one's sense of direction; however, I accomplished the manœuvre somehow. The conversation was purely formal.

Not long afterwards I was invited to luncheon at the Palace. This was arranged in European style, including the dresses of the ladies. I sat next the Empress Dowager, who was friendly and full of conversation, asking many questions about my family. She spoke nothing but Japanese, and, in accordance with etiquette, in a whisper, addressing her remarks to a lady-in-waiting who sat on my left and interpreted in French, that being the foreign language most used at Court.

After this came my visits to my diplomatic colleagues, the most remarkable of whom was Dr. Solf, the German Ambassador. Solf had been Foreign Minister at the time of the Emperor's abdication and while telling his master to 'fly all is lost' and declaring that he would not stay if His Majesty went, nevertheless did remain, as the Emperor is said to have remarked with some bitterness.

It was understood that Dr. Solf was somewhat weary of exile in the Far East and would have welcomed an appointment at Geneva, but after leaving Tokyo two or three years later he obtained no further employment. He was a big man in person and a biggish man in character, and was always friendly in manner.

Some time in July, 1926, I had a conversation with Dr. Solf in which he referred to the wave of chauvinism which was passing over Japan. I had myself been told that these waves had come and gone at regular intervals ever since the country was re-opened to foreign intercourse, and there was, as Dr. Solf said, a 'revulsion of the heart against western civilization.'

A different sidelight on this question comes from a conversation which I had with an American musician who had paid several visits to Japan. I asked him whether the Japanese were taking any real interest in European

J

music. His reply was that there were certainly larger audiences now than formerly, but that they came as students to hear what the music was like: out of curiosity, that is, not admiration. I had myself noted that at the last concert I had been to, the theatre was three parts filled with young male students. The same phenomenon had been recorded recently in some paper, and in writing to a friend at the Foreign Office I observed that it expressed the attitude of Japan to Europe at the present time pretty well.

The French Ambassador was Monsieur Paul Claudel, the distinguished French dramatist. His work was unfortunately too mystic and above the heads of most of us, but he had an Air Attaché who was said to comprehend his style, and these two went for immense walks together during the Chuzenji season. M. Claudel did not entertain very much and I never knew him well, but I did once by some accident have a walk with him, in the course of which, far from indulging in anything highbrow, he told me how much he appreciated English nonsense verse. He had just been reading some collection and quoted with great gusto:

> '*Nebuchadnezzar when he saw this food*
> *Said it may be wholesome but it is not good.*'

Madame Claudel never came to Tokyo while we were there, nor did the wife of Claudel's successor, M. de Martel, nor did the wife of the French Ambassador ever come to Rio in our time, although she had been there earlier: an unfortunate habit of French diplomacy I should say.

The Belgian Ambassador was my old friend Albert de Bassompierre, the American, Charles McVeagh, a man of great charm but with no diplomatic experience, being the lawyer of the United States Steel Corporation. We became great friends.

There was also a whole series of visits to the Imperial Princes and Princesses to be worked through, although owing to the great number the business was never quite completed. Most of these visits were paid after my wife had arrived. We sat on straight-backed chairs facing the Prince and Princess and answered questions about our family and the climate; at least I believe this account would cover pretty nearly all of them, except perhaps Princess Higashi Fushimi, a widow not very nearly related to the Emperor, who was full of friendly conversation. Princes and Princesses in Japan are not, as a matter of fact, always what one would expect in European countries. For instance, the Emperor's sisters by different ladies of the Court, were brought up as Princesses.

One of my first excursions was to Kamakura to see the Great Buddha, a colossal figure in the open air on the site of a former temple. The Buddha is seated in the usual attitude of contemplation. An English friend told me that some years previously he had come out to Japan to do some business and gone to consult Sir Claude Macdonald, the then Ambassador, as to what steps he should take to accomplish his purpose quickly. Sir Claude's advice was that before anything else he should go to Kamakura and spend an hour gazing at the Great Buddha. This he did, and having satisfied himself that to the Buddha time meant nothing, he came back to Tokyo prepared to exercise infinite patience.

One of my first dinners in a Japanese house was with Baron Mitsui, the head of the great banking and business house of that name. The dinner took place in a huge hall built for the occasion of the Prince of Wales's visit and used for entertaining Ambassadors and visitors of distinction, this being considered, apparently, Baron Mitsui's duty. Neither he nor the Baroness spoke any English, and as there was no interpreter one did not get much beyond smiling. After dinner we went into some more or less Japanese rooms, but with chairs and sofas to sit upon, and admired some of the wonderful art treasures.

An ordinary Japanese house, of course, contains practically no furniture at all; here and there there may be a picture or a vase or some other precious object, these being changed from time to time.

Once when dining with the Mitsuis just before going on leave the picture on view represented swallows, because swallows go away and return again; a charming compliment.

At a garden party given by a rich Japanese where there was an English house adjoining the Japanese house, I was taken all through the latter, seeing some thirty rooms. In one was a low table; otherwise all were empty; in the bedrooms the bedding would have been found in cupboards to be brought out and laid on the floor at nightfall.

Among my first European visitors were Lord and Lady Willingdon, on their way to China in connection with the Boxer Indemnity Commission. They only spent a day in Tokyo and lunched at the Embassy, but that was long enough for one to fall a victim to their brilliant charm and I account it a happy fate which brought them to Tokyo.

My wife and eldest daughter arrived on May 21st. That same day came Sidney Peel on his way home from Peking, where he had been our representative at the Tariff Conference. We had been in College at Eton together and it was a delight to see him. I should rate him very high among my contemporaries for straightforward ability, courage and humour. I was surprised that although in the House of Commons for a few years he made no mark there.

At the end of May we paid a visit to Nikko. I had been there before with Davidson and my son in order to inspect the Embassy summer quarters on Lake Chuzenji. My predecessor, Sir Charles Eliot, who did not care about the simple life, never went there and one of the secretaries had occupied the so-called Embassy house. The staff were very anxious that I should go back to Chuzenji and I was soon as delighted to do so as they could wish.

Chuzenji is some two thousand feet or more higher than Nikko, itself two thousand feet above the sea, and on that first visit we three walked up

the hill, there being then no service of cars, and no private cars having
begun to make the journey. The roadway was good, but there were about
thirty hairpin bends, and when cars did venture on the road, ours being
among the first, it was necessary for one or two to back in order to get round
the bend. In backing our wheels went to the very edge of the precipice,
which was somewhat hair-raising.

Our house stood in a sort of clearing among the trees on the shore of the
lake, but well above the water. It was a two-storeyed building in Japanese
style, with shutters instead of doors and windows, containing a series of quite
small rooms, and a big verandah. We looked straight across the lake to
Nantai-san, a mountain of some eight thousand feet. When the sunset
began there was a path of gold across the water which was wonderfully
beautiful. The lake was some six or seven miles long and in places perhaps
a mile to two miles wide.

Nikko itself has often been described in books on Japan; the succession
of temples, shrines and mausoleums in red lacquer on a hill covered with
cryptomeria trees of immense age and size: the sacred bridge also of red
lacquer across the river which divides the main town from the temple area,
and the avenue of cryptomerias several miles in length by which the place is
approached.

The mausoleums are those of the great Tokugawa family, who for two
centuries ruled Japan in the name of the Emperor, with the title of Shogun;
the most important being those of Ieyasu and Iemitsu, both of whom died
in the seventeenth century.

Apart from our visits to Nikko itself we often passed through the place
on our way to and from Chuzenji. When we decided to take our car up
for the first summer stay some of the old inhabitants, such as the German
Ambassadress, declared that we should spoil the place; however, a public
service began the same year so we did no harm. On one of these journeys
I was accompanied by the Italian Ambassador; having gone to Nikko
by train we had to wait an hour before the motors were able to start, the
hill being a one-way road. While waiting we heard that there had been a
motor accident near the town, a car having fallen over a small precipice.
My Italian colleague was most anxious to see what was to be seen and
rushed out of the hotel dragging me with him. Not knowing in the least
where the scene of the accident might be and unable to speak a word of
Japanese, he hurried hither and thither crying to everyone he met: "Where
is? Where is?" a procedure which has become legendary in my family.
Happily, if that is the word, I knew enough Japanese for our purpose, and
having caught my friend up I led him to the scene of the disaster, where after
all there was nothing to see but a car on its side.

One of the earliest ceremonies which I attended this year was the
dedication of an Anglo-American Law Institute founded by a Mr. Masusjima.
The American Ambassador took the chair and Judge Putnam had come from
America to represent the American Bar. This was one of those occasions

about which we make a tremendous parade of Anglo-American-Japanese friendship, but which do not in practice carry us very far.

Mr. McVeagh, the United States Ambassador, spoke in the most eloquent way of this 'unique and impressive occasion', of this 'wonderful foundation' and of the 'wonderful contribution made by Mr. Masujima towards spreading the knowledge of the Common Law and insuring a greater fidelity to its principles.'

Dr. Baty, the English Legal Adviser to the Japanese Foreign Office, made a speech and accepted the title of 'Recorder' of the Institution; then Mr. Masujima himself made a speech in the course of which he read a translation of a Chinese classical poem composed by him in anticipation of the occasion.

He began by telling us that "here ten of Ako's loyal men (that is, the forty-seven Ronin famed in Japanese history) fell upon their swords after they had avenged their Lord, and still about the place there lingers the fragrance of their memory." Actually in a home of English Law this sounded a rather strange note. He also told us that "here Nogi among the myriads only he, faithful and patriotic, followed his Imperial Master to the Heavens," that is, he committed hara-kiri.

He told us in this poem that the craft of his family was the teaching of archery, an art wholly depending on right aim, "wherefrom also virtuous conduct springs." (After the dedication we saw an exhibition of archery with the long bow.)

He also declared that the Anglo-American Bar transcended the Bar of all other nations; weaving "justice with fact as warp and law as woof."

Towards the end of the poem he asked members of the Oriental Bar why they did not themselves rear the citadel of justice on its own foundation and follow its principles with integrity and independence. "Why not yourselves declare political offenders disgraced? Why stain the sacred sword of the Samurai?" Official parasites and bookworm professors abused the law to serve the needs of the passing moment.

"Once let justice prevail to hold politics in check, and the whole world will enjoy the blessings of peace."

Unfortunately the general sentiments of his countrymen differed a good deal from his.

Then came an address by Judge Putnam referring largely to the history of the Temple in London, and after that the planting of memorial pines, of five years growth. The Japanese, we were told, associated the word *Matus* (pine) with the verb *Matsu* (to wait) as promising a reward for patient lingering under its boughs.

Then came the Archery. Altogether a typical Japanese ceremony with an admixture of European culture.

A very different gathering a little later in the year was a dinner at the Brazilian Embassy in honour of Princess Higashi Fushimi. At this or some subsequent dinner there in her honour the Princess was placed opposite her host, with the Prime Minister on her right. To the uninstructed eye this seemed quite suitable, but we observed that the Princess and Minister never spoke to each other. Afterwards some Japanese friend explained that belonging to entirely different circles (if one may use that word of the Imperial family) they naturally would have nothing to say to each other.

Some years later we dined again at the Brazilian Embassy with a new Ambassador, whose wife belonged to a well-known Bolivian (or was it Peruvian?) family, owners of a great silver mine. Consequently everything in view was of silver; not only the table decoration, the dishes and the plates were silver, but we had silver mugs instead of wine glasses and silver coffee cups. At the parties in the same house my hand has ached with carrying about a heavy silver plate, teacup and saucer.

A caller about this time was Mr. Keith Murdoch, the well-known Australian journalist. He spoke of the anxiety widely felt in Australia as to Japanese intentions in regard to their country; adding, however, that from what he had seen and heard in Tokyo he was inclined to think this anxiety exaggerated. I told him of a discussion in the Japanese Diet in the course of which the speakers appeared unable to distinguish between Austria and Australia, and either he told me or I told him of the surprise expressed by Japanese at the excellent English spoken by an Australian, when his native tongue was, of course, German.

Even highly educated people may make odd mistakes owing to the difficulty of recognizing Japanese characters when reading. I sat near a friend in the train once, a Japanese who had been to Cambridge; he was reading his newspaper and presently told me there seemed to have been terrible happenings in Madrid: a little later after more cogitation he came to the conclusion that the word was Moscow.

Among my guests at lunch and dinner one of the first was Mr. Edmund Blunden, who was teaching English at one of the universities, but we never persuaded him to return. My first big dinner was for the Minister for Foreign Affairs and Baroness Shidehara; other guests on the occasion being the Minister of Marine, Admiral Takarabe, with his wife and daughter, Prince and Princess Shimazu, he being the head of the great Satsuma clan, and a number of other Japanese, both men, including Prince Tokugawa, and ladies, the German Ambassador and Madame Solf, the Siamese Minister and his two daughters, the Dutch Minister, the daughters of the Italian Ambassador, and several members of my own staff—thirty altogether. This still looks to me a very good mixture.

One curious question arose before dinner when our experts heard who were coming. Prince Shimazu was a Commander in the Navy, subordinate therefore to the Admiral, but he was the Admiral's feudal chief, the Satsuma clan being specially associated with the Navy. Which then would bow the lowest? Japanese, by the way, when they meet in Society do not shake hands but bow, and it is very important for the person who is lower in rank to make a more profound bow than his better.

We all watched and we came to the conclusion that it was the Minister who bowed lowest.

May 11th. Lady Ravensdale, who was on a visit to Japan, came to lunch. She sat next the Vice-Minister for Foreign Affairs and in the course of conversation told him she had been travelling for some time as she had had a hunting accident and had to give up riding for the time.

He asked what she hunted. "Foxes," she replied. "And rabbits," he asked.

May 18th. Sir Arthur Yapp of the Y.M.C.A. lunched. During his stay he had an audience of the Prince Regent, to whom he had been presented during the Prince's visit to England. Sir Arthur went to the Palace prepared to give an eloquent and carefully prepared account of the doings of his Association. The conversation was something like this:

The Regent: "Have you just arrived in Japan?"

Sir Arthur: "Yes, sir."

The Regent: "I hope you will enjoy your visit. Good-bye."

On June 7th we had a dinner for the Prime Minister and Mrs. Wakatsuki; Count Makino, Count Chinda, a former Ambassador in London, Countess Chinda and others of all nations were among the guests.

We made a point of asking Japanese ladies and I believe they liked coming, but, as a rule, only those who had had a diplomatic training talked at all, even if they sat next a Japanese man. Women (except Geishas whose business it is) are not expected to talk in public.

Once a prominent Japanese gentleman and his wife had accepted an invitation to dinner. A few days before the date of the dinner I met the lady and said I was looking forward to seeing her at our house. She said she did not know whether she would be able to come as her husband had been away for a day or two. Two days later the husband wrote regretting that his wife was not very well and could not accompany him. When he arrived I made it quite clear that I did not believe a word of this.

An interesting report was issued this year of the reconstruction of the Library of the Imperial University which had been destroyed in the Great Earthquake; a loss involving seven hundred thousand volumes.

The contributions towards this reconstruction of the Library received from institutions and individuals at home and abroad numbered by 1926 four hundred thousand. Mr. John D. Rockefeller, Jun., had subscribed four million yen—about £400,000. In England a committee had been formed at the British Academy under the chairmanship of Lord Balfour, and had sent some thirty thousand volumes, while Parliament had voted £25,000. Many other British institutions and private persons had sent contributions. A fine new Library building had now been completed. All this suggests that the tragedy of the earthquake did evoke real sympathy in England.

I was called upon this spring to address the Tokyo Women's Club (British and American, I think). Apparently they wanted me to talk about

Parliamentary Law, but, being ignorant on that subject, I talked about the importance of everybody, man, woman, and child, studying history, and learning what are the probable consequences of certain actions. I also urged them to remember that all the details of family history were likely to become useful in later years in filling up the gaps in men's picture of the past. As to this I quoted some old account books which had been in my room at the Foreign Office: one contained a charge for conveying the Secretary of State's mattress to Hampton Court (when he went to attend Queen Anne), and another a charge for replacing the King's Messenger's watch and chain taken by highwaymen when he was on his way to Culford in Suffolk with despatches for Lord Cornwallis. Finally I told them each to take a period and make herself entirely familiar with it.

We moved to Chuzenji early in July and spent a very happy summer there. The great amusement was sailing, races being held about twice a week in which a dozen or more boats belonging to various members of the diplomatic body took part. All the boats except ours were known as 'Larks,' built locally, fourteen feet long. Our boat that year was a relic left by some predecessor, and known as the *Ark*: it was twice the size of the others and much slower, and was sailed for us by my son, who had been for a time in the Navy. The rest of the family went out as crew or passengers. The races not only occupied the whole morning and sometimes more, but gave rise to a great deal of discussion and general conversation afterwards.

Apart from sailing there was not much to do but walk, and walks were limited to the two sides of the lake. The village was at one end and then the road down to Nikko began, so there was no long walk to be taken that way. On our side of the lake there was a path through the wood to the end of the lake: when one wanted a really long walk one could follow that path till one came to the road which ran along the far side of the lake, and then past a fine waterfall, and alongside a torrential river, to another smaller lake and eventually to Yumoto, where there were hot springs. One could also at one point on our side cross the hill and go down to the copper mines at Ashio: that too involved a very long walk. Facing our house, as I have said, was Nantai-san, a great mountain and a place of pilgrimage. Pilgrims no doubt were fewer than in the past, but there were still a good many who climbed the mountain and viewed the rising sun: all men, be it said, the place being too sacred for women.

Another attraction, for the Japanese especially, is the great waterfall of Kegon, with a height of some two hundred feet, at the Nikko end of the lake. It is a great place for suicides. Disappointed lovers, or, less romantically, students who had failed to pass in their examinations, were very apt to choose Kegon for their suicide. One summer while we were in Japan there were great floods; when the waters went down twenty corpses were found at the bottom of the falls. Sometimes people committed suicide in the lake itself. One man took for the purpose a boat belonging to one of our staff, pushed out into the lake (said, by the way, to have a depth of ninety fathoms, or by more credulous people, to be bottomless), filled the sleeves of his kimono with stones in accordance with tradition and threw himself into the water. That summer another man drowned himself from the garden of the French Embassy, and a third higher up the lake.

One of the joys of these walks was the flowers. There was a stretch of flattish open ground at one point on the way to Yumoto which was a great place for irises. I have a list of flowers picked on the plain and beyond that on the way to Yumoto towards the end of July. The list includes pink spiræa, tiger lilies, a small campanula, white and purple orchises, wild geranium, a flower much resembling the sun flower, a yellow spiræa and a Canterbury bell, both queried on my list, and a variety of flowers which were unknown to us. Also there was monkshood; we once picked a quantity of this and brought it into the house to the horror of our 'boys,' who begged us to let them throw away at once this poisonous and presumably unlucky plant.

I see that I have omitted one amusement which attracted some of our staff, namely trout fishing in the small rivers running into the lake; the trout were largely the so-called 'Parletts,' imported originally from Canada through the good offices of Sir Harold. . The fishermen unfortunately suffered terribly from mosquitoes and had to wear veils all the time.

The great feature of the season was the arrival of the Crown Prince and Princess of Sweden, the latter being, of course, English, the daughter of the Marquess of Milford Haven. They came up to Chuzenji for a day, took part in one of the sailing races and lunched with us. Unfortunately the rain came down in torrents, and as our house was approached by a long footpath from the village, or by boats and a climb up the hill, most of the guests arrived wet through and had to be dressed in our clothes, notably the French Ambassador. The Princess wisely brought a change with her. We crammed a good many people in. Dr. and Madame Solf, Claudel, the Italian and Swedish Ministers and most of our own staff, and everything went well.

The Royal guests I believe thoroughly enjoyed this unconventional day.

Having mentioned the footpath to our house, I may say that at the gate was a notice put up by some Japanese authority to the effect that here were a high British Official and a fierce dog (an Alsatian). Beyond our gate the path led through the wood, down to the lake-side, and then to a biggish temple with a fine red *Tori* (sacred Arch). On the arch were generally a number of stones put there by pious folk who by so doing saved a child's soul from destruction.

Before we got to the temple we passed a small carpenter's house; the family bath (the usual barrel) was on the opposite side of the path and sometimes we were so fortunate as to see the head of the grandfather emerging from the water and possibly a little boy held up at his side.

On one occasion when walking along the path I heard a curious rustling noise; stopping to investigate I found that it was a man on his hands and knees looking for something: ferns I believe. He jumped up when he saw me and coming forward announced that he was an O.B.E. One does, of course, find O.B.E.s in many places, but not often sprawling in a Japanese wood. As a matter of fact he was a Belgian who had done uncommonly good work for us during the war.

We had no sooner got back to Tokyo for the autumn than we had a State luncheon for the Crown Prince and Princess of Sweden; Princess Higashi Fushimi came to meet them, also the Minister for Foreign Affairs and Baroness Shidehara and a number of big Japanese, both politicians and nobles, as well as many of our Diplomatic colleagues.

We also dined and lunched with the Crown Prince and Princess and met his Royal Highness at dinner with Princess Higashi Fushimi.

Their expedition to the Far East had no connection with politics and was entirely concerned with Oriental Art and Learning.

On September 29th I note that Miss Riddell came to luncheon. Miss Riddell was a most remarkable lady who had founded a leper colony, and lived there herself. Those who were sufficiently fit lived, we were told, in little bungalows and helped each other, making up each other's deficiencies in respect of limbs. They were said to live very happily. The worst cases were in a hospital. Miss Riddell had a young Englishman to help her and a Japanese doctor. From time to time she raised subscriptions in England as well as Japan and contrived by her own efforts to keep this wonderful institution going.

About a year later I heard from my brother that he had met Miss Riddell at Cambridge and been thrilled by some of her stories. He had seldom met a lady with such an impressive presence and so fascinating a voice. She had a meeting in aid of her leper colony at Cambridge and made, my brother said, an admirable speech.

In the course of the autumn my wife and I paid a visit to Nara to see the famous temples and the park, but the most memorable feature of our stay was a mushroom-picking expedition made at the invitation of the municipal authorities. We started off early in the morning in a special tram with the Mayor, the Chief of Police, a schoolmaster to act as interpreter and several minor officials and police. At a distance of some miles from Nara the tram line ended and we were met by three cars, one containing a posse of police. A short drive brought us to what was obviously the scene of action, a wooded hill close to the road with flags flying among the trees and a smart little tent at the top. Leaving the cars we found a path through the wood carefully cleared and roped off, and half-way up we came to the mushrooms.* Then my wife was invited to take a seat with the mushrooms at her feet and we were all photographed. Someone stayed to collect some mushrooms and the rest of us went on to the top of the hill to have refreshments in the tent. Then down again and back to Nara in time for luncheon. Truly rural.

At the end of October a great Pan-Pacific Science Congress was opened in Tokyo under the presidency of our friend Professor Sakurai. In his opening address he said that its primary object was to study the scientific

---

* See illustration, facing page 82.

problems of the Pacific by co-operative effort, "those problems do not concern one or two only, but many if not all branches of science." He explained that the problems to be studied were specifically limited to those affecting the Pacific, and he also declared that these Pan-Pacific Congresses were distinguished from all others by the genuine warmth of feeling which pervaded them: each and all were eager to cultivate mutual friendship and respect.

He also laid stress on the fact that English was accepted as the language of the Pacific.

There was a good deal more to this effect, but I fear that most of it was wishful thinking.

English, by the way, came quite naturally to Professor Sakurai, and he once told me that he often wrote letters in English rather than in Japanese to save time. He had studied a good deal in England and had received various academic honours in this country and if he had had half a chance would have been a valuable friend. He came over during the Coronation year and lunched with me at the Athenæum; I asked several distinguished people to meet him, but he said practically nothing, which was disappointing. He died not long afterwards.

At the final banquet of the Pan-Pacific Congress he made an effective speech telling the story of the first Japanese experiments in anatomy as taught in Europe. In 1771 two Japanese doctors came across a Dutch book on anatomy and found from the illustrations that the organs shown were quite different from those described in Chinese books, the only books they otherwise had. People whom they consulted replied that Europeans were differently made from Japanese. They had white skins and no hair; they sat on chairs because their knees did not bend and wore heels on their shoes because they had no heels of their own. A little later an opportunity arose for dissecting a Japanese criminal and the doctors were astonished to find that the organs were just like those in the Dutch book.

Professor Sakurai drew the moral that the heart of man is the same whether he has a white or a yellow skin, and whether his knees do or do not bend. Oneness of heart, he argued, was at the root of the success of all international undertakings.

The British Empire was extremely well represented at the Congress; Britain, Canada, Australia and New Zealand all sending distinguished delegates.

Dr. Marshall, the New Zealand delegate, and his wife dined with us one night, with two or three others of whom one was Miss Lenox Conyngham, the daughter of the English delegate. We were presently reminded of the episode in Brazil when we met our friend from Maybole. Dr. Marshall, when asked about his English origin, said he came from a small and almost unknown village in Suffolk. We were able to tell him that that village was only two or three miles from our own, and that a few miles off in the other direction lived some of the Lenox Conyngham family.

The Canadian delegate, writing on his way home to thank me for hospitality, expressed great admiration for the way in which the Japanese had managed the Congress. In all the speeches at the various dinners and social gatherings the same note was struck and reference was made to the long-standing friendship and cordiality which existed between the speakers' various countries and Japan.

I have suggested earlier in this book that such speeches mostly mean very little, but I assume that the members of the Pan-Pacific Congress had really the idea of friendship in their minds; unfortunately the Japanese members were probably outside the class which was the dominating factor in Japanese politics, and they were after all making a natural effort to show their country to the best advantage.

In the middle of November we had a visit from Prince George (the late Duke of Kent) who was on his way home from Hong Kong, where he had been stationed for some time. He and a brother officer occupied our little guest house for a night and some of the staff came to dinner and lunch to meet him, but the visit was, at his own request, strictly incognito. He made use of the opportunity to make a brief tour of the island and really to see many interesting things without ceremony and doubtless much more thoroughly than would otherwise have been possible. On one of his excursions, when Japanese police were always attached to him, he had the idea of taking a walk of a good many miles; the two policemen started walking in a stately way, one ahead and one behind. At the finish both were trotting far behind H.R.H. in a state of exhaustion.

Some people might be astonished at the idea of Japanese men being exhausted by any imaginable exertion, but I was frequently told that their stamina was really poor. Considering that their diet is for the most part limited to rice and a little fish and other odds and ends this is not wonderful. Undoubtedly they make up for the deficiency in part by great determination. I have heard of regiments undertaking some long march at a prodigious speed and the men collapsing at the finish. My Russian colleague once told me that he had watched a man working on the road; he was moving a large paving stone, a job properly speaking beyond his powers, but he moved it to the required position and then he, too, collapsed. To fail in any task is dishonourable. Hence the suicides at Kegon Waterfall. Again, while we were in Japan some Olympic games were held for Oriental countries. Indian athletes took part and one of them told me that he had seen with surprise a young Japanese runner dissolved in tears; at first he was shocked at such weakness, but later he was told that the youth was weeping because he had failed his country by not winning some race.

Considerable efforts, by the way, were made on that occasion to dissociate the Indians from Britain; efforts which I hope I counteracted by ostentatious patronage. The Indians themselves came to the Embassy and were very friendly: one, indeed, was a Eurasian.

At the end of November the Bishop of London arrived on a visit and occupied our guest house for some days with his friend Mr. Blyth. We did not for some time learn the name of the latter as he had always been described in advance simply as 'the layman'; he was therefore known to us as the Bishop's layman.

The Bishop was making what I suppose should be called a pastoral tour, visiting missionaries and Anglican congregations in the States, in Japan, China, and finally Australia. The Anglican community, both British and American, was very enthusiastic about his visit and we had a service in the English church at which a considerable number of Americans were welcomed. They surprised us by laughing aloud in the course of the Bishop's sermon when he made some reference to religious unity which struck them as humorous, though it was not so intended. We were assured that in the States this sort of thing was quite usual, and I suppose at the time of the *Mayflower*'s voyage it would not have been unusual in England.

We had a large dinner for the Bishop to which a Japanese Bishop, two American Bishops and another English Bishop came: also two or three Japanese Christians and some other Japanese dignitaries such as Prince Tokugawa, as well as the American Ambassador and Mr. McVeagh. The English Bishop, who came from Kobe, was known to us as Bishop Basil, it being for some reason the habit in Japan for Bishops to use their Christian names instead of their surnames or the name of their see; which is rather a confusing practice. Mrs. McVeagh asked Bishop Basil why he did it, and he, not knowing who she was, replied that it was to prevent people from thinking he was an American.

The Bishop of London was a delightful guest and, as everyone who knows him would expect, full of life and vigour. He was entertained by various Japanese bodies and his visit was no doubt full of encouragement to the Anglican congregations, but the Japanese Protestants were even then well on the way to take over all responsibility for their own religious affairs, much on the same theory which was inducing them to eliminate English teachers from the schools and universities. I suspect that their own religious pastors and masters are not much better qualified for their work than the Japanese teachers of English.

The Bishop afterwards addressed a long letter to *The Times* eulogizing Japan and the Japanese in most enthusiastic terms. With one at least of his arguments I should certainly be disposed to disagree. He thought that Japan was not going to be a danger to the peace of the world if only she had fair play from other nations. It was, however, for the League of Nations to think what was to be done with over-populated strong nations, and he argued that Hokkaido was no good for relieving the pressure, being too cold for a race which clearly loved warmth. I, on the contrary, whenever I have been talking about the population question in Japan (not that I ever did so publicly in that country), have always said that it was absurd for the Japanese to complain when they left a large part of their own country half empty. I still think it is absurd. Every other race makes the best of its own country first before it begins to overflow into other people's countries, and I can think of none which refuses to do so, even in the case of much worse climates than that of Hokkaido.

CHAPTER XI

ON DECEMBER 25TH THE EMPEROR DIED. WE HAD NEVER SEEN HIM AND for some years he had been living in complete seclusion, the Crown Prince acting as Regent.

The first ceremony in which the Diplomatic body took part was a visit to the Palace to pay our respects to the Spirit of the late Emperor. We formed up in one of the halls of the Palace, and Bassompierre, the Doyen, stepped forward facing the Imperial Remains, which were, I think, behind some kind of curtain, and addressed to them a short farewell speech, after which we all passed by and bowed.

To address a speech to an invisible presence with any dignity is not, as I know by experience, very easy. I had to do it once at the tomb of Will Adams at Yokohama, and standing there with the rest of the party out of sight behind me I felt that I was doing something very strange. However, Bassompierre was fully equal to the occasion.

More than a month later came the Emperor's funeral at some distance from the capital. The ceremony took place at night. The diplomats gathered in a building, where some refreshment was provided, and at the appointed time took their places in a vast open shed. As there was a hard frost some of the company were highly tried, particularly as at the most sacred moments we were asked to remove our overcoats, or, in the case of the ladies, fur coats. I was all right as an Ambassador's uniform is thick and heavy, but the American Ambassador next me in a dress suit was not so well off. One lady positively refused to take off her furs on the ground that she had a cold already.

The arrival of the funeral procession was most impressive. The coffin was drawn by a team of sacred oxen, the wheels of the catafalque making a weird creaking noise, and the advance was slow and solemn. The only light was that of occasional torches. There were several thousand persons in the procession, many in ancient Japanese dress, and every movement was in accordance with regulations.

When the procession stopped the oxen were led away and the catafalque occupied the foreground in front of us. Then came the ritual offerings, made to the accompaniment of solemn music: water, salt, rice, wine, rice cakes, fish, pheasants, ducks, fruit and sea-weed, representing the fruits of the sea, the land, the mountains, the fields and the forests. This took a long time as the offerings were passed by many Court officials from hand to hand until they reached the Chief Ritualist. The offerings, I understood, were intended for the use of the Spirit on its way to the next world. After the offering came prayers and then an address by the new Emperor to his father's Spirit. It was nearly midnight when we started for home.

February 28th. We had a farewell dinner for Captain Guy Royle, our Naval Attaché, and Mrs. Royle. Royle, a very able officer, is now, in 1942, in command in Australia. I might observe here that several of my staff in Japan have since reached Ambassadorial rank. Cecil Dormer, who was a great stand-by during most of my five years, is Ambassador to the Polish Government; Peterson was until lately at Madrid, and Charles is now in Rio, all admirably fitted for their posts. Being, as a Director of the San Paulo Railway, still closely connected with Brazil, it is a great pleasure to me to think of Noel Charles installed at Rio. Leslie Hill, our Military Attaché, was another member of the staff who was a most loyal supporter during most of my time, while Hubert Graves and Philip Broad were admirable Private Secretaries.

In the early part of 1927 the rising anti-foreign feeling in China induced our Government to send a considerable force to Shanghai, a battalion of the Coldstream Guards among them.

On January 21st a statement was issued by our Foreign Office to the effect that the one object of their military and naval dispositions was to protect the lives of British subjects; and there is no doubt that this protection was required, for several foreign Concessions had been invaded and in some cases looted by Chinese mobs. The Chinese Government, on January 31st, responded with a note to the British Legation protesting against the despatch of troops and next day they dismissed Sir Francis Aglen, the Inspector General of Customs.

I pressed the Japanese Government to take measures similar to ours, but while expressing general sympathy they refused to send any troops. If necessary they could do so at any time. Although Mr. Wakatsuki's sensible Government was still in office, I take it that they did not lose sight of some ideal unity of the Far-Eastern peoples in face of the European—a sort of Monroe Doctrine.

In the spring of this year the abortive Naval Conference at Geneva was going on, but did not give us much trouble in Tokyo. I had a letter from Bridgeman (afterwards Lord Bridgeman) thanking me for some information I had given him, and expressing his fondness for Japan, as, indeed, he often did, and telling me that for some reasons he envied me my job. What led to this love of Japan I do not know, but after all Will Adams, the English sailor who in the early part of the seventeenth century was ship-wrecked in Japan and settled there as advisor on shipping and other matters to the Shogun, said of the Japanese people that they were "good of nature, courteous out of measure and valiant in war." Surface courtesy and valour go a long way towards making friends, and induce a belief in the 'good nature' of those possessing such qualities which is not invariably justified.

Towards the end of April Mr. Wakatsuki's Government came to an end, and he was succeeded in office by Baron Tanaka, the leader of the opposition, who was a soldier by profession, and having begun life, so I was told, as a policeman, had risen to the rank of General and been Minister of War. He spoke no foreign language except a little Russian, and hearing this I exclaimed to my Soviet colleague: "*Quelle propagande vous allez faire.*" My friend did not think the Premier's knowledge was going to carry him very far.

One personage who was reported to be delighted at Baron Tanaka's accession to office was Marshal Chang Tsolin, the Viceroy of Manchuria: it was said that they had been friends in the past and that the Marshal clapped his hands on hearing of the new appointment.

His joy was a little premature, for it was while Tanaka was Premier that the Marshal's train was blown up, it was said by Japanese, and he himself killed.

I had a charming letter from Baron Shidehara to whom I had written a regretful farewell. After speaking truly of the agreeable relations both official and personal that we had always had, he went on to say that in private life he would continue to take keen and abiding interest in the growth of Anglo-Japanese friendship.

I met Mr. Wakatsuki, the retiring Premier, at a dinner party given by Viscount Saito, the Governor of Corea, and afterwards himself Prime Minister, who was on the eve of his departure for Europe to take part in the Disarmament Conference. The guests included the retiring Minister of Marine, the Vice-Minister for Foreign Affairs, several Admirals and three diplomats besides myself; I being the only Ambassador.

In the course of the evening it became very evident that Mr. Wakatsuki was, in the elegant phrase invented by a cousin of mine, 'very delighted.' Presently one of the Japanese guests came up to me. He said I had probably noticed Mr. Wakatsuki's condition, but he hoped I would think nothing of it as it was natural in view of the fact that Mr. Wakatsuki had that day gone out of office.

I may say that a newspaper which gives a long account of the new Premier, Baron Tanaka, mentions quite as a matter of course that he 'is said to be a great drinker and a liberal patron of Geisha establishments.'

Baron Tanaka was expected to take a stronger line towards China, particularly in regard to the troubles which Japan was experiencing over her Treaty Rights in Manchuria. It was also thought that he would, in consequence, be more ready to co-operate with us in Chinese affairs. Personally I felt quite sure that Japanese co-operation would always be severely limited to plans which would facilitate her own aims and intentions.

I may say here that heavy drinking in Japan is an accomplishment to be proud of and the quantity of drink consumed is often enormous.

A Japanese Admiral once told me of a dinner which he had recently attended in honour of a man who had just received a great appointment.

The party consisted of five friends and they drank ten gallons of *sake* and a bottle and a half of whisky, the host only drinking water.

Again I find in my diary that after the death of Count Chinda, a former Ambassador in London, Baron Matsui, one of his successors in that post, told reporters that the Count was noted as a heavy drinker of *sake*.

I visited another university in May, the Tokyo University of Commerce, where there were two English teachers whom I knew, and addressed the English class or classes.

I described to them the life of an undergraduate at Cambridge and succeeded in making them laugh. At the time I did not know whether they were laughing from amusement, though it seemed unlikely that their English was good enough for that, or from politeness. Laughing comes a good deal into play where Japanese manners are concerned. It is bad manners, for instance, to distress your friend; therefore when you tell him a tale of horror you laugh over it. To the foreigner, therefore, it is by no means always easy to understand a laugh.

In this case the Students' Magazine subsequently reported that 'His graphic accounts were here and there punctuated with light jokes and pervaded with slight humour, and what with his warm personality of a born diplomat, we were held in thrall throughout the whole address.' I ended, it seems, by urging them, as I had urged the teachers elsewhere, to take any opportunity they could of visiting England as their Prince Chichibu was then doing.

In May, also, my wife and I made an expedition to the Southern Islands in order to unveil a monument erected at Hirado to commemorate the establishment of a factory by a party of Englishmen who arrived there in 1613.

We stopped on the way at Kobe, where we attended an Empire Day luncheon arranged by the local branch of the Overseas League, to whom I made a speech, and in the afternoon children's sports. We also visited an English school. Later we went on board the boat for the voyage down the beautiful Inland Sea, arriving at Beppu on the Island of Kyushu at ten o'clock next morning. On arrival at our hotel we were visited by the President of the Municipal Council. He and I, my wife and the hotel keeper stood round a little table while he made a speech of welcome and I replied: this was almost as bad as making a speech towards space.

At Beppu we seemed to be in a sub-tropical climate; at any rate it was exceedingly hot; but the country was pleasant apart from the hot springs. These were on a considerable scale and rejoiced in formidable names, the 'Green Hell,' the 'Red Hell,' and so on. One of the largest pieces of water had a figure of a fierce-looking devil emerging from it, making the whole thing look a little artificial. The Japanese who showed us the sights told us that some of the delegates to the Science Congress had visited the place, but as it was thought that they would be shocked by such a name as the 'Green Hell' they were told that it was called the 'Emerald Pool.' Whether

K

it was a compliment for diplomats to be considered less squeamish than scientists is an open question.

From Beppu we crossed the water again for a night at Shimonoseki and next day crossed back to Kyushu and arrived at Nagasaki on May 28th. That evening we were entertained by the Governor at a great dinner in true Japanese style. A great room in a hotel was filled with low tables of red and black lacquer. At each of these were places for four guests all seated on the ground.

Next day we crossed in a destroyer provided by the Japanese Government to the little island of Hirado, not far from the Kyushu coast. We were met at the pier by Mr. Matsuura, the eldest son of Count Matsuura, our real host. Our Count Matsuura was the lineal descendent of the Count Matsuura who in 1613 as the Daimyo of Hirado welcomed the English settlers.

The Count himself was kept away by mourning for the Emperor, and his son and the party accompanying him were all in the deepest black, frock coats and tall hats with high *crêpe* bands. In spite of the mourning, however, we were most generously treated and a splendid Japanese banquet was provided in Count Matsuura's house for a party of eighty. It was explained to us that his dinner service was just big enough for the purpose. The service in question consisted of a series of small red lacquer trays each having three or four red lacquer bowls containing rice, soup, raw fish, sweetmeats and the other usual dishes provided for a banquet, so that it was anything but a small one.

In the grounds of the castle we watched a sham fight between large parties of soldiers in ancient Japanese armour, the soldiers being tenants or servants of the Count.

At the unveiling of the memorial speeches were made by the Mayor of Hirado, by Mr. Mullins on behalf of the British community of Kobe, by Mr. Paske Smith, our Consul at Nagasaki, who, with his usual energy, had interested everyone in the memorial, collected the necessary funds, had the memorial in the shape of a Cenotaph designed and executed and arranged the ceremony of unveiling, and by myself.

In my speech I spoke, as usual, of the need for Anglo-Japanese friendship, and of the fact that at the moment there were no clouds on the horizon. I ventured to remind my hearers at the same time that to some minds peace and quiet is dull, and there were always writers and speakers who liked to stir up troublesome questions; I only hoped that these would be ignored. I said it was common sense that we should be friends and contrary to common sense that we should not.

Here at Hirado, as at Nagasaki, I was speaking to men of the sea, and it was from Kyushu that many of Japan's greatest seamen, such as Count Togo, had come, and there were many other great traditions of the sea gathered round this part of Japan. I drew some comparisons between Hirado and the Isle of Wight, one lying close to the great naval station of

Sasebo (forbidden ground to the foreigner) and the other to our great naval station of Portsmouth. Hirado was doubtless as dear in the eyes of their seamen as the Isle of Wight was in the eyes of ours.

I also gave them a personal message from Prince George, who had sent me a private letter speaking of his visit to Nagasaki which he had much enjoyed.

I was pleased to learn from a friend that my reference to the greatness of England and Japan on the sea had made a great hit with Japanese seamen. Officers had been seen copying out extracts and others had been talking of the comparison between Hirado and the Isle of Wight.

Before leaving Hirado I ought to say that the settlement there was maintained by the English East India Company from 1613 to 1623; the leaders being Richard Cocks (an ancestor of Lord Somers), Will Adams, the Master Pilot to whom I have already referred, and John Davis, Commander of the *Clove*. There were eight others described as Merchant Adventurers. They seem to have got on very well with the Japanese, and especially with the Daimyo, but after ten years the East India Company, in process of reducing its expenses, insisted on closing the English house at Hirado.

We had another dinner given by the Mitsubishi Company at Nagasaki on the 30th, and then returned home.

Nagasaki itself, though of less importance as a port than it formerly was, has several points of interest. One is that there the Christian Religion secretly survived in certain families from the time of its supposed extermination by the Japanese Government in 1638, as being subversive of the peace of the country, to the time in 1865 when Catholic missionaries returned to Japan. As I was told, fathers of families performed Christian ceremonies, such as funeral offices, after the public Japanese ceremony was over; figures of the Virgin and Child were preserved under the disguise of figures of the Goddess Kwannon, and various Christian traditions were carefully kept alive. One curious fact was that when the priests returned these crypto-Christian families refused to have anything to say to the Saints that had been 'invented,' as they considered, during the two intervening centuries.

In October we had a visit from our friends the Clementis and their children on their way home from Hong Kong, of which colony he was Governor and from which he was about to be transferred to Singapore. The Prime Minister gave a luncheon in their honour and we took them to a Japanese theatre, where we were invited to go behind the scenes and were photographed in a group with Baiko Onoye, the great impersonator of female parts, although himself a grandfather. Made up in the traditional style and dressed in woman's clothes he makes an odd pendant to us in the photograph.

We also gave a big dinner for the Clementis to which the Ministers for Foreign Affairs and Marine, Viscount Saito, the Governor General of Corea, and Viscountess Saito and a number of others came.

Talking of make-up it is doubtless well known that all Japanese women are carefully made up, and it would be thought improper for them to appear in public without any make-up. They all show glossy black hair, though sometimes the natural colour is much lighter, and do not allow the grey hairs to appear till they are sixty. As the style, or rather the colour, of their dress also varies according to their age they have not much chance of dissembling. Happily they no longer blacken their teeth, though I did notice an old woman sitting beside me at a railway station with her teeth all carefully blacked.

The remainder of the year was normal. There were the usual diplomatic entertainments, a few Japanese entertainments, a quiet Chuzenji season, some visits to the Japanese theatre, some speech-making, some visits from English friends.

One speech of mine was made at the dedication of a new building at Yokohama for the Y.M.C.A., the body at whose invitation I went there being the 'National Councils of the Y.M.C.A.s of the U.S.A. and Canada,' and I spoke not only as the representative of Canada but also as the representative of England, for, as I reminded my audience, the Y.M.C.A. was founded in England.

I took the opportunity also to remind them that the three great beneficent Associations, which had spread their influence over the whole world, the Y.M.C.A., the Salvation Army, and the Boy Scouts, were all purely of English origin. I had it at the back of my mind that a good many people might suppose that one or other of these great societies was of American origin and I thought it as well to claim the credit for ourselves.

As to the Japanese theatre, I wrote, but never sent, the following letter to a friend giving some account of an average play.

February 22nd, 1927.

Have you ever been in a Japanese theatre and would it amuse you to hear anything about one? It happens that my wife and I went last night to one of the two principal theatres and that the most Japanese of the two. Theatre-going as a rule is impossible because of the high prices: our stalls were sixteen shillings each.

To begin with the theatre is an oblong. A stage some hundred and fifty feet wide, and an auditorium the same width with a depth of only sixty or seventy feet. Nearly all the seats are on the floor of the house—but there are shallow galleries facing the stage and lines of boxes along the sides each holding four persons sitting on their heels. Many of the ladies in the stalls sit on their heels on their chairs. There was an audience of—say—three thousand, among which we were the only foreigners.

The first 'piece' began at four but we only arrived at five-thirty, just before a half-hour interval. The second piece was a sort of ballet with three principal performers, a young man, a beautiful girl, and a comic man, with about a dozen men in attendance whom you might perhaps call the chorus. The dancing was really posturing, mainly done by the girl. The next piece was a sort of fairy-tale about a giant spider who is finally slain by a body of soldiers (dress medieval and gorgeous). Then came thirty-five minutes during which we had dinner. After that the last piece beginning at eight-thirty and ending at nine-thirty. It was a sort of melodrama, date just before the 1868 revolution, but the manners more one's idea of the sixteenth century. Scenery very good: one in the Yoshiwara in a Geisha's room: others of a river with trees, bridges, etc. The stage is a revolving one, and in the last act it revolved rapidly to show a pursuit.

The star performer was a gentleman of sixty who recently lost his grandchild. He appeared in turn as the beautiful girl of the first piece, the Spider of the second piece, and a villainous middle-aged female in the third. He is wonderfully made up, as we could well see, for our stalls were next the 'flower walk' leading from the back of the theatre to the stage by which the characters came on and on which some of the action takes place.

Of course we did not understand a word, but an English synopsis is provided and the acting is very realistic so that one can follow pretty well.

The actors all talk in a conventional high-pitched voice, the fighting and all movements are conventional, and there is hardly any expression on the actors' faces; as a rule those who are not acting remain quite impassive.

An attendant in black squats behind the principal performers to alter their dress, remove things which they no longer require and hand them what they do require.

The programme was very popular and there was a good deal of applause, and hoarse gurgles when favourite actors came on.

Altogether as different from our theatres as anything could well be. There is an orchestra who sit at the side with instruments on which they make a noise something like humming, and they also hum or croon a sort of song and make something like cat-calls at intervals.

Yours ever, J. T.

Court entertainments were, owing to the mourning, absent from our programmes for some time, but as in all other years they were of an unvarying character I give a brief account of some here.

They included banquets, garden parties and duck-hunts, although at the latter only junior members of the Imperial family were ever present.

There was always a great banquet, Japanese style, at the Palace at the beginning of the year, when a huge number of people, running into thousands, were invited. It took place at midday.

The foreign diplomats sat in the principal room over which the Emperor presided. His Majesty sat at a table by himself on a raised platform, the Ambassadors below him on the right. On the first and even second occasions when I was present I hardly attempted to eat anything and went home to lunch. Before I left Tokyo I made an excellent meal on these occasions, shovelling rice and soup into my mouth without ceremony, and making quite good play with the chopsticks.

There were two garden parties during the year, one, the most famous, known as the Chrysanthemum Garden Party. I was somewhat disappointed with this as the chrysanthemums were pot plants shown in a series of tents. Great regard is paid to the number of flowers on a plant and their regularity, and in some cases there were four hundred blossoms in even circles round the plant: more wonderful than beautiful. Other plants shown had enormous flowers, often supported on sheets of paper with the petals pricked out: again more wonderful than beautiful.

The duck-hunts were like nothing else. A party of diplomats were invited to spend a day at the decoy; 'hunting' was carried on before and after a sumptuous luncheon. The party take it in turns to 'hunt,' about a dozen at a time. Armed with something like butterfly nets they take their places, six on each side of a small piece of water with a high embankment at one end and a sluice gate at the other.

Before the party takes up positions the wild duck have been lured in numbers to the decoy. At the right moment the gate is opened, the duck sail through and on seeing the hunters rise from the water to escape over the high embankment. The hunters endeavour to catch them in mid-flight with their nets. I once caught two and generally managed one; my younger daughter succeeded in catching three. When one has caught the first duck one jerks the net back and an attendant releases and kills the duck; if this is quickly done one has another chance.

In the special train on the way home a Court official announces the catch and distributes the birds; five to an Ambassador, four to a Minister and so forth.

It would be difficult to maintain that the hunt is in accordance with our ideas of sport, but it is amusing in a way, because queer.

In December also we had a visit from Admiral Tyrwhitt, the Commander-in-Chief of the China Squadron. We had a man's dinner for him to which Prince Takamatsu, the Emperor's third son, came as well as the Minister of Marine, a number of Japanese Admirals, some of Tyrwhitt's Staff and some of our own.

Our Admiral made great friends with some of the Japanese and we greatly enjoyed his visit.

On another occasion we had a visit from General Luard, who was then commanding at Hong Kong. I had a similar dinner for him with Generals instead of Admirals, but it was not so pleasant an evening as hardly any of the Japanese soldiers spoke English and they were less inclined to be friendly. Indeed, I hardly met any soldiers during my five years in Japan, except in a purely formal fashion, and I was told that the sentiment in the Army was mainly pro-German.

During the autumn my elder daughter had become engaged to Captain Jermy Gwyn, an officer of the Indian Army who was among the language officers attached to the Embassy for the purpose of learning Japanese.

He being a Roman Catholic and my daughter having also joined that

Church, they were married on January 7th in the Catholic Church by the Apostolic Delegate. One of the features of the wedding which interested people was a group of four little Japanese girls in bright Japanese dresses among the bridesmaids. They all behaved beautifully. One was Miss Matsuura, a grand-daughter of our Hirado host, who wrote to me as it happens not long ago to ask after the bride whom she had attended.

The children had been brought to tea at the Embassy by their fathers and mothers not long before in order to rehearse their duties, and both mothers and daughters were at first a little scared at what was before them. What scared the mothers much more was the fact that the fathers, seeing me waiting on my guests, did the same, for the sensation of having their husbands waiting on them instead of their waiting on their husbands was novel and alarming.

After the ceremony in church we had a wedding breakfast to which Prince Chichibu and Princess Higashi Fushimi came; they were described in the *Japan Advertiser* as having 'entered into the festive spirit of the occasion with the utmost zest and informality,' and, indeed, they really did so in a way very unusual in members of the Imperial Family. Prince Chichibu was specially interested in the cutting of the cake by the bride with the bridegroom's sword.

We managed to get a number of leading Japanese and all the foreign representatives into the house where Baron Tanaka, the Premier, proposed the health of the bride and bridegroom.

Some three hundred more were provided with a sit-down breakfast in marquees leading from the house, and Dormer, the Counsellor of Embassy, proposed the health to them there. Our Japanese cook made light of the work, borrowing no doubt other people's servants right and left for the occasion. As our own kitchen was extremely small the cook asked that a little tent might be put up beside one of the marquees on the lawn, with a stove of sorts in it. With this minimum of equipment thirty-six roast turkeys were produced.

The bride received quantities of Japanese presents, including some beautiful gold lacquer.

Baron Tanaka spoke in Japanese, which presumably my son-in-law, who replied, was able to understand.

My own conversations with Baron Tanaka and those of all the foreign representatives were conducted through an interpreter, and he received us generally in a kimono. Conversations of this sort are ordinarily much less convincing than conversations in which the speakers have some common language. We heard a delightful account of a conversation between Baron Tanaka and the Roumanian Minister, who had been sent to Japan especially in order to induce Japan to sign the Bessarabian treaty. This treaty had been drawn up after the war and had been signed by all the parties to it except for some reason the Japanese. The Roumanian Minister had spent a year in Tokyo before; not being of Ambassadorial rank, he was able to secure the desired interview.

It was therefore a great day. He set forth his case most eloquently. It was then translated into Japanese by the interpreter, a process which always takes a long time, Japanese being a prolix language. Then Baron Tanaka delivered his reply in Japanese. At last the interpreter began the French version, the Minister all attention. *"Le Premier Ministre espère que Madame trouve le climat de Tokyo agréable."* This was the only material sentence and was quite reminiscent of Sultan Abdul Hamid.

I think it was about this time, 1927–1928, that Chiang-Kai-shek appeared in Japan, where he had as a matter of fact received part of his education. He had, according to a Japanese paper, fled to escape the confusion in his own country. No great fuss was made about him and Japanese officials told me that they did not consider him of very great importance, but they did not say so with very much conviction.

Shortly after my daughter's wedding we went home on leave, travelling on a very comfortable Japanese boat. On the way we landed at Suez and had a fine drive across the desert to Cairo, where we spent a night and a morning before rejoining our boat at Port Said.

We had time to dine with the Lloyds, and in the morning to drive out to the Pyramids and have a look at the Tutunkhamen exhibits in the museum.

On the last day of our voyage we had an extra fine luncheon with a huge and wonderful cake covered with a model in icing sugar of a castle, or something like that, which the Captain kindly sent after us to our temporary house in London. What to do with it was a serious conundrum. However, to go back to the luncheon, as soon as we had finished we went ashore at Marseilles, and were met by the Consul-General, who announced that he had luncheon waiting for us and a small party to meet us.

The same thing once happened to us at Smyrna. We had had an excellent lunch on board our boat as we came into harbour. Coming on deck we saw the Vice-Consul, who was in charge of the Consulate at the moment, waiting for us with a small boat. He called up that he had lunch waiting for us and we felt bound to eat it. That, too, was a good but oddish lunch, for he had found his cook acting as boots at a Han at Aleppo and had himself taught him to cook with the help of Mrs. Beeton.

I am not sure that both of these efforts of ours were not beaten by our Military Attaché at Tokyo. He had received and accepted an invitation to a banquet given by the Minister of War. Then he received another invitation for the same night to a banquet at the Foreign Office, to which I and most of my Staff were bidden. He thought that loyalty to me required him to be there, and as one dinner was at six-thirty and the other at eight this was possible. What he had not reckoned with was that the menu was the same for both dinners and cooked by the same cook. When one has just finished a dinner of eight courses it requires great courage to begin at the first again, but one qualification for the diplomatic service is undoubtedly the stomach of an ostrich.

During our stay at home one of my pleasantest days included a visit to Lord Balfour, as he had become. I had been charged by the Imperial University with messages of thanks to the English and Scottish Universities which had contributed books for the reconstruction of the Great Library. Cambridge and Edinburgh, of which Lord Balfour was Chancellor, were among the donors, and he invited me to lunch in order that I might convey my message personally. He was very frail at the time and this was the first day after his illness on which he had attended to any business, but he was quite ready to talk about Japan. He was still in Carlton Gardens and I was happy to have this chance of seeing him again, though for the last time.

I also paid visits to the House of Lords and the House of Commons. In the House of Lords I exercised my privilege as a Privy Councillor of sitting on the steps of the Throne, a privilege which I fancy is generally exercised only by Ministers. I know that my identity puzzled several people, but Lord Faringdon, whom I knew, evidently thought I had become a Peer and consulted me as to the side of the house on which we should sit.

In the House of Commons I was lucky enough to hear Mr. Lloyd George and Mr. Maxton, but the scene did not please me as much as one which I attended when I was in the Foreign Office. I had gone to the Private Secretaries' Gallery—or box is it?—to provide the Government Representative with information if necessary. There were three or four members in the House. One of these on the opposition side was speaking with tremendous eloquence and expressive gestures. "I know that I shall carry with me every member of this House when I say," he cried, quite regardless of the then state of the House. Let us hope that his constituents were impressed if, and when, they read his speech.

While at home I went to the Office of Works to see the plans for the new Embassy House, which, alas, was not finished in time for us to occupy. At the first glance I observed that there was a magnificent ballroom where several hundred people could dance in comfort. I said to the official who was showing me the plans: "Of course, we shall only give one Ball." "Why is that?" he asked. "What do you mean? I don't understand." "Well," I said, "you have got a room to hold three hundred or four hundred people with only one door. That would be bad enough anywhere, but in a country where you may at any moment have a panic caused by earthquake it is impossible." I then pointed out that the ballroom was at the extreme opposite end of the house to the dining- and drawing-rooms, so that the circulation which is an essential of a big party was impossible. The distance was greater than it otherwise would have been because to evade the full shock of earthquake the house was long and narrow from north to south, the line of the shock. There was also a space between the walls of the principal rooms for the same reason. The whole house would not fall together.

I am glad for my successors' sake to say that the plans were entirely altered and the ballroom and other reception rooms brought nearer together; but at the first attempt the ballroom was again given one door. I protested and they took away the whole side of the room, so that in the end they did the thing thoroughly.

As to earthquake panics, I believe the instruments record about ten a day; I used to reckon on feeling about one a month on the average. Only twice while we were in Japan did we feel a shock strong enough to make us take any action. Once I felt a fairly powerful shock in the middle of the night, but while I was looking for my slippers I came to the conclusion that it was not coming to much and went back to bed. My wife had got up too and walked into the passage; thought it would be wise to go back and out on to the verandah and came to the same conclusion as myself. On another occasion we were standing on the edge of the Palace moat at the top of a steep bank going down about fifty feet to the water. I felt what I thought for a moment was a passing tram, realized what it was and hastily left the bank, remembering stories of people who had been precipitated into chasms and never seen again.

One is always, so to speak, expecting earthquakes, and one talks about earthquake weather, instead of thundery weather. When my dentist made me what is politely called a new plate he begged me to keep it by my bedside at night in case of earthquakes.

Most of the ruins left by the 1923 earthquake were cleared away during our time both in Tokyo and Yokohama, only our own compound and some of the other Embassy compounds remaining desolate.

I suppose that the average person would expect to hear that the taller buildings collapsed most readily; this was not so, some of the big steel and concrete houses stood up well. In Tokyo itself most of the damage was done by fire.

Tokyo, it should be remembered, unless it has changed during the last ten years, is mainly a Japanese-style city; street after street is bordered by little houses of wood and paper and only in the business quarter did one see European-style houses. I once read an account of Tokyo in an English newspaper which gave a very different impression: readers must have imagined that Tokyo was much like Chicago. To me it would have been obvious, even if I had not known the facts, that the writer had spent one night in the hotel and was describing the route from the hotel to the station, which was all he had seen.

Some American journalists once asked their Embassy where the second-hand market was, believing there to be something like the Caledonian Market in Tokyo. They were told there was none, but if they wanted local colour, etc., etc. Their answer was: "We can get that at home all right."

We returned to Tokyo in September, travelling via Canada and the United States.

After a day at Quebec and a night at Montreal we arrived at Ottawa to spend three days with Lord and Lady Willingdon, a wonderful host and hostess who took endless trouble on behalf of their guests.

The most striking point about Ottawa seemed to me to be the magnificence of the public buildings and the general design of the city, which are meant to be worthy of the great capital of such a great country as Canada will in future years become.

From Ottawa we went to Toronto in order to see Niagara. We found that Lady Willingdon had written to the Canadian Commissioner at the Falls to tell him of our coming and he kindly met us and took us to lunch at his house. From his garden we had what must be the best view of Niagara, for his shrubs were so arranged as to shut out the hideous factories on the American side.

From Toronto we went on to Chicago, our first experience of American railways. My wife and I had a drawing-room car (I hope that is the right name), a sort of miniature cabin with two berths, one so high as to be almost inaccessible. My younger daughter, who was with us, had a berth with green curtains in the ordinary sleeping car. Neither arrangement was by any means comfortable, but the food was good.

At Chicago the Consul-General took us to his flat for a bath and breakfast. Here was another surprise. We supposed anything to do with bath-rooms in the United States was superlative in quality; not at all. Although this was a fairly expensive flat the bathroom was tiny and the bath only big enough to sit in and not to lie down in.

However, we had a very good view of Chicago during the day and were taken for a long drive and to tea at one of the beautiful villas on the lake. Somehow, although I had read many books, mostly, I fear, detective stories, about Chicago, I had never thought about the beauty of its situation on the shores of a vast lake. This beauty, much more than skyscrapers and millionaire villas carefully guarded against attack by gangsters, greatly impressed us.

From Chicago we went on to San Francisco. The arrangements at the railway station seemed to be extremely primitive. As in old days in France we were not allowed to go on to the platform to wait for the train, but were kept on a sort of immense balcony above the platform. When the time for our train arrived a gate was opened and we rushed down only to find that no one knew whether it was the right train or not. At last I got hold of an engine driver who said it was not the train. Something had happened somewhere and the right train was not coming, but another train would probably start soon. Back on to the balcony and after a time another rush down and this time a train which was really going our way.

At San Francisco we were to spend the day and I was to attend a public luncheon, but we had all the difficulty in the world to extract our luggage. The luncheon was in an hotel, and though no drinks were allowed in the dining-room we were given cocktails beforehand in another room. The luncheon was in aid of the American Hospital at Tokyo and I had been persuaded by Mr. McVeagh, my American colleague, with whom we were going to stay in California, to attend and speak.   Everyone was extremely friendly and hospitable and I had an excellent reception, even when I said that having spent three days in New York some years earlier and one day in Chicago and a few hours in San Francisco now, I felt that I had seen the United States pretty thoroughly.

We went on that night to Los Angeles, where next day Mr. McVeagh and I were to attend a similar luncheon at the Biltmore Hotel.   There was this much difference that no cocktail could be served in the hotel where the luncheon was to be held, so on the false assumption that I could not do without cocktails I was hurried off to a house a mile or so away, where we were given the supposedly necessary drink.

Many people have written and spoken about the absurdities of the Prohibition years, so that I need not dilate on them.   They could hardly be exaggerated.   Among other things I was told that the negroes who act as servants on the trains were particularly disgusted because they were never allowed a drink, while white men all round them drank night and day. Negroes, I understood, were not only forbidden to touch alcohol, but were forbidden (by custom, not by law), at any rate in the south, to vote at elections.   I heard some discussion as to whether on a particular occasion the ban on their voting ought to be raised.   In theory no doubt, in the U.S.A. as in Brazil, there is perfect equality between the races; in practice even less in the States than in Brazil.   While I was in Brazil one negro was by some accident elected to Congress; the question was whether the election should be cancelled or whether it would look better to let it stand.   The latter course was followed.   Also I once saw a negro in the stalls at the Opera and my host of the evening gave me an explanation, which I have forgotten, of this phenomenon.

From Los Angeles we went to Santa Barbara for a delightful week's visit to the McVeaghs.   They, or their family, had had a villa there for many years and remembered the days when Santa Barbara was not yet a fashionable resort, and visitors hitched their horses' reins to the gate-post.

The weather was still warm and we were able to enjoy our first morning on the verandah before the house.   I noticed one man come to the front door and one man only.   He turned out to be a bootlegger who had seen a notice of our arrival in the morning paper and had come up to see whether any wine or spirits were wanted.   Being an official of the States our host thought it right to be dry (or nearly dry).

During our visit we were hospitably entertained in all directions, luncheons and dinners every day, including one in the beautiful Montecito Country Club.   Some of the villa gardens were on the grand scale, especially one great Italian garden.   One at least of the luncheons was alfresco, the guests fetching their own provisions from the house.   McVeagh took us for a long drive over the hills to a country inn where we had lunch and, on that occasion, a drop of whisky which he had brought with him.

On the way home we stopped for tea at a ranch belonging to an Englishman; he had a partner, away for the moment, who turned out to be a Fonnereau, a representative of an old Ipswich family whose home, Christchurch Mansion, is now the Museum.

I could not help being amused during this visit by American ideas of poverty. I was told of one poor lady recently widowed "if she has a million dollars it is all she has." Still, rich or not so rich, everyone we met was overflowing with kindness.

From Santa Barbara we made our way to Vancouver and thence to Yokohama by the *Empress of Britain*, with the McVeaghs as companions.

Towards the end of October I took part in an interesting ceremony at the Waseda University, namely, the opening of a Museum of *dramaturgy* built in the form of Shakespeare's 'Fortune' Theatre. The ceremony was held specially in honour of Dr. Shoyo Tsubouchi, Dean of the Faculty of English Literature in the University, who was celebrating his seventieth birthday. Tsubouchi had just completed, after thirty years of labour, the complete translation of Shakespeare's Works in thirty-nine volumes with one volume of commentaries. He was good enough to present me with a set of these volumes, which I in turn presented to the School of Oriental Studies in London.

I am afraid the number of Japanese readers was likely to be extremely limited, and the production of European plays, even modern plays, had made little headway in Japan. I once attended a performance by Japanese students of one of Lord Dunsany's plays (*The Glittering Gate*) in which two drunkards are found outside the gates of Heaven. It was characteristic of Japanese students to attempt something very difficult, but they appeared to have little or no comprehension of the play.

Eighteen months after the opening of the Museum I attended a performance of *The Merchant of Venice* given at the University by members of the Tokyo A.D.C. It was notable for an excellent performance of Shylock by Mr. Medley, a leading member of the British community, who had for many years been a teacher of English in Tokyo.

That performance was held, not in the Fortune Theatre, but in the Okuma Memorial Hall of the University.

Count Okuma, a great patron of the Waseda University, was a brother of the Count Matsuura who entertained us at Hirado. He and several of his brothers had been 'adopted' into different families; a regular practice in Japan, where there is no other son of the house, but one which makes it as difficult for foreigners to remember who is who, as the practice of dropping surnames in Brazil, or for that matter, I suppose, the practice in regard to our own House of Lords.

The President of the Shakespeare Association was Professor Ichikawa, who had received several Academic honours in England. We once invited this gentleman to lunch; the invitation was accepted and Professor Ichikawa was announced. We were surprised to find that he spoke only a little English and that with great difficulty and seemed to have no real interest but marine biology, of which we were all profoundly ignorant. Ultimately it turned out that he was Professor Ishikawa instead of Ichikawa. Altogether a trying meal. The real Ichikawa came a week or two later. In return for his efforts on behalf of English Literature I secured his election to the Royal Society of Literature.

CHAPTER XII

EARLY IN NOVEMBER THE ENTHRONEMENT CEREMONIES BEGAN AND ALL the Foreign Representatives, with some of their Staff, went off to Kyoto, where we were the guests of the Japanese Government.

The three great ceremonies were those of the Kashikodokoro, the Shishiiden, and the Daijosai.

The Kashikodokoro is the shrine of the Sacred Mirror. This Mirror is a replica of that sent down from Heaven by the Sun-Goddess Amaterasu-Omikami, Ancestress of the Emperors, to her Grandson Ninigi-No-Mikoto when she placed him on the Imperial Throne, telling him he was to regard this Mirror as Herself, the ceremony at which the Emperor worships before it was elaborated by the Emperor Meiji after the Restoration.

The Shishiiden is the Hall in which the Emperor ascends the Throne (Takami-kura). The enthronement ceremony is based on that which was celebrated for the first time by the Emperor Jimmu in 660 B.C.

The Daijosai is the ceremony at which the Emperor presents the offering of sacred rice and *sake* to the Imperial Ancestors. He does this in the evening and again in the morning, passing the intervening night in solitary communion with the Sun-Goddess and the Imperial Ancestors.

The sacred mirror with the sacred sword and sacred jewel, likewise sent down from Heaven, are the symbols the possession of which proves the right of the Emperor to his Throne.

All the surroundings in which these ceremonies take place are of an archaic and simple character.

The Kashikodokoro is placed in a simple wooden building. The Shishiiden is not specially imposing and the small pavilions used for the Daijosai are quite primitive. They stand on piles and are built of wood and bamboo with floors of split bamboo; the pillars being simply trees in their bark and the roof a thatch of straw. I was told that they resemble the buildings of a Hawaiian village and are evidence of the Polynesian origin of the Japanese.

We were commanded, not invited, to attend the Kashikodokoro and Shishiiden ceremonies and the members of our staffs and their wives were (in a postcript) permitted to attend.

The Kashikodokoro is hung in a sanctuary built for the purpose called the Shunkoden and the Emperor enters this sanctuary to offer prayers to the Goddess Ancestress, Amateresu Omikami, for the perpetuity of the Imperial Dynasty and the happiness of his subjects. He is accompanied only by the Imperial Family and two or three high dignitaries.

Meanwhile the Court and other officials and the Diplomatic Body waited in an open pavilion erected at some distance from the sanctuary, and as the ceremony took place in the early morning we were as bitterly cold as we had been at the funeral of the late Emperor, particularly the ladies in *robe décolleté*, at moments when the fur coats had to be taken off. We could not, of course, see the Emperor while he was at prayer.

The scene was extraordinarily picturesque, as the Imperial Family and all the Japanese officials and attendants were in ancient Court dress, of the most voluminous kind. The Princesses wore very long trains folded under their feet, and must have been through much practice in order to walk with as much dignity as they did. They wore scarlet skirts with trains of white silk and their hair was arranged in long plaits. The Court ladies wore yellow skirts. The men wore robes of black brocade with wide sleeves, white *hakkama* (trousers), large heavy lacquered sabots on their feet, very difficult to manage, and on their heads black caps rising to a high peak at the back.

The Princes, like the Princesses, managed their dresses admirably, so well in fact that at one moment when the ceremonies were in progress we were surprised to see Prince Chichibu and Prince Takamatsu indulging in something like a wrestling match.

The second ceremony took place later in the day in the Shishiiden, an open pavilion faced by a large open square courtyard. The diplomats were seated to one side of the pavilion and the Imperial Family and high officials filled the rest of the building. In the centre were two erections something like pulpits, with curtains in front of them to conceal the occupant until the correct moment. The square before us was filled with officials and guards.

After we had waited some little time we heard the Imperial procession approaching from behind us; presently the curtains of the pulpits were drawn and the Emperor and Empress were revealed to the public. His Majesty then read the Imperial Rescript in a strong voice and impressive manner, after which the Prime Minister, advancing from the courtyard to the steps of the pavilion, read his reply: the reply in fact from which I quoted in the last chapter. After that came the cheering, the shouting of *Banzai*.

This is the description of the cheering given in a handbook issued by the Prefecture of Kyoto: 'Every member of the throng will, with all powers of lung and voice, join in a tremendous chorus of Banzai. . . . At the pre-arranged signal, every man, woman, and child in the Empire, even those beyond the seven seas, will, with single heart and voice, rend the air in happy concert, shouting "Long live the Emperor." ' The cheering before the Shishiiden was, in fact, splendid.

Subsequently there were two banquets; one in the middle of the day on the sixteenth in Japanese style, and one in the evening of the seventeenth in European style. The first was attended by some two thousand persons, the second by some two hundred.

The Japanese banquet took place in a vast wooden hall highly decorated and hung with silk. As nearly all the uniforms were covered with gold lace and the Japanese ladies wore kimonos of vivid colours, no black being allowed, the scene was really gorgeous. The Emperor and Empress sat at separate small tables on a dais; below them the Princes on the right and the Princesses on the left with the Ambassadors behind the Princesses. We were given cups of black *sake* and white *sake* made from the sacred rice grown for the occasion. These were very thick and anything but alluring to drink, and after one or two sips I was relieved to find that they evaporated or soaked into the earthenware cups in which they were served. The food was of the usual Japanese style, soups, mixtures of rice, chicken and peas, little bits of cold meat, raw fish, the bark of some tree which I did not try; also a whole fish and sweetmeats made of beans, jellies and so forth which were sent after us to the hotel.

During the first and after the second banquet some wonderful dances were executed by girls in red and white dresses of historical style. One of these had its origin in the following tradition. One day while the Emperor Jimmu was playing the *koto* in his Palace, some beautiful girls attracted by the harmonious music came down from Heaven and danced before the Emperor, making the long sleeves of their dress whirl round five times. This dance has always been executed by the daughters of Dignitaries and on this occasion was performed by daughters of Court Nobles.

On the second occasion after the dancing there was supper at small tables. At my table were Admiral Prince Fushimi and Princess Kaya, of the Imperial Family, the Soviet Ambassadress and the Swiss Minister, both newcomers. Five (not six) makes a set in Japan. The Prince and Princess both conversed with me, but neither spoke a word to the other two, or appeared to take any notice of them, the reason I think being merely shyness on both sides.

We remained about a week in Kyoto after this and were offered every kind of entertainment: banquets, excursions, including the shooting of the rapids on the river, garden parties, theatrical and 'No' performances, and a wonderful puppet entertainment for which Kyoto is, among other things, famous.

One of the banquets which pleased me most was that given by the Prefect or Mayor: the great hall where we dined was very high and was surrounded by a gallery: all along the railings of this gallery were arranged plants of the hanging chrysanthemum and long trails of flowers fell like a great piece of tapestry round the hall.

CASTLE OF WAKAYAMA

Marchioness Tokugawa in Japanese dress: Marquess Tokugawa between Lady Tilley and Miss Tilley

AUTHOR SPEAKING AT PAN-PACIFIC CLUB
Prince Tokugawa on his left
Mr. Debuchi, Vice-Minister for Foreign Affairs, on right of picture

One marked difference between these Enthronement ceremonies and those of the King's Coronation was the treatment of the crowds. They were kept at a considerable distance from any route along which the Emperor was to pass and there was no cheering when he did so. In fact it is bad manners to look at all at the Imperial carriage, and the proper attitude is, if not prostration, a low bow with both eyes fixed on the ground.

There were, however, two innovations as compared with previous Enthronements. The crowds were permitted to wear greatcoats and put up umbrellas in case of rain when Their Majesties were not actually passing. Even more remarkable was the fact that Their Majesties were present at a vast gathering in one of the Parks where the Emperor read a rescript.

Another difference between the Enthronement and the Coronation was the extreme remoteness of the Emperor and Empress even from their guests, which after all we were. Although at the banquets they shook hands with us as they passed in, they never spoke. No doubt this is in keeping with the theory of the Emperor's Divinity.

Finally there is the striking fact that the Emperor ascends the Throne not by the grace of God, still less by the grace of men. He is there by the grace and favour of his own ancestress, though it is true she was, not a god, but a goddess.

From Kyoto we returned to Tokyo to resume our ordinary life.

There were, however, still some ceremonies connected with the Enthronement; there was a great Naval Review at Yokohama, where we spent the day on the *Suffolk* with Admiral Tyrwhitt. We enjoyed the day but the review suffered considerable interference from the extremely rough sea. In the course of the afternoon the Admiral went off in a small launch, or some other small boat, to pay his respects to the Emperor on board the Japanese Flagship and we wondered a good deal whether he would ever get there. Some of the other visiting Admirals stayed prudently in their own ships.

Our party went ashore in another small launch at the end of the day. We should have done pretty well had we not had a Japanese officer on board who was going back to his ship. We had to make several frantic efforts before we could get alongside, and as a result I believe every member of our party, except myself, was very ill.

The Italian Embassy party stayed on board their Flagship all night and the Americans waited till late in the evening when the sea had gone down a bit.

Next day I returned to Yokohama to pay my official visit to the Admiral; luckily the sea was fairly smooth. I lunched on board and then rushed back to Tokyo in order to call on the Vice-Minister for Foreign Affairs at his request. From the Foreign Office I had to hurry back to the Embassy to receive the Prime Minister, then to the American Embassy to say good-bye to the McVeaghs, then to a dinner given by the Minister of Marine to the Foreign naval officers, at which I, for some reason, had to reply

L

impromptu to his speech, and then home for our own Ball for the naval officers. Prince and Princess Chichibu came to the Ball and were very cheerful.

On December 6th we went to a garden party given by the Japanese to the naval officers, where, after watching one or two Japanese dances, we were invited to sit out in the garden and eat plates of stewed meat, cold turkey and beef sandwiches washed down with tea and whisky at 3.30 p.m. of a December afternoon. Here again was a call on the diplomatic digestion.

I heard from Admiral Tyrwhitt after he had left Japan that he had had delightful letters from some of the Japanese Admirals, all vowing eternal friendship and suggesting an alliance between Great Britain and Japan.

The Admiral tells me that when he got home he reported this personally to Sir Austen Chamberlain, but was told that our relations with the United States made consideration of such an alliance impossible.

The final Imperial entertainment was a luncheon at the Palace given by the Emperor and Empress to the special Ambassadors who had received their credentials for the Enthronement; this included myself and most of my regular colleagues. We each had a few words with the Emperor, and it was on this occasion, I think, that he was afterwards found to the general surprise in animated conversation with my younger daughter on the subject of lawn tennis.

I say most of my colleagues, but the American Ambassador, who was resigning his post, had already left for home. I always thought this a great mistake, and matters were made rather worse by the fact that the United States Government did not appoint a successor for the best part of a year.

The Emperor talked a good deal and His Majesty told me how he had prayed for the recovery of King George during his recent illness.

On the 8th we had a farewell lunch for Dr. Solf and in the evening I went to a dinner in his honour at the Tokyo Club, at which there was a very big gathering, largely Japanese but with many English and Americans, and at the end of dinner 'For he is a jolly good fellow' was loudly sung.

There were several more 'Enthronement' entertainments, including a reception by the Prime Minister, with four thousand guests, but too thoroughly 'organized' to be altogether satisfactory.

At the end of November we had had a farewell dinner for Mr. and Mrs. Matsudaira, he having just been appointed to the Embassy in London. Among other guests we had four former Ambassadors to London: Marquis Inouye, Count Uchida, Count Chinda and Baron Matsui.

I also attended among other farewell parties a big dinner given at Yokohama in Mr. Matsudaira's honour by the Japanese branch of the British Association of Japan. Mr. Matsudaira made an admirable speech on which I congratulated him. I added that I sympathized with him when I remembered that this was not the only speech which he would have to make in English before his departure and I was afraid some hard work was entailed. He said not at all; he could only learn one long speech and he should repeat in Tokyo what he had said in Yokohama. This seemed odd at first, but after all I suppose it is what parsons often do.

Mr. Matsudaira, with great help from Mrs. Matsudaira, was a most successful Ambassador in London and made many friends. His eldest daughter, who had been at school in the United States, had recently become the wife of Prince Chichibu, and Mrs. Matsudaira's sister was also married to an Imperial Prince.

By way of wedding present to Prince Chichibu, of whom I had really seen a good deal, I brought back from England a picture by my old friend, Sir Charles Holmes, of the Pillar rock in the Lake District which the Prince had climbed when in England. Holmes had been in college with me at Eton and we were in sixth form together. I was able to tell him that his picture was highly appreciated and in reply he sent me an amusing letter written when he was experiencing the first 'wonderful relief' at release from his official troubles as Keeper of the National Gallery.

I liked his story of having been awakened one morning in a New York Hotel by a voice on the telephone saying: "Miss Ada Clark." Quite unprepared to receive this lady he pressed for explanations, to find at last that this was the American for "It's eight o'clock."

When Holmes died I and others of his friends gave to the school one of his water-colours which had recently been exhibited, and I went down to Eton to present it officially to the Provost. Holmes certainly deserved a memorial at Eton, which has not been strong in painters.

On December 18th we had a tea-party of eighty ladies in honour of Miss Macdonald, a Canadian who had done wonderful work for many years in the prisons, and was among a very small number of foreigners to receive from the Emperor on the occasion of the Enthronement a distinction in the shape of a silver cup. I read her a telegram of congratulation from Lord Willingdon which gave great pleasure.

Here is a story of her prison work.

While we were in Japan burgling was very rife. In many houses an appropriate sum of money was left in the hall for the burglar, but this was not always enough for him. One night a burglar broke into the house of Mr. Nitobe, a Japanese well known at Geneva, whose wife was American. No money had been left out and the burglar demanded five hundred yen. Mrs. Nitobe argued at length and in the end successfully for fifty yen. Later on she was horrified to find that she had only given the man forty, so she took the balance to Miss Macdonald, who promised to hand it to the man when he next came to prison.

Owing to the prevalence of burglary I argued with the Foreign Office that the Embassy compound should have a decent wall built round it when reconstruction work began. The Office of Works put up a wall between two and three feet high on the inner side and about six feet on the outer side. I maintained that though they spoke of it much as one speaks of the Great Wall of China it was not good enough. I told them of a time in Ayrshire when the police warned us to be on the look-out because an old burglar was coming down from London to burgle in the neighbourhood; he came, burgled and returned to town. I always pictured him as a little frail old man on his last burgling legs, but even he could have surmounted the Great Wall of Japan. Whether this had any effect I never knew.

On December 21st Baron Okura came to luncheon, a young millionaire who had been educated at Cambridge and who had offered to defray the expenses of a lecturing tour which we were trying to arrange for Laurence Binyon, the Treasury having refused to do anything for us.

In the evening we dined with Prince Shimazu. Prince Shimazu, as I have said before, is the head of the great Satsuma clan to which so many naval men belong. The Satsuma men fought against us at the battle of Kagoshima in 1869, since which time there has been a sort of special friendship between them and the English. I write this in 1942 when I see that Shimazu is to be in charge of the arrangements for British prisoners of war.

I note that we went at this time for a week-end to Atami, on the coast about seventy miles from Tokyo with a Riviera climate, the last ten miles being along a corniche road passing among orange groves. It took us an hour and a half to do the first twenty-two miles and four and a half hours to do the seventy miles as the road was congested with cyclists and pedestrians showing no thought of trying to avoid cars.

I note that I attended two more gatherings in December at which speeches had to be made. One was a luncheon arranged to celebrate the 200th meeting of the Pan-Pacific Club. This was a body formed to work for the promotion of peace and good understanding between the various nations of the Pacific and was the favourite child of Prince Tokugawa.

I ought to say a few words about the Prince with whom we were on the most friendly terms. He was the representative of the great family whose chief ruled Japan for two hundred years with the title of Shogun, and the Prince himself, as a child, was Shogun when the Restoration took place. He spent some time in England as a young man and spoke excellent English. On returning to Japan he took his place as the premier nobleman of Japan, became President of the House of Peers and was always regarded with something like veneration by his fellow-countrymen, except perhaps the extremists. I had a letter from him a few years ago expressing horror and alarm at the recent murder of prominent statesmen by men of that party.

In my own speech I urged people to remember that while being loyal to their Pan-Pacific creed, they should also be loyal citizens of the world, for peace in the Pacific was chiefly desirable as tending to the peace of the world. I also said a word for James Cook as the great pioneer of Pacific exploration.

At another Pan-Pacific gathering on the anniversary of Cabral's discovery I took occasion to refer to the fact that this happened to be a 'moon watching' day in Japan. No day could be more suitable for thinking about the Pacific, seeing that, according to one theory, the Pacific Ocean filled the hole made by the moon when she was torn out of the earth by some cataclysm of Nature.

The second gathering was the dedication of the new library of the Imperial University, built out of Mr. Rockefeller's donation. I told the audience of the great interest shown in the reconstruction of the library by Lord Balfour when I saw him during my holiday.

In the course of the proceedings we were taken round the library and in one room saw on exhibition specimens from the various gifts. One of the most comic, put there perhaps out of malice, was a second-hand copy of the Globe edition of Chaucer given by an Australian University. There were also some second-hand volumes of Everyman's Library. The Parliamentary Journals attracted attention. One volume happened to be open at a page which recorded the passing under Queen Elizabeth of a bill directed against the 'Family of Love.' I told Shidehara it was doubtless a bill to prevent the birth of illegitimate children, information which he passed on with great glee to others. The glory of our collection was a Kelmscote Chaucer. About this time I was also engaged in obtaining for the Emperor from England a small reproduction of a statue of Darwin which he had seen in the Natural History Museum in London. Natural History was, I believe, his great interest. Incidentally, when he visited Cambridge and was taken round Christ's by the Master, what pleased him most was the sight of some mummified rats which the Master had found when the Lodge was rebuilt.

Another matter with which I was involved was the institution of a 'Shakespeare Medal' to be given for annual competition at the Imperial University. The idea was originally propounded to me by Professor Arundell del Ré, an English teacher of part Italian birth, who was also responsible for suggesting to Laurence Binyon that he should come to lecture in Japan. Of Binyon's visit I shall speak later. The idea of the Shakespeare medal was taken up by the Japan Society, who agreed to provide the necessary funds, and the competition has been held ever since, sometimes producing quite a good essay, although those that I saw were rather concerned with technical points than with more spiritual values—which I thought a pity.

On January 10th we had a dinner party. One of the guests was Prince Konoye, who 'talked a lot and was very pleasant and is ambitious.' This is the Konoye who became Prime Minister during the war.

Among the other guests were Mrs. and Miss Ozaki. Mrs. Ozaki was more than half English and had written books in English, but was not devoid of Japanese superstition. She once told us that at the house to which they had moved in the country everything seemed to go wrong. She consulted a soothsayer, who pointed out that she had approached the house from south to north and she should go back to Tokyo and return to the house in a southerly direction. This she did with the result that the family health improved and her daughters who had been tiresome began to behave much better.

On January 19th I attended a great funeral. My part consisted in joining a long queue, taking a twig of bay from a priest, laying it on a heap before the ashes, bowing, bowing again to the widow and her son and so out. A double row of distinguished personages lined the hall of the shrine, including Baron Shidehara, Count Uchida, Barons Matsui and Hayashi. The whole thing took two minutes.

CHAPTER XIII

TOWARDS THE END OF JANUARY, 1929, MY WIFE AND MY DAUGHTER EDITH and I set off for an expedition to Formosa.

We slept three nights at Kobe, the port from which we were to sail, where there was a considerable British community. For this visit we stayed with Mr. and Mrs. Ross at their house over the Hong Kong and Shanghai Bank of which he was manager. It was a place of vast rooms, in which Mr. Ross allowed no curtains or carpets, but it was extremely comfortable.

Next day Mr. Royds, the Consul-General, came for me at nine-thirty and took me on a round of official sight-seeing, to the British Athletic Club, the British and Foreign Bible Society depôt, the Canadian Academy, the Missions to Seamen's Home, and the cemetery with the British war monument.

At the Canadian Academy I was asked to say a few words to the junior class, about thirty children of eight or nine, then to the next class and so on until I had delivered five patriotic speeches including a longish one to the senior class, consisting of boys and girls of sixteen to eighteen. There were about two hundred and fifty pupils, about half British and half Japanese.

After this well-spent morning we all three went to lunch with Mr. Jonas, a very leading British subject, belonging to a Bagdad Jewish family which acquired British nationality in Burma. His mother was a Japanese and so was his wife, but he was brought up in Scotland. We spent some time before lunch in examining his fine collection of netsukes (defined by Chamberlain as ornaments for the tobacco pouch carved out of wood or ivory). Mr. Jonas is the great authority on these ornaments and has published a valuable book on the subject. After the netsukes came cocktails, the lunch starting with oysters and stout and proceeding in five courses accompanied by sherry, champagne, port, and liqueurs, so we did pretty well. After lunch we inspected Mr. Jonas's fine orchids and then drove a few miles on to the villa of the Sumitomo family, which they had offered to lend us. It was a magnificent Japanese house in a beautiful garden, but we never had time to stay there. Then back to Mr. Jonas's house for an elaborate tea. His house was so close to the sea that we could see nothing at all but sea from the ground-floor windows: I had never seen houses built so close to the sea.

After tea we returned to Kobe and had to dress for dinner given in our honour by the British Association. Over a hundred guests turned up, including several Indians with whom I had a very friendly talk. There were the usual speeches and then a concert and a small play written by a member of the community. Quite a successful evening.

In my speech I said that I had recently seen in some, I suppose 'left', book that British merchants who went to foreign countries ought not to expect protection from their Government; they ought to stay at home. I said I thought this would be a very poor rule for the world to follow. I also impressed on them the anxiety of the Foreign Office to help them through the Consular Service, an anxiety which was not always appreciated. Some years ago people used to say that if they went to the Consul they got no help; now people said that if they did go to the Consul they would get no help, and so left the idea untried. I also told them of a place where the British community wished they had a Consul like the American Consul, while the American community were wishing they had a Consul like the British.

I told them also that our Government were determined to have no more wars if they could help it, and I supposed the quarrels of the future would have to be settled through the persuasiveness of diplomats, which made me rather glad that I was approaching the age limit.

Next morning Paske Smith, our Osaka Consul, and Sansom, the Commercial Councillor of the Embassy, called for me and we went off by car for Osaka, where I attended a Rotary lunch of about sixty people. There were speeches and rather feeble American songs. I made a speech of the usual sort about economic co-operation. I also dropped a brick here as I had understood the Japanese chairman to say he was an actor and made conversation accordingly, to which he replied smilingly but vaguely. It turned out later that he was an architect; but had added a syllable to make it pronounceable for him and slurred over the 'r' as a Japanese would. After lunch we went to the Cotton Exchange, noisy but interesting, and then to the offices of the Osaka Asahi newspaper. We also visited one of the largest cotton mills. This visit had a curious aftermath. Some time after I had left Japan the Federation of British Industries sent a mission to Japan. They expressed a wish to see a cotton mill, but were told that this was quite impossible. Subsequently, when a leading Japanese business man was calling at the Embassy someone asked him the reason for this refusal. He said it was due to the fact that when the Ambassador (myself) went to Osaka he took an expert with him who was probably trying to discover Japanese secrets. The answer, of course, was that I had no expert with me, but I do not suppose it made much impression. All that I can imagine is that I, who know nothing about machinery, asked simple questions while Sansom or Paske Smith asked more intelligent questions.

We next went to the villa of a Mr. Yamada, a leading cotton merchant, to dress for the banquet which was to be given in my honour by Osaka business men. Mr. Yamada had a fine European house and the first thing I noticed in it was a good picture by Corot.

There were some sixty people at the banquet, all but half a dozen being Japanese, and including the governor of the Prefecture and the Mayor of Osaka.

Here is the invitation :

> 'Hearing that Your Excellency is shortly visiting Osaka certain well-wishers would like to have the opportunity of hearing your lofty words and offering you a rough and ready repast. We realize that we are bothering you, but we should be highly honoured if you would come to the Sakai-u-ro in this city.'

The dinner was in Japanese style, the guests being seated on the ground at low tables for five each. After the cold eggs and a little *sake* the speeches began. Rather trying as they were delivered from the middle of the room facing the squatting audience, as if one were addressing a school-treat; the children being represented by hoary men. Kneeling by each was a Geisha or two to make conversation for the guests. Owing to the necessity for translation, the two speeches, that of the gentleman who proposed my health and my own, lasted about an hour.

The speaker who proposed my health took the opportunity to mention two grievances, the Indian tariff and its effects on the Japanese cotton trade and the disabilities of Japanese in South Africa, both matters which had been well ventilated. At the same time he urged co-operation between our two countries in general and in particular in the help to be given to China in her process of reformation.

I did not discuss his grievances, which were somewhat controversial for such an occasion, but I did point out that as regards the cotton trade Japan had been fortunate in learning by our early mistakes and avoiding Lancashire's tragic apprenticeship. I agreed that co-operation between our two countries was eminently desirable, and mentioned that, as Mr. Matsudaira and I had recently said at Yokohama, and as Baron Matsui and I had said in London, there were no serious questions at issue between us.

The Governor of Osaka, who sat on my left, was one of the most extraordinary figures I ever saw: about five feet high and four feet broad with bandy legs and a very large egg-shaped head, perfectly bald except for a Newgate fringe. The dinner lasted for three rather tiresome hours, with practically no conversation, but some good Japanese and European dancing. We got back to Kobe about ten-thirty. Next morning we made a very thorough tour of the Dunlop Rubber Works, employing some one thousand five hundred people, and about to make a fresh start with new and larger buildings. We went straight from the factory to the quay.

Our boat, the *Asahi Maru*, was a ten-thousand-ton steamer bought from the Italians: as the *Dante* she had been an emigrant ship travelling between Genoa and New York. We had the Governor-General's most comfortable suite and our voyage was a most excellent and uneventful one. Part of our cargo was a consignment of Berkshire pigs destined to improve the Formosan breed. The first night a Japanese musical troupe came and gave us a sort of concert of European music, one man singing very well.

Extract from Diary.

We arrived at Keelung soon after lunch on the 29th, and a number of officials and others came on board to meet us and we were regaled in the saloon with claret, there apparently being no champagne. Cowley, the Acting Consul, and Mrs. Cowley were of the party and presently we all went by train to Taihoku, about an hour's journey. The road it seems is very bad between Keelung, the principal port, and Taihoku, the capital, although a great deal of money has been spent on it; at times it is impassable: lately a quantity of loose stones has been thrown on the surface in some places to enable cars to pass. Arrived at Taihoku we went straight to the hotel; a very large one in rather the tropical style, big rooms, verandahs and wide spaces, and quite comfortable except for rather indifferent food. In the evening we were given a dinner by the Governor-General, Mr. Kawamura, a very cheery person. Among the guests were a brother of Baron Shidehara, who is President of the university; the Dutch Consul and his wife, the American Vice-Consul, an Englishman who represents Sale with his English wife, and a large number of Japanese, both men and women. The excitement was that this was the first time that ladies had been included in such a banquet. It was a very friendly gathering.

Next day we spent in sight-seeing in Taihoku, the Monopoly Bureau, with its camphor factory, the opium factory, the Botanical Gardens, and a fine Chinese temple with charming little figures on white wood, landscapes, figures, flowers, etc., all round the cornices and in other suitable places, but in which none of our guides would take any interest. After lunch we did the tobacco factory (Havana tobacco) very thoroughly: the cigars are very good but fairly expensive, some being sold at ninety-six yen a hundred (nearly two shillings apiece). We also saw the Museum with a good Natural History collection, and the Research Institute, including several snakes and experiments in snake poison. As to opium, the number of licences to buy is gradually being reduced and the officials profess to hope that in a few years there will be no smokers left.

Taihoku is built on rather a grand scale, wide streets with avenues of trees, and colonnades, and imposing Government buildings: much red brick is used.

After dinner we left by train for the south, travelling all night, changing

trains in the morning at Takao, and at ten-thirty exchanging the train for
cars in which we drove about sixty miles to Garambi, a lighthouse at the
extreme south point of the island. After the first few miles the scenery was
delightful, the sea on one side, the open hills on the other; road good;
much of the country quite wild and the villages very primitive. The houses
appeared to contain two rooms apiece and no furniture: the beds consist
of mats thrown on the floor. Some of the villages had remains of old
brick walls which once served as a protection against savages. About
ten o'clock we stopped to picnic on the shore, a novel proceeding for our
escort. Koshimura, the interpreter sent with us by the Japanese authorities,
said this was the first time he had had such an experience. The picnic was
delightful except that we had not reckoned on the carrying power of a dead
whale which we had passed a quarter of a mile back. The whale had been
caught that morning and was being cut up. Prodigious quantities of flesh
had been extracted and dragged up the little pier, but the back view of the
whale was still solid. After lunch we went on to the lighthouse, where the
keeper regaled us with excellent *papaw*, tea and biscuits, and then showed
us the building. It is at the angle of the island, with blue sea on two sides and
natural lawns and shrubberies sloping down to the shore. After an hour
at the lighthouse we retraced our steps some thirty miles and then turned
off to a little village called Shizukei, in the hills, where there is a hot spring.
There was a small hotel with an annexe behind and above it which we
occupied. Except for the lavatory arrangements, which were horrible,
the little bungalow was delightful and we could step out on to the hill. We
had chicken *sukiyaki* (titbits fresh cooked) for dinner, with fruit and bread
and butter and cheese sent with us by Mr. Cowley. Next morning we
left early, about seven-thirty, to drive back to the railway. Half-way
we stopped to inspect some savages. Very tame savages, and while the chief
wore some sort of skin cap with horns and his wife also wore a strange head-
dress, another man wore a chauffeur's cap. Though their clothes were
unusual they were all well dressed. Having returned to the railway we found
the Governor-General's saloon car waiting for us, a very comfortable refuge.
We then proceeded to Heito, where we stopped to see the sugar factory, had
lunch with the general manager and inspected the miraculous bamboo
grove, which sprang from the buds that sprouted on a dead bamboo pole
after the Prince Regent had touched it with his sweaty hand.

We arrived at Takao early in the afternoon, and after a drive round the
town, and in my daughter's case a bathe in the sea with an American,
Houghton by name, representative of Brunner Mond, we were taken to a
sort of municipal guest house reserved for princes and other distinguished
guests. It was a large and very delightful Japanese villa. We had tea, and
a walk to the Shrine higher up the hill which commanded a fine view of the
town and harbour. According to Houghton the harbour is destined to take
the place of Keelung, as more convenient for ships coming from China,
and when properly dredged larger and safer. We found our Japanese

style bedrooms quite comfortable. At Shizukei I had suffered from the fearful weight of bedclothes: at Takao I only suffered from the difficulty of keeping my pillow close to my *futon* (quilt), so that I passed a good deal of the night with my body on the floor and the pillow two feet away from the mattress. In the morning we saw the cemetery, where among others the wife of Sir Pelham Warren is buried.

We reached Tainan early and our first visit was to the English Presbyterian School, where I was expected to address first the boys and then the girls. I addressed the boys as of the Canadian School, but before I reached the girls remembered that the Canadians are at Taihoku and the English Presbyterians at Tainan. The school was started in 1865 and is very flourishing but teaches no more English than any other Japanese middle school, and no Christianity except that the Bible is read and hymns sung. Possibly the fact that many of the pupils are boarders makes some English influence possible. They have good buildings and were trying to raise £10,000 for endowment. There is also a hospital, but we had not time to go into the wards. We visited one of the community houses of which they have several and very good, and had tea and cakes with the ladies, who seemed to be a very cheerful party. After that some of them went with us and our official guides to see the salt pans. We were struck by the great quantity of salt. Some time later we learned that it had been specially brought there for the occasion. "*Para Ingles ver*," as the Brazilians say. Then to Anping, a deserted place where we saw the remains of the British Consulate and the ruins of the Dutch fort, and back through a particularly pretty park to the Governor's house, where we had luncheon (and speeches) —European style. Then back to the railway and so to Kagi, where we were taken to see the timber mills—very interesting, and the cutting up of camphor trees, and then to the hotel, which boasted two European beds. Next morning about seven we started off again for Lake Candidius (otherwise Jutsujetsutani); first train, then trolly car (*alias* push cars) for four or five miles along the side of the mountain stream, and then four or five miles on foot for my daughter and me and in a carrying chair for my wife. It was a delightful walk through the woods, sometimes very steep, so much so that my wife insisted on walking, and finally over an alarming suspension bridge on to the plain bordering the lake.

Lake Candidius is so called after a Dutch missionary, Georgius Candidius, who discovered it in 1627. It is about two thousand four hundred feet above the sea and ten miles round with bright green water. It is said, I do not know on what authority, to be one of the oldest lakes in the world, the lowest estimate of its age being fifteen thousand years, and it is predicted, again I do not know on what authority, that it will last another two thousand years. On three sides it is surrounded by hills, the highest six to seven thousand feet. The highest peak in this part of the island is nearly fourteen thousand feet.

We crossed the lake to the 'Savage' village, where the women came out and made music for us by hammering on a stone with great pestles of different lengths. The houses had merely bamboo screens for walls and no floor or furniture except an oven and a cupboard of sorts, and the pigs, dogs and chickens ran in and out. The women were good looking and well dressed. The men were away road making. Each house was flying a Japanese flag at half-mast in mourning for the death of a Japanese Prince, which detracted a little from their savage appearance. The whole party then went on to the inn, at a place called Kampekiro, where we were to spend the night. I say 'whole party' because besides my wife and myself there were by now a whole crowd of officials, some in uniform and some in plain clothes, police and coolies; some twenty in all. They all slept about on the floors of the inn, some in the hall; none had any luggage, but Japanese inns provide night kimonos and tooth brushes. Talking of night kimonos, I may say that English travellers, including once a large party of men and women on some charitable or missionery enterprise, often buy night kimonos without knowing what they are, and amuse the populace by walking about the streets in their nightdress thinking that they look quite Japanese. In the course of the afternoon my wife and I thought we would go for a short walk. No sooner had we left the inn door than police sprang from behind every bush and wished to accompany us; but as we were only going for a walk of half a mile or so we managed to dissuade them from following.

Next morning at six the 'savage' women came and danced and sang for us in front of the hotel, dancing and singing having been out of the question the day before, which was the last day of National mourning. I do not think that at that hour, before breakfast, we were at our best for appreciating the treat provided for us. When breakfast did come it consisted of cold boiled ducks' eggs, which we did not appreciate very much either. I do not know how savage the savages are, but they are undoubtedly the aboriginal inhabitants from the time before the Chinese occupation. There are also real savage head-hunters in the interior of the island, securely fenced in with barbed wire and watched over by armed guards, but of these travellers see nothing.

At seven we started on our return journey to Taihoku. On the following day we had a long programme and the usual calls on the digestion. After breakfast we went to visit the English Presbyterian Mission, which has been doing good work for many years, the present hospital having been built in 1900. There were forty beds for women in the modern ward, six for women with babies (lying in), and sixty-eight beds in the older wards for men. I gathered that the work was greatly appreciated by the people and the only trouble was that the patients generally insisted on going out for the Chinese New Year. There was also a tubercular ward to which the Japanese Government had subscribed and twenty beds in private wards. I am not sure whether it was this or another British institution which was doing work among lepers. The staff entertained us at breakfast at eleven o'clock, or a cross between breakfast and luncheon, a meal to which we endeavoured to do justice. Then we went on to Tamsui, where we had a Vice-Consulate. Before reaching that destination we visited the Rising Sun Oil Depot, when we were entertained with champagne and sandwiches, and at one the Vice-Consul gave us a fine old English dinner of soup, fish, roast beef, turkey and pudding.

Tamsui is some twelve to fifteen miles from Taihoku by road and we heard afterwards that before we went there the police had searched every house on the road. The fear apparently was 'that the natives or Chinese might make some sort of attack on us in order to create an incident which would give the Japanese authorities trouble. Although the Japanese may be efficient I gathered that they were by no means popular. One of the sights that pleased us most as we drove along the road was that of the water buffaloes. These animals are said to dislike the smell of foreigners and go for them; we heard of one man, though I rather think he was a Japanese, who had been pursued by a water buffalo for a considerable distance across paddy fields, the worst possible ground for making good time.

From Tamsui we went back to Taihoku for a Rugger match got up in our honour. Next day we went back to Keelung and thence to Kobe.

We enjoyed our tour immensely and saw an enormous amount that was interesting. Formosa is full of a number of things, so that the Formosans ought all to be as happy as kings. They are certainly making progress and in Mr. Koshimura's MS. of a new handbook on the island I was delighted to see in a passage about the improvements in the well-being of the savages that some were so far advanced as to pay taxes. Certainly the Japanese are making the most of the natural riches of the island. We stayed two days at the Bank house at Kobe in Ross's absence. One day the Royds lunched and we went for a charming drive among the hills to Arima and then down to the Opera House and playgrounds at Takarazuka, a sort of half-way house for Osaka and Kobe, to which thousands of people go daily. The Opera House holds three thousand people at a uniform price of thirty sen and gives good shows; the profits being made out of the tram fares, the tram company having provided the theatre, etc. Next day we lunched with Paske Smith at Shioya, and had a delightful walk among the hills that side. So home.

[End of Diary].

In the spring we went off on another expedition to stay with Marquess and Marchioness Tokugawa at Wakayama in the south-east, in the country of which the Marquess's ancestors had been daimyos. We were taken all over the old feudal castle, but the family were living in a more modern villa with some rooms furnished in European style. The Marquess had been a good deal in Europe and was always most hospitable to English visitors. We made a number of beautiful expeditions from Wakayama and enjoyed ourselves very much. In the town of Wakayama we went to see a newish public garden; in one part of it were flower beds in the nature of an English herbaceous border. The Marquess sniffed at this a good deal—obviously 'the garden of a *nouveau riche.*'

Japanese gardens are largely affairs of landscape; arrangements of trees and water, bridges and big stones for which large sums, one hundred pounds or more, are sometimes paid. Apart from the landscape effects there is usually some one flower to which the garden is devoted; azaleas, peonies, or whatever it may be, but no mixture of flowers, so that for a good part of the year they are apt to look a little dreary to our eyes. The proper Japanese way to enjoy a garden is to go there at the azalea-viewing time, if azaleas are its feature, sit down and spend an hour or two in silent contemplation of the flowers.

May brought the Duke of Gloucester's Mission with the Garter for the Emperor.

The *Suffolk*, in which the Mission came, reached Yokohama on May 2nd, when the Duke was met there by Prince Chichibu, as well as by myself and my staff, and the Japanese staff attached to him. We came on almost at once by special train to Tokyo. The British staff was headed by Lord Airlie and the Japanese by Baron Hayashi. I noticed these two in animated conversation, but although Hayashi spoke excellent English there seemed to be some hitch. I listened to their talk and was surprised to observe that Airlie talked exclusively of naval matters, and Hayashi, a former Ambassador in London, answered in a deprecating sort of way. At last I disentangled them and discovered that Airlie believed himself to be talking to the great Admiral Togo.

At Tokio station the Duke was met by the Emperor and other members of the Imperial Family, after which he was escorted to a Palace that had been placed at his disposal.

In the afternoon we had a rehearsal of the investiture ceremony which actually took place the following morning. It was carried out with great dignity and made a splendid impression on the Japanese present. These included only a very limited number of Dignitaries and Household Officials, and no ladies were present. The Emperor was seated on a Throne facing the door of the hall with Imperial Princes, Ministers, and great Officials of the Court to his right, and myself and my staff to his left.

The various members of the Mission advanced from the end of the hall bearing the insignia and were announced by me with their full titles.

They were Mr. Hugh Lloyd Thomas, acting Secretary to the Most Noble Order, carrying the address, and Captain Howard Kerr, carrying the Hat and Mantle.

Admiral Meade and General Ellis, carrying one the Collar and the other the Garter.

The Earl of Airlie, carrying the Riband and George with Star. Finally came the Duke of Gloucester in Garter Robes, bearing the King's autograph Letter and the Warrant. The Duke handed to the Emperor the autograph Letter and Warrant and made a brief address, 'Declaratory of the object of the Mission,' as the Ceremonial Programme has it, to which the Emperor replied. H.R.H. then invested the Emperor with the Garter, buckling it round his knee, the Riband and George and Star, the Mantle (Blue velvet), Collar and lastly the Hat (a towering mass of feathers) which the Emperor placed for a moment on his head, and then set down beside him. The Duke then retired backwards to the door, a feat which he managed with great skill; having taken the precaution to see that his mantle was a short one.

Everything was done with great solemnity and without any sort of theatrical effect. It was in fact a wholly successful ceremony and Count Makino considered it an excellent lesson for the Japanese. The succeeding days were filled with entertainments of every kind at the Palace, the Embassy and elsewhere. We gave a dinner party of seventy on the 4th, an afternoon reception for the British community on the 7th, when we had about four hundred guests, and a Ball on the 8th. The visit lasted three weeks, but during part of this time the Duke was making a tour of the island.

I noticed that perhaps the most enthusiastic public welcome given to the Duke was at the theatre, when the whole audience turned to the Imperial box and cheered. One of the most splendid entertainments was a banquet given by Baron Mitsui followed by a 'No' dance in which the dresses of the performers were most magnificent. The 'No' dance is a theatrical performance of archaic character, in which every action is based on long tradition. Every movement and gesture of the actors has some meaning which is only intelligible to experts.

The entertainment which probably pleased the Duke himself more than most, was a visit to the Cavalry School, where a sham fight took place, as well as all sorts of exercises and *haute école* performances in the Riding School. At a football match, where there were some ten thousand spectators, largely students, the Duke had a splendid reception, as he had also when he visited the Imperial University.

I need hardly say that during the visit, speech after speech dwelt upon the traditional friendship between our two countries and the excellent relations which so happily existed at that time. It was, in fact, true that these relations had been of a remarkably friendly character in the past and that not only had we no quarrel of any sort, but there was no apparent reason for any change apart from our abandonment of the alliance. Even that could have been taken as a recognition of the fact that in days when peace was the prime objective, alliances were out of fashion, for in practice all alliances are really designed against some specified or unspecified opponent. On the other hand, if one considers who these opponents would have been in the case of an Anglo-Japanese alliance, one has to recognize that whereas Japan thought she had most to fear from Russia, and also had a serious grudge against the United States on account of the Immigration Law, we were most likely to experience trouble in the Pacific from China. The position might therefore have been uncommonly difficult. Japan was also in bad trouble with China over Manchuria, but she could never have been really anxious for us as a partner in dealing with China considering the views which doubtless even the most sensible Japanese entertained about the East for the Easterners.

Altogether I do not think that the prospects of a renewed alliance were very promising.

I might add that from time to time I was asked whether I thought that there was a secret treaty in existence between Japan and Russia, which presumably would have been directed against China with whom both were having trouble at the time. I suppose it might even have involved hostility to us. My reply always was that I did not believe in any such treaty, but I thought it possible that there was some sort of understanding between the two countries, that in spite of frequent alarums and excursions on the Siberian frontier they would not go too far.

The Garter Mission over, we returned to a normal life.

Almost our first visitor was Sir Rabindranath Tagore, who lunched with us one day. He was a most imposing figure, and one could believe anything good of him, but although he made himself very agreeable I cannot pretend that we had any very deep conversations.

It must have been in the course of this summer that one of the Japanese papers, *The Japanese Times*, published in English, excelled itself in tendentious invention. There was a feeling among the Japanese Nationalists that Britain was putting pressure on Japan in order to obtain her help in China. I, having gone to Chuzenji for the hot weather, made up my mind to remain there and not go down to Tokyo once or twice a week as I generally did, so that no one could say that I was harassing the Foreign Minister. Nevertheless, the *Japan Times* not only reported that I had had an interview with the Minister for the purpose of obtaining Japanese co-operation, but actually gave details of our conversation; what I had said, what he had replied, what I had then urged on him, his further answer and so on.

Happily, before I could take any action the Minister himself published a contradiction.

Soon after this came the forerunners of the Canadian Legation, the establishment of which had just been announced. Mr. Herbert Marler, the Minister, did not arrive until September.

I may say at once that we were excellent friends from the beginning: he was entirely loyal and never showed any desire to separate his interests from ours. It always seemed to me, however, that there was something lacking in the argument for a Canadian Legation. It was doubtless natural that Canada should wish to have her own representative, but exactly what matters he could deal with, apart from trade questions for which a Commercial Mission would have sufficed, was not quite apparent. I once ventured to ask the Minister what he would do if Japan made herself really nasty about immigration and even threatened hostilities. The only answer possible was that he would come to me. Up to now political questions have always involved some idea of force in the background, remote though that background may be.

By this time the Tanaka Government had fallen for no apparent reason and been replaced by a new government with Mr. Hamaguchi as Premier and Baron Shidehara back as Foreign Minister. We had our old and genial friend, Admiral Takarabe, as Minister of Marine, and he came to dinner to meet Admiral Waistell, who had succeeded Admiral Tyrwhitt on the China Station. We also had a dance for the officers who came with Admiral Waistell.

In October came the British Delegates who had represented the Institute of International Relations at the conference held at Kyoto by the Institute of Pacific Relations. This delegation was a very strong one, headed by Lord Hailsham and including Mr. Malcolm MacDonald, Mr. Lionel Curtis, Mrs. Alfred Lyttelton, Canon Streeter, Miss Eileen Power and others. Lord and Lady Hailsham stayed in our guest house for two or three days, and we had a big dinner to give them an opportunity of meeting Japanese notabilities. Mr. Malcolm MacDonald, unfortunately, did not come to Tokyo. The British Japan Society—mixed British and Japanese— also gave the delegates a great banquet at which Lord Hailsham and I made speeches. Altogether the party saw a great number of leading men and most of the sights of Tokyo in the short time at their disposal.

In view of the strong feeling between Japan and China over Manchuria, the proceedings at Kyoto were, I believe, very difficult and at the outset an explosion was imminent. Happily peace was preserved. I have no doubt it was all very successful, but I felt that for countries which did not thoroughly understand English ways it might be difficult to believe that the delegation did not really represent the British Government. A delegation of leading Japanese acting independently of their Governmeet would of course be unthinkable. I do not mean to say that our delegation expressed views which were distasteful to our Government, merely that the position is a little misleading to strangers.

During the autumn we had a visit of a very different kind and one that met with popularity quite beyond our expectations. I have already referred to the arrangements for bringing Mr. Laurence Binyon to give a series of lectures at Tokyo and opening an exhibition of English water-colours under his supervision.

Binyon came, saw and conquered. His first lecture was very well attended: many hundreds crowded the lecture hall. We thought this might be an instance of the Japanese coming to see what it was like; not at all: the numbers if possible increased as the series continued and at the sixth and last lecture hundreds were turned away for want of room. His subject was Landscape in English art and poetry and his eminently beautiful diction was as remarkable as his subject matter. He afterwards travelled through Japan and saw a number of great art collections in a way which is seldom

M

possible. The Japanese were impressed with the fact that he was a genuine lover of art and genuinely interested in oriental art, and, that being so, they brought out for his inspection treasures which would otherwise never have been revealed.

The exhibition of water-colours was a great success. There were drawings by Gainsborough, Towne, Girtin, Cotman, Constable, Turner, DeWint, Rowlandson (one lent by Mr. Ramsay MacDonald), David Cox, and other more modern artists, and they attracted great interest and admiration from Japanese art lovers, who had probably never had such an opportunity of appreciating English art of any kind; and this was particularly English art.

The *Japanese Advertiser*, in a very good article on the exhibition, said: 'There is not a single picture that the lover of pictures would not linger over with pleasure.' Among those which the writer specially mentioned was 'the fine Pillar Rock of Sir Charles Holmes,' lent by Prince Chichibu, to whom I had given it as a wedding present. Among the best features of the exhibition, so far as organization went, were its coherence and its admirable arrangement.

The writer whom I have quoted referred to the beginning which was being made by Japanese artists to attempt our European style of painting. Anything I had seen myself in the way of pictures and still more of sculpture in this style seemed to me indescribably hideous, and I found difficulty in saying anything civil about it to Count Makino, who was a great patron of the new school. The writer whom I have just quoted said of the foreign section of recent Japanese exhibitions that there was 'an atmosphere of inspissated gloom, suitable perhaps for some of the more intensely modern of the new cafés, but out of keeping with a happy home.' He described Japanese art as still full of vitality, but sitting uneasily on two stools.

Sir Charles Holmes had at one time been very anxious to arrange a temporary exchange of pictures between the National Gallery and the Imperial Collection, but this fell through. The trustees of the National Gallery did not feel able to let their pictures go out of the country, and the Japanese, though they might have been willing to take the risk, thought it dangerous. Count Makino, as Lord Privy Seal, had a controlling voice in the matter, as the pictures to be sent would have been Imperial property. He explained to me that he would have to send a very large number; I think, he said, three times the number of the English pictures, as the Japanese paintings could not be exposed to the light for very long.

Another international affair this autumn was a great Engineering Congress, which was attended by a number of eminent engineers from our country. They, too, considered that their meeting was a great success.

We had a dinner for them at which Prince Chichibu was present and made himself most agreeable. Sir Alexander Gibb and Sir Richard Threlfall were among our representatives. When I think of all these gatherings which took place during my term of office, and of the really remarkable response which Britain and the British Empire made to every opportunity offered for showing friendliness and appreciation to Japan, I do feel that in this respect we left nothing undone which could have contributed to the maintenance of peace and amity. Unfortunately the Japanese with whom our visitors made friends were the cultivated class, men with wide views of human affairs, whose influence in their own country was diminishing in favour of the ultra-nationalists, who cared nothing for co-operation, intellectual or otherwise, with Europeans, unless it could contribute to the aggrandizement of Japan. Aggrandizement, too, has its appeal even for the wisest.

Our next visitor was the Maharajah of Kapurthala, who came with two aides-de-camp to lunch at the Embassy and accepted an invitation to dinner to meet various dignitaries. My wife was away at the time and my younger daughter, aged twenty, was acting hostess. The Maharajah told her he supposed he should wear ordinary evening dress at dinner. She at once told him that would not do at all: she would expect to see him in his most beautiful clothes. Accordingly he played up and he and his suite came in gorgeous brocades. It was a very mixed dinner. Among the other guests were Mr. Wakatsuki, the former Premier, and Admiral Takarabe, who were just going to England for the Naval Conference. We also had some of the Institute of International affairs party, including Miss Eileen Power and Lady Craik, the Brazilian Ambassador, the Danish and Polish Ministers and three other Japanese couples.

Just before these gatherings we had been guests of the management of the Kabukiza Theatre, who gave an evening's entertainment of classical plays, with dinner in one of the intervals, for the Diplomatic Corps, as represented by ourselves and the Soviet Ambassador and his wife. I think I may say, incidentally, that we were on excellent terms with Mr. and Madame Troyanovsky.

The manager of the theatre made a little speech at dinner thanking us for our presence and adding: "I shall be gratified if I can contribute a widow's mite to the promotion of international understanding and friendship."

I might say, while on the subject of theatres, that our Tokyo A.D.C. during those years was a very active society, one very ambitious effort being a performance of *St. Joan* for some Japanese cause. We—I say we because I was President of the Society and took part in the committee meetings— also gave several plays in lighter vein, such as: *So this is Geneva* and *So this is London*. To some of these I invited Japanese students whose acquaintance I had made in the course of my many visits to places of education, and they expressed great appreciation of this opportunity of seeing something of the English theatre.

I think it was about this time that Count Chinda died. He had been Ambassador in London and, after his return to Tokyo, Grand Chamberlain to the Emperor. He and Countess Chinda were very good friends of ours and had liked English life. She told us that when they came back to Japan they expected to go on living a European life, but they soon found themselves relapsing into Japanese habits, and by the time we arrived in Tokyo the only difference they made was in eating a little more meat at dinner than the normal family.

Towards the end of November my daughter and I set out on an expedition to Corea, and thence by way of Mukden and Dairen to Peking, where we were to stay at the Legation with the Lampsons; my wife coming back from Europe was to meet us at Tientsin.

Our visit to Corea was most interesting. The adjective which is always in my mind when I think of that country is 'Improbable.' It is the most improbable country that I know. The appearance of the men, tall figures stalking about the countryside in long white coats like dressing-gowns and miniature top hats of black gauze, is the most improbable thing of all. We were hospitably entertained at Seoul, the capital, by the Consul-General, Oswald White, and Mrs. White, and he kindly gave an afternoon party to which he asked the whole British community. These numbered eighty-one, of whom eighty were missionaries. They were all introduced to me, but the Consul-General, being a newcomer, did not know the histories of all of them quite correctly. He would say: "Sir, this is Mr. Jones, an Australian Baptist." "No, no," said Mr. Jones, "a Canadian Congregationalist." Then: "This is Mr. Cameron, a Scots Presbyterian Minister." "No, no. I am an English Methodist," and so on. I tried to follow their affairs with interest, but it was not very easy.

Corea is a sort of paradise for missionaries, being all divided up into sectors between the various British and American bodies, though I am afraid Christianity does not yet go very deep among the Coreans. We ourselves, the Anglicans, have a Bishop and a Cathedral, but not, I fancy, a very large congregation.

With Mr. White we saw all the sights of Seoul, including the Palace of the former sovereigns and various temples. I also asked to see a private house and was kindly invited to that of a rich Corean. We were received by our host in a large room almost devoid of furniture, as a Japanese room would be, and well heated from a stove below the floor. Afterwards we went round the large compound. The long one-storeyed house where we had been received had two other houses behind it: the middle one for the children being educated, the third for the ladies of the family, who were in fact peeping through chinks of the door. On the outer side were godowns and stores of various kinds. As we came round to the front again I noticed a row of somewhat dilapidated buildings on the edge of the compound. I asked what they were. "Those are for the poor relations." I liked the idea of having a rim of poor relations to one's grounds.

I gathered that the submission of the Coreans to Japan is of a sullen nature. The Coreans are not great fighters, but they did give culture to Japan and on that account may well think themselves the superior race, although quite unable to give effect to their superiority. To the Japanese they are a race to be bullied with ease, although as a matter of fact some of the Governors-General have been very good men. Fortunately for the Coreans their climate is too severe to attract many Japanese settlers, so that they have not been ousted from their land, and the Japanese in the country are mainly officials. Before we left we lunched with Admiral Viscount Saito, the Governor-General, a charming gentleman who was afterwards Prime Minister and was murdered as being insufficiently Nationalist.

From Seoul we went on to Mukden by night train on the South Manchuria Railway. At midnight I was woken up to receive the Japanese official who was to take charge of our tour through Manchuria; rather an officious as well as official person, but very polite. At Mukden we dined with the Consul-General and met Mr. Wellington Koo, who was acting as Minister to the Young Marshal, and Mr. H. Donald, an Australian, who was his Adviser, and, I believe, a very capable one. The Young Marshal was Chang Sueh Liang, who had succeeded his father, Chang Tso-Lin, as Viceroy; he was quite a young man; as nearly independent as may be of the Chinese Government and not on good terms with the Japanese. For that reason I did not ask to be received by him although he was in the habit of showing hospitality to English travellers. All I saw was the electric wires which fenced the grounds of his Palace and the course where he played golf; for he lived in constant fear of assassination, presumably by Japanese agents. The character I heard of him was on the whole good, but by the Japanese he was regarded as an adversary who was trying to rob them of their treaty rights in Manchuria and of all the fruits of their labours there.

That Japan, in acquiring the South Manchuria Railway from Russia, really had obtained extensive rights in Manchuria, had invested an enormous amount of capital in the country and had so far provided order and prosperity that Chinese from other parts of China had immigrated by the million, is apt to be forgotten.

The great sight of Mukden is the Mausoleum of the Manchu Dynasty, approached by a splendid avenue lined with colossal stone figures of animals.

From Mukden we went to Dairen, the capital of the leased Kwantung territory. There we lunched informally with the President of the South Manchuria Railway. There was nothing noteworthy about the lunch except the oysters. Seeing them on our plates as we came into the room I had a spasm of anxiety about their quality, but I ate them and enjoyed them. After luncheon we went with our Consul, Cunningham, and Mrs. Cunningham, who put us up most hospitably, to Port Arthur, where we were able to realize the extraordinary feat performed by the Japanese troops in climbing the hill and storming the fort.

We were also entertained at luncheon by the British Chamber of Commerce and attended a St. Andrew's Day dance at the Dairen Club.

Next morning we embarked on the *Tencho Maru*, a boat of 1,200 tons, for Tientsin, a voyage normally of twenty-four hours. We had not been at sea very long before a typhoon, or something like one, started. By the evening there was a tremendous sea. I, being a good sailor, went down to a solitary dinner, stumbling over a young American who was lying frightfully ill at the top of the hatchway. That night things got worse and next morning there was no attempt at giving us any food. I went on deck and somehow late in the morning got hold of the Captain. He, poor man, said he was "very sorry": he did not know where we were: he had lost, or never had, his wireless apparatus: he supposed we might be sixty miles from Dairen and he hoped we might be able to get back there. Things did not look like our getting anywhere except to the bottom of the China Sea, but I insisted on having some food meanwhile, and eventually a seaman brought me a bowl of soup and stood facing me with the basin clutched in his hand while I lapped it up. Fortunately, in the course of the evening the weather mended; we got some sleep and in the morning all was peace and we were arriving at Taku at the mouth of the Pei-ho river. At breakfast most of the passengers appeared calm except an American lady who was furious because the waffles were too hot or not hot enough. Her husband silenced her by observing that as they had barely escaped drowning it did not perhaps matter very much about the waffles. She then told us how distressed she had been during the first night by the recollection that she had made no will and that she had a trunk full of souvenirs at Kobe which were not labelled, so that nobody would know for whom they were intended.

Eventually we arrived in good order at Tientsin and the officials of the line came on board, apologized for the behaviour of the sea and presented my daughter with a large bouquet. They said that they had been in a great state of nerves as they could get no news of the *Tencho Maru* and had even telegraphed to the Admiralty at Tokyo for assistance. Very likely if we had been drowned, the Captain, if not the Chairman of the Line, would have felt obliged to commit suicide.

At Tientsin we stayed two nights and went out with the Consul-General to the British Club—a vast place. We met my wife at the station and so on by train to Peking, where we spent a week with the Lampsons. I had a Japanese servant with me, but they thought it safer not to put him up at the Legation where the Chinese servants might have made serious trouble about his presence.

The British Legation at Peking, constructed out of an old temple, was an altogether delightful place, with a very big compound, and one can well imagine that no Minister could do otherwise than grieve over the necessity of moving to Nanking, where no good quarters were to be had and the surroundings were altogether disagreeable. The Lampsons were most kind to us and we had as a fellow guest Bill Astor, who had also been one of the Kyoto Conference party.

We did all the great sights of Peking pretty thoroughly, the Forbidden City, Temple of Heaven, Summer Palace and so forth, but they have all been repeatedly described by experts and I will not dilate upon their beauties here. One delightful afternoon was devoted to a long ride across country, starting from the Lampsons' villa some miles out of town; near the villa, by the way, I saw the first 'business' camels I had met since Constantinople days.

We dined one evening with a former Chinese Minister in Rio who gave us a regular Chinese dinner of some twenty courses; my hostess helping me all the time to titbits from the dish in the middle of the table. We all drank wine with each other continually, but I altogether declined to empty my glass each time in the approved fashion; not that this was really a more serious undertaking than a dinner at the Swedish Legation in Rio, where a similar practice was kept up.

While we were in Peking my daughter and I debated whether we should have the courage to go back to Japan by sea, or whether we should go round by land at the risk of finding the train uncomfortably full of Chinese soldiers. We decided that it could not be so rough again within a week, nor was it, but the difference was not very great.

We went by train to Taku, the most god-forsaken place I ever saw, where an Englishman who made such kindness his business took charge of us and gave us hot baths and tea and toast. Our boat was late in sailing and, as we afterwards heard, was the only one that ventured to cross the bar that day.

It was a most disagreeable voyage. One cabin contained an American with his wife and two children; she put the lifebelts on them so as to be ready for the worst, but he took them off on the ground that in the cold China Sea it was better to drown quickly.

Eventually we reached Shimonoseki all safe and sound and got back to Tokyo in time for Christmas.

To finish the year's entertaining we had a big Christmas dinner for our staff and the Canadian Minister and his staff, to whom were added Mr. Noel Coward and Lord Amherst, who were travelling together. Noel Coward added greatly to the fun of the evening, and though he had some other engagement, stayed till all hours, most of the time playing nursery games.

Almost our first visitors of 1930 were a party of English singers making a world tour. They sang in the Elizabethan fashion sitting round a table, and unaccompanied, their songs being nearly all of the sixteenth and seventeenth centuries, though there were also some folk songs arranged by Vaughan Williams. The English part of the audience enjoyed it immensely and the critics were full of praise. We persuaded Prince Takamatsu, the Emperor's second brother, to be present at one performance, he being musical and interested in art of all kinds. I did not hear from him what he thought of the concert, but Prince Chichibu told me his brother thought it 'very funny.' Though he did not appreciate this concert I understood that he did greatly appreciate our Exhibition of Water-Colours.

Our next excitement was Prince Takamatsu's marriage to a young lady of the great Tokugawa family. The Prince was the adopted heir of one of the richest of the old Japanese families connected with the Imperial House, the Arisagawas, and the bride's mother was a daughter of Prince Arisagawa. She herself had been brought up to be the wife of an Imperial Prince. Prince Takamatsu was not only rich, but said to be both clever and artistic, which I can well believe: he was certainly attractive. It was arranged that they should visit England later in the year. The Japan-British Society had a dinner for them, and the Cambridge and Oxford Society had a dinner for him, at both of which I presided. The Cambridge and Oxford Society, composed of elected members educated at one or other university, both British and Japanese, was always very insistent on putting Cambridge first, which of course suited me. The Prince was a little nervous on these occasions, but made quite good speeches in a clear voice. The wedding itself was only attended by the members of the Imperial Family and high Court officials and the ceremony was carried out in traditional style: the bride's dress is described as 'a five-fold robe of gorgeous colours of dark green, crimson and red and a cream court train hanging from the shoulders and falling three feet on the floor.' Prince Takamatsu wore the usual black court robe with white trousers and sacred baton.

We were all invited to a great luncheon party at the Palace.

There had been two sporting events during the autumn and winter to which I have not alluded.

One was a duck hunt arranged for us by Marquess Kuroda at his country place, Haneda, a little way from Tokyo. The Marquess had been educated at Cambridge and was actually at King's during my first year there, though I hardly knew him; consequently he was very ready to make friends. He was head of one of the great Japanese families and had been President of the House of Peers. His eldest son, Mr. Kuroda, was a distinguished ornithologist.

The duck hunt was on the same lines as the Imperial duck hunt; and although the decoy had not been kept up very elaborately it was the parent hunt, the Imperial Household having copied its traditions. The flocks of ducks amounted to over twenty thousand and from two to three thousand could be captured in a season. The duck included Wigeon, Shovellers, Teal, Mallards, and Pintail. Others that had been occasionally taken were Merganser, Mandarin duck, Spectacled Teal, American Wigeon, Gadwall, Pochard, Tufted duck, Eastern Scarp duck, Goosander, Red Breasted Merganser and Siberian White-eyed duck. The list is taken from a pamphlet written by Mr. Kuroda.

It seems from the same pamphlet that the old feudal lords had their own duck-hunting grounds because the Shoguns did not allow any hawking on the open plain except by their own people. Even in the duck-hunting grounds the duck were taken by hawks until the 'scoop net' system was invented in comparatively recent times. The Haneda ground where we enjoyed the sport was only constructed in 1887: before that the Kurodas had a decoy at their Tokyo house, a fact which suggests the great size of the parks surrounding such houses in former days.

One of the strictest rules is that of complete silence, the decoy man giving all necessary directions by signal.

I had a good deal of correspondence with Mr. Kuroda about birds, and among other things he gave me a list of eighty-eight species which had been recorded in Tokyo itself, including a considerable number of water fowl, the green pheasant which breeds in the Imperial Gardens, the Hondo Ural Owl, Hondo Great Spotted Woodpecker, Shrikes, Hawfinch, and others whose relatives would not be found in London. My own notes of birds seen were too amateurish to be of value, but I did observe a considerable number of species.

One feature of our Haneda visit illustrates Japanese ways of life. After the first 'hunt' we were given an excellent luncheon in a house on the property which did not seem to be in regular occupation. We were waited on by three Japanese women whom I supposed to be maids brought from Marquess Kuroda's Tokyo house. Afterwards we discovered that they were the wife and daughters of the Marquess's agent, a well-known member of parliament who had been educated at Cambridge, and had come with us from Tokyo.

The other 'sporting' event to which I referred was an attempt to introduce the Eton 'field game' of football, which Count Maeda had seen and admired while in England in attendance on Prince Chichibu.

With some difficulty I procured for him a copy of the rules, after being mendaciously assured by an old Etonian in Tokyo that there were no printed rules. Count Maeda was highly pleased and collected two elevens, but, unfortunately, the only ground he could get was about half the proper size. Consequently, as the field game is played with a small ball and the 'behinds' kick as hard as they can, the ball was much oftener out than in; and moreover the game being a very fast one the players went from one end of the ground to the other in no time. Not, I fear, a success.

Then, of course, there was the racing, especially at Yokohama, of which I have said nothing, though as President of the Club I was a fairly regular attendant. The racing was not of a very high class and there were few good horses, but things were gradually improving and the Club built a very fine Grand Stand and other accessories during our time.

We were surprised that at the first meeting after this stand was opened the entrance money taken amounted to very little, although there seemed to be a large crowd. Eventually we discovered that some ingenious Japanese had forged a vast quantity of tickets and sold them cheap: as a matter of fact, most of the Japanese crowd squatted near the betting booths and never looked at the horses.

During the first months of 1930 the Naval Disarmament Conference was in progress in London.

Mr. Ramsay MacDonald had delivered an address before the Council of Foreign Relations in New York on October 11th, 1929, in the course of which he said: "Public opinion in Europe to-day tells its political leaders that it knows there are risks in peace: that it knows that the assumption made between one nation and another, that they are to conduct their affairs in sincerity and justice, does lay the believing nation open to a certain amount of risk. I will take it. I will take it!"

The Naval Conference was summoned in this spirit, but the Treaty signed at the end of April was no great cause for congratulation. The proceedings did not much affect the Embassy beyond the delivery of occasional messages to the Japanese Government; but I believe the Chauvinists thought that Britain, in collaboration with the United States, was putting undue pressure on Japan, and there were rumours of an intended anti-British demonstration, but it came to nothing.

The Americans having been some time without an Ambassador sent Mr. Castle, the Assistant Secretary of State, to be at Tokyo during the Conference, and withdrew him again when it was over. Before his departure he was entertained at a farewell banquet by the Japanese Government and the usual speeches were made about the traditional friendship between the two countries. The harmony of the evening was, however, somewhat disturbed by a late speaker with some such innocuous toast to propose as the health of the chairman. This speaker had been Ambassador in Washington and he told the gathering that after listening to all this talk of amity he wished to say that there was nothing in it, that Japan would never forgive the immigration laws and talk of friendship was useless while they remained in force. When I heard of this outburst I remarked to the Vice-Minister, in a more or less jocular way, that no doubt the speaker had been primed by the Foreign Office; he appeared, and I really believe was, horrified at the suggestion and said he and the Minister did not know which way to look.

It is true that we sometimes painted our 'traditional friendship' in rather bright colours, but we had no obvious reason for anything but friendship, and there was really a large amount of admiration and goodwill for Japan among English people who knew anything of foreign affairs. I do not think this could with veracity be said of the United States.

During the rest of this our last year in Japan we led a quiet life.

One of the sad incidents was the death of Colin Davidson, who during the four years of our stay had become a close friend. His loss to the Embassy staff was a severe one, for although the Japanese had latterly become more reserved towards English people, he had still many excellent and even intimate friends among the leading men of the country and was an admirable guide for myself and my predecessors in the intricacies of Japanese social life.

We had several visitors, particularly, as it happened, from Australia, for first came the De Chairs on their way home from the Government of New South Wales, and then Lady Stonehaven, wife of the Governor-General, known to me long ago in the Foreign Office as Johnny Baird, and a life-long friend.

One luncheon guest I may mention, namely, Professor Voronoff, of monkey-gland fame, if only to suggest the singular variety of the guests who came to our house. He appeared to be very much in earnest about his work.

Then there was one other expedition which we made during the early summer to Gifu to see the cormorant fishing on the River Nagara. This is conducted at night by the light of flares, the cormorants being attached to the boats by a sort of leash: the birds have a band round their throats to prevent them from swallowing the fish which they catch, and when they have caught a certain number are pulled into the boat and made to disgorge. The whole scene is decidedly picturesque. We had been taken for a cormorant-fishing expedition once before on the Tamagawa, the river of Tokyo, we being in a motor launch; but it was a daylight entertainment and by no means equal to Gifu.

A different set of visitors who came to us in the summer at Chuzenji was a party of British boy scouts, the Cathedral troop from Shanghai. They lunched with us and were taken for a sail on the lake by Colonel Simson, our Military Attaché. My daughter—she was herself a cub mistress in Tokyo—and I dined at their camp and had an excellent dinner prepared by six of the boys: boiled salmon trout and mayonnaise sauce, salad, fried egg plant, pancakes and fruit. Afterwards there was much singing. Count Sano, a leader of the scout movement in Japan, was one of the guests.

The last ceremony that I performed in Japan was the laying of the foundation stone of Christ Church, Yokohama, built to replace the church destroyed in the earthquake.

In my speech I emphasized the importance of a church to a British community and observed that, as Chairman of a Committee on British communities abroad, not long before I left the Foreign Office I had signed a report emphasizing that opinion. I thought of English churches abroad as being among other things places of spiritual refuge for the community, just as in mediæval times they had often been places of refuge in the literal sense; in both cases much needed. I spoke, too (as many people are speaking to-day), of the immense need for some spiritual foundation for the life of any community and I ended by quoting a message which Lord Balfour, as I had somewhere read, had sent from his death-bed to Bishop Talbot, 'that he kept to the old things.'

The service was conducted by Bishop Reifsnider, one of the American bishops working in Tokyo, and before I finally left Japan I had a most generous letter from him, speaking in the name also of the other bishops, thanking me for what I had, he said, been able to do for our church while I was in Japan.

Before we left Japan there was a long series of farewell banquets, at all of which we had the kindest of receptions and every sort of evidence of genuine friendship. There was a luncheon at the Palace, dinner with the Yokohama branch of the British Association, at which Baron Shidchara was present and spoke, also the Mayor of Yokohama; luncheon with the Pan-Pacific Club, dinner with the Minister of Marine, Prince Tokugawa, the Cambridge and Oxford Society, the Tokyo Club, the Japan British Society, the Brazilian Embassy and many others.

I ventured to warn the Pan-Pacific Club against any idea that the Pacific stood apart from the rest of the world; much less was it true that, as a speaker at one of its banquets had said, the rotten effete civilization of Europe was being overwhelmed by the pure and beneficent civilization of the Pacific. I urged that all the countries in the world were interdependent. The happy country was that which had no news value. If a country had news value the fact of a small boy getting his ears boxed became 'further horrible cruelties.' I regretted that more of the people of Japan and Britain could not visit each other's countries: I did not believe that money really made the world go round, but it did make people go round the world and some way was wanted of enabling people to go round without it.

The last gathering of all was a great dinner given by our kind friend Mr. Marler, the Canadian Minister, at which one hundred and twenty-five members of the British and Canadian communities were present. There was a really splendid display of cordiality to bring my mission to a happy conclusion.

We left Tokyo on October 18th, 1930, with many regrets. Britain and Japan were still good friends, but it was becoming clear that Japanese ambitions and Japan's determination to go her own way might make difficulties in the future, although I do not think we, any of us, foresaw how great the dangers would be.

One of the more odious features of the time in Japan was the increasing influence of the extreme Nationalists. We were beginning to hear much of the Black Dragon Society, a terrorist organization whose policy was to exterminate opposition to its creed by murder if necessary. The world was soon to learn by fearful evidence that political murders were regarded by a large party in Japan not only as necessary and permissible but as deeds of patriotism, and the killing of eminent statesmen in cold blood went almost or quite unpunished.

From our point of view, and probably from the point of view of many sensible people in Japan itself, the sad thing for that country is that she has learned many lessons in both military and industrial spheres, has developed their teaching by her own genius to a high degree, but has failed almost completely to learn or develop any corresponding moral values. Public morality in Japan has reached but a very low standard.

I might add a few words about Bushido, the theory of chivalry professed and doubtless practised by the Samurai, the feudal warriors of old Japan. Tales of the Samurai make good reading, and fifty or sixty years ago when Europeans began to take an interest in Japan as a quaint and unreal country they readily ascribed to the 'little' Japanese all sorts of virtues as well as all sorts of amusing fashions, and accepted the chivalry of the Samurai with everything else.

The Japanese have consciously, or unconsciously, followed suit, and now expect the world to believe that they as a nation profess and practise the virtues which the Samurai are said to have practised. These were, chiefly, loyalty, courage, courtesy and endurance.

Loyalty meant loyalty to the feudal chief: I do not think it has any particular application to the life of to-day.

Courage in the sense of indifference to death the Japanese certainly have, as the Samurai had. Unselfish courage I doubt. If death does not matter, why bother to save a man from drowning or burning? Political and civic courage they have not. In proof of this it is enough to recall the gangs of ruffians who will rush into a house and murder an old man in his bed without incurring any special public condemnation, not because no one does condemn them, but because no one has the courage to say so.

Courtesy implies compliance with certain traditional formalities: for instance, bowing with the right degree of politeness or humility or laughing while telling a sad story so as not to distress one's friend. Otherwise there is no special courtesy between man and man, and no courtesy at all is shown to women, or thought to be called for in their case.

In fact, when the Japanese speak to-day of Bushido as a national characteristic they are really taking advantage of the fancy portrait drawn of them by foreigners during a previous generation.

CHAPTER XIV

WE HAD DETERMINED TO SEE AS MUCH OF THE WORLD AS POSSIBLE ON our way home, and we were going to begin by Indo-China. We therefore took a French boat from Yokohama to Saigon. The food the first day was very poor, and when we called at Kobe and told friends there about it large presents of food were sent on board for us. This seemed to stir the pride of the Captain, or the cook, or someone aboard, and from Kobe to Saigon the food was much better.

We stopped at Shanghai for a day, staying the night at the Consulate-General, and said good-bye to our friends there. We went to lunch with a former Turkish colleague, and to an afternoon party at which Count and Countess Ciano, then on a tour of the Far East, were present; Count

Ciano struck us as insignificant: she caught the eye more. We also lunched with Ingham, the Counsellor of Legation, who was living in Shanghai, the Minister hovering between Peking and Nanking: this was the last phase before the Legation, or Embassy as it soon became, moved definitely to the south. Ingham had his Japanese colleague to meet us, they being on excellent terms.

From Shanghai we went on to Hong Kong, where we stayed a night at Government House with Sir William and Lady Peel, and met a large party at dinner. Thence on to Saigon. Going up the river we passed a string of American destroyers who punctiliously saluted us, much to the surprise of some French naval officers who were on board our boat, till they espied my Ambassador's flag which we were flying.

We arrived early in the day at Saigon, which looked exceedingly tropical—palms and heat. We were met by our Vice-Consul and the Governor-General's private secretary and taken to the Governor-General's palace, where we were put up for the night: a very palatial palace with a fine garden. We spent the day quietly with the Vice-Consul and in the evening dined with the Acting Governor of Cochin China, the Governor-General and the Governor of Cochin China being at Hanoi for the meeting of the Assembly and also, no doubt, to cope with a revolutionary movement which was going on in Annam. The Annamites, we learned, were both fiercer, richer and more advanced in civilization than the Cambodians. The revolution was said to be communist and directed from Moscow— but then unpleasant behaviour is apt to be ascribed everywhere to the machinations of some foreign power. It was also said, probably untruly, to be directed against the richer classes of their own people rather than the French.

The dinner, which included the Belgian Socialist leader, M. Emile Vandervelde, and his wife, was pleasant, and we were struck by the fact that the Frenchmen present seemed unexpectedly contented and by no means hankering after Paris, while there were quite a number of ladies. They had a hill station and a sea-bathing place within reach of Saigon; golf, tennis and dancing; in fact, every joy.

We left Saigon at six-thirty next morning in a car kindly provided for us by the authorities and driven by a young Annamite presumably in their service. We had no excitements beyond crossing the Mekong in a ferry and passing with all four wheels over a very big snake which stretched all across the road. We were congratulated afterwards on our good luck, for if the wheels had only crushed the tail end of the snake his head would undoubtedly have been reared up and poked in at our window. This would certainly have been disagreeable. The first and last few yards of the transit of the Mekong have to be rowed, but a steam tug takes the ferry across the main part of the river. From the Cambodian frontier on I was struck by the increasing number of birds. This was later explained to me by the fact that the Cambodians are stricter Buddhists than the people of Cochin

China and therefore do not take animal life. Cranes, herons, ibises of all sorts, gorgeous kingfishers, jays, shrikes, great brown and white kites were among those I noted. The country was mostly marshy; the road excellent.

We reached the Residency at Pnom Penh at eleven-thirty, rather dirty and weary after a five hours' journey begun so early in the morning and eager for a wash and brush up, but we were met at the door by our host, who told us that we were just in time, all the guests assembled, *déjeuner* about to be served, and we could go straight in. Our host was the Political Adviser, the Résident Supérieur being away. He had been thirty-two years in Indo-China and his son was soon coming out to follow in his foot-steps. His wife had been born there, and his daughter, though not born there, had lived there all her eighteen years except for two holidays at Toulouse, which she had not enjoyed because none of the girls could speak, or even understand, Cambodian, and her own French was poor. Our host had been till recently Resident at Battambong and had got himself moved to Pnom Penh so as to give his daughter the advantages of society. Madame was of an old Colonial family, of authentic noblesse, had had ancestors in Canada and others in Pondicherry. She thought Indo-China much better for girls than France, the life much freer and out-of-doors instead of immured in a school. On her last journey out she had been at Madras and thought the Indian habit of going naked except for a loin-cloth (also the habit of the Japanese farm-workers in summer) *dégoûtant*, and their hovels miserable in the extreme. I suggested that Cambodia was, so far as I had seen, not very different, but she pointed out proudly that every man had his own culotte, which was true, though the children go naked. As to the houses, nothing could be more primitive than some of the bamboo shacks we saw, many with their legs planted in the water.

We had to stay two nights at Pnom Penh because the Vanderveldes were at the Angkor Residency and the hotel there was shut. On the third morning we started off on our three hundred and twenty kilometre drive to Angkor, stopping for lunch at the Residency at Kompong Thom. We were received by a pleasant Adjoint who had been in England, but presently the Resident himself, who had been occupied with some official ceremony, appeared in full uniform and a complete set of gold teeth. During lunch the Resident asked about our car and what chauffeur we had. "*C'est l'assassin*," said the Adjoint equably: however, it seemed that it was only the Resident that he had twice nearly killed, possibly by accident. We thought him quite a good driver, and he spoke French well.

The rest of the drive was mostly through forest: at one place we saw a flock of hoopoes on the road, and at another we admired an old Cambodian bridge said to be a thousand years old, with the piles so near together that there was hardly any space for water, and a balustrade in the form of a serpent. The road was also frequently enlivened by passing Bonzes (priests and theological students) in saffron, primrose or amber silk togas, walking always single file.

We reached Siem Reap, the seat of the Angkor Resident, at seven and were met by a most hospitable little Resident, living *en garçon*, with his house very dirty and board beds, which in view of the heat had their merits. With him we passed some happy days.

We made an early start the first morning for the ruins of Angkor, accompanied by the Resident and Dr. Parmentier, one of the Directors of the Archæological Institute and a great enthusiast. We passed by Angkor Vat, the most famous of the monuments, in order to begin with the Bayon, the temple of Angkor Thom, the great city of the Khmer race, a city of three hundred thousand inhabitants in its day. Parmentier was an excellent guide and showed us all the most striking of the carvings with which every inch of the walls is covered: representations of battles on land and sea, hunting, palace scenes, markets, and domestic life.

The temple is built in three tiers: the first one hundred and sixty metres by one hundred and forty, the second eighty-two by seventy, the third smaller again, and it has fifty-one stone towers. It stood at the centre of the great city. The first and second tiers are surrounded by galleries covered with bas-relief, those of the first tier representing Cambodian life and history in the tenth century; and those in the second, mythological subjects.

From Bayon we went past the terrace of the King's Palace—over three hundred and thirty metres long, at either end of which is a marvellous procession of stone elephants—to see two or three of the smaller temples, all in the same style of architecture but still surrounded by the dense forest amid which the ruins were discovered in 1860 after a sleep of some four hundred years. Angkor Vat and Bayon were cleared in 1908 and subsequent years and now stand in wide open spaces.

Owing to the heat we had to stay in the house in the middle of the day, but in the afternoon we were able to pay our first visit to Angkor Vat, the most famous of all the ruins. Indeed it is not so much ruined as partly damaged by exposure and decay.

The temple is approached by a causeway five or six hundred yards long, and like the Bayon rises in three tiers, the top tier a mass of conical towers, the central tower containing the principal shrine.

Climbing from storey to storey is a hair-raising business as the steps are only four inches wide by about fourteen inches high, and one has to, or at any rate I had to, go up sideways and come down backwards, feeling giddy even then.

Angkor Vat was built and dedicated to Vishnu in the first half of the twelfth century, and is of huge size. The moat which surrounds it is five hundred and fifty metres long, and the wall inside the moat one thousand and forty metres on the north and south, and eight hundred and twenty metres on the east and west. Like the Bayon the galleries on the first and second tiers are covered with bas-relief. As a more prosaic detail I may add that the whole of the ceilings of these galleries were festooned with sleeping bats.

The second morning was devoted first of all to another temple built on a steep mound. Near the base we were met by an elephant, the only survivor of three formerly attached to the Residency, and he pining for his recently deceased wife. The higher authorities had refused to allow the purchase of another elephant. My daughter and I rode the elephant up the hill and my wife and she rode it down. I have never before felt quite so helpless, and expected every moment that we should all fall together over the edge of the narrow path: however, he walked so deliberately, carefully placing one foot before the other, that to my surprise we reached the top safely.

M. Parmentier explained to us that the work of building all these temples was done by an immense number of slaves, chiefly prisoners of war, and this method proved the ruin of the Khmer Empire, not only through the prodigious waste of money, but because the infuriated labourers eventually turned against their masters and joined the Siamese invaders, who destroyed Angkor.

One little difficulty in trying to comprehend the history and general plan of this place was caused by the fact that M. Parmentier and the Resident differed *in toto* on nearly every point. The Resident pointed out a wonderful effect of perspective and Parmentier said it was merely a matter of convenience. The Resident told us that the vast artificial lake was constructed to provide a reserve of fish: when I repeated this to Parmentier, he exclaimed: "Where did you hear that nonsense? It was made entirely for irrigation purposes." When I asked the Resident if I had understood him to say 'irrigation' he replied that there were no traces of any irrigation work. "There are panthers in these woods," said the Resident. "There are no panthers here," said Parmentier. But they were excellent friends.

In the afternoon we drove out to see the great lake, which is some ten miles from Angkor. On the shore at one end is a little country club where we had tea and fed some tame cranes. Next day we came again and my daughter and a doctor and his wife bathed.

That night we had a dinner party. Parmentier, the doctor and his wife, very much interested in English literature, particularly Katherine Mansfield; and a native Cambodian official. The latter was a very uninteresting young man, and only woke up when he accompanied us for an after-dinner drive and saw a rabbit, when he gave vent to wild tally-ho's.

The third night we went to see the ruins of a monastery buried in the forest, the trunks of huge trees being all mixed up with the remains of the walls: as seen by moonlight it was ghostly to the last degree.

That ended our visit, which had been of enormous interest. It seems almost profane to add that the food was indifferent, and that we have evil memories of a goose which we saw hanging about the back door before making our evening meal.

N

So far as we could make out the people of Cambodia were well off and contented; the only obvious thing to criticize being the sight of fettered prisoners strolling about with a guard in attendance. The Resident said that no guard could be found to look after unfettered prisoners, so there it was.

Early next morning we started off by car to a point on the river some ten miles off from which a small steamer was to carry us westward to Battambong. The voyage was an affair of eight hours, mostly over flooded land; first a stretch of river, then floods, than a lake, then more floods, then a river again, in places so narrow that we had to be kept off the bank with poles: in other parts quite wide, with villages built on piles along the banks and in the river itself. Men, women and children slid perpetually into the river and out again. We passed numbers of barges with wood, fruit and other cargoes, the whole life of the place being in and on the water. Our steamer was very comfortable and we were given an excellent luncheon. The province was taken from the Siamese in 1907 by the French on behalf of the Cambodians, who had lost it in the fifteenth century, and the French officials all spoke of it as if they had reconquered a second Alsace.

Battambong is a place of considerable importance with some twelve thousand inhabitants, and the Residency had been the Palace of the Siamese Governor. The Resident and his wife were as hospitable as their colleagues and entertained us well. We had a vast bedroom, my wife and I at one end and my daughter at the other, with a good many bats in between.

We started again at six-thirty next morning for a seventy-mile drive to the Siamese frontier, where we took the train for Bangkok—a nice breezy drive with wonderful bird life: blue jays, kingfishers, herons and cranes all the way. At the station we had half an hour to wait and a half-caste Siamese-English took charge of us, gave us breakfast at the rest house and saw us into the train, forgetting, by the way, to give us a considerable amount of change due to us on our bill.

We arrived at Bangkok after a comfortable day's journey and there spent a week at the Legation with Cecil and Lady Mary Dormer, who had been so long with us at Tokyo.

I said that Corea was the most improbable country that I had ever visited, but Siam runs it close. Whereas the Corean men go about in night-gowns and toy top-hats, the Siamese of the higher classes appear in white jackets and sky-blue satin knickerbockers: really rather pleasant to the eye. We did not see much of the Siamese ladies except some of the Princesses, to whom I will return presently, but the Siamese men were intelligent and agreeable, and so, in fact, I have found their Ministers in other countries. Many of the Royal Family have been educated in English public schools, and some in universities, and they speak the English language uncommonly well: one who was Minister of War was particularly good and idiomatic. "Do I not?" he said when someone asked if he remembered some mutual acquaintance.

When Air Vice-Marshal Sir Geoffrey Salmond, who was then command-ing the R.A.F. in India, flew over for a brief visit to Bangkok he found an old Woolwich friend in the War Minister, but very properly addressed him as Sir. "Not so much Sir," said the Prince.

While on Princes I am reminded that Prince Damrong, who had lately been on a European tour with some of his family, dined one night at the Legation, bringing three daughters with him. I asked the one next to me if she had been with her father. No, she had to stay and look after the family. Afterwards I idly asked someone what the family consisted of. "Well," he said, "when I first came here I went one night to the cinema, and observed that the first row of the balcony seemed to be reserved for ladies. I asked whether this was so, and was told that it was not generally reserved, but these were Prince Damrong's daughters. In the end I learned that H.R.H. had forty-five daughters and twenty-six sons."

One night while we were there there was a reception at Court. We, with the Dormers, had places in what corresponded to the entrée room, and instead of our passing before the Royal Family, the King and Queen with another Prince walked round the room and stopped to say a few civil words. They were preceded by the Lord Chamberlain walking backwards. In the course of the evening I happened to refer to this ceremony, and I was then told that a lady of our Legation not long before had, soon after her arrival at Bangkok, wished to pay a visit to the hairdresser. Having ascertained who was the best artist in that line she went off to his shop and was somewhat taken aback to find herself in the hands of the Lord Chamberlain.

We saw, of course, all the sights of Bangkok: a very interesting historical museum—managed by another Prince—and one or two rather gorgeous temples: but the most improbable of them was one built of concrete inlaid with pieces of broken plates and saucers of ordinary European patterns. Whether they were brought whole and broken *ad hoc*, or whether we beheld the fruits of the ordinary labours of many kitchen-maids, I never discovered.

One of the drawbacks of Bangkok was the mosquitoes. We had netting and curtains of all sorts and sarongs to put round our legs at dinner, but there were mosquitoes lying in wait everywhere. Also it was exceedingly hot, not hotter perhaps than Pnom Penh, where I slept mostly on a hard sofa, or Siem Reap, where I slept on a bed of boards, but still very, very hot.

It would be better if the authorities cleaned up the little canals with which the town is threaded, for there were a good many smells: still, this did not prevent us from spending an amusing hour or two in a small launch going up and down the streets; while on the river, the Menam, an excursion was very pleasant.

On the whole Bangkok seemed a nice easy-going place, and I believe the Siamese, if left to themselves and not called upon to fight, would do very well. I have known several Englishmen employed in Siam who liked the life.

I believe we have officially gone back to calling it Siam, after a few years of Thailand: why we should bother to change our name for some countries and towns and not others I have never understood. I observe that some people nowadays, after speaking for fifteen hundred years (themselves, or their ancestors) of Constantinople, affect now to speak of Istanbul, and we try to talk of Iran instead of Persia, though not of Hellas instead of Greece. Rather foolish, I think.

From Bangkok we made our way to Singapore. Our train reached Kuala Lumpur in the early morning, and as the acting Governor had kindly sent his own train to take us the rest of the way, we had time for a drive round the town and surrounding villas, which looked delightful. We stayed two nights at Government House at Singapore and went on by one boat to Rangoon and then by another to Calcutta. At Rangoon, too, we had a pleasant drive through the beautiful suburbs.

On the boat for Calcutta we had a captain who was a great story-teller: roughly one good story at each meal; afterwards he gave me the book of them, for he had had them printed; this was a new experience in the matter of story-telling.

At Calcutta we only spent a day on this occasion, for Lord Irwin had said that if we wanted to see them in 'Lutyens' masterpiece' we must go straight to Delhi, for they were themselves moving shortly to Calcutta. So to Delhi we went, and spent three or four days with Lord and Lady Irwin in the Viceroy's house.

Lutyens' masterpiece is a splendid achievement. There is one objection. From the outer gates there ought to be a long gentle slope up to the house; there is not: two great Government buildings have been erected half-way between the gates and the house, obscuring the view altogether. After passing these buildings the road descends, and from the bottom of that slope one does at last look up to the Viceroy's house, but too late.

In the house there are many fine rooms: the great dining-room I should have thought rather too narrow, and the ball-room allows no space for the Viceregal party to sit in state and survey the scene. We had a fine suite, but it consisted of a very large sitting-room and two smallish bedrooms, whereas large bedrooms and a smallish sitting-room would have been more convenient. However, the whole result is splendid. The gardens were only just born; I hope by now there are trees. I suggested to someone that they should buy full-grown trees as is done in Japan and plant them straight away. I was told it would be too expensive, though it seemed to me that considering the great cost of the house the moving of some trees would be a mere flea-bite.

We duly saw the sights of Delhi and the neighbourhood, and thoroughly enjoyed our visit. From Delhi we went back to Agra. We told the Vice-regal party and household that we were going there: they hoped we should see the Taj Mahal at its best and that we should all meet again somewhere. Next day at Agra we went, of course, to the Taj Mahal, both morning and afternoon. In the afternoon we did notice that presently there were very few people about, and then a guardian came up and asked if we would mind leaving as a very important person was just going to arrive. English or Indian, we asked. English. Leaving the grounds to go back to our hotel, we saw troops and police in all directions, and we soon learned that the important person was the Viceroy. Next day we saw an English doctor and observed that so sudden a visit must have caused a great commotion in Agra. "Oh," said the doctor, "we all knew a fortnight ago that the Viceroy was coming." Not a very well-kept secret.

At the time we were in India there was a good deal of trouble and anxiety about Indian extremists and there were very few tourists; practically no Americans, we were told; the management of the Agra hotel consequently almost fell on our necks. We had ourselves been warned by an A.D.C. at Calcutta or Delhi: "If anyone spits at you for goodness' sake don't spit back or there will be a row at once." Actually we saw and heard nothing to cause us the slightest anxiety, apart from the knowledge that some few arrangements had to be hastily altered for the biggest people.

From Agra to Lucknow where, among other things, I was introduced at the Club to a gentleman who as a baby had been in Lucknow during the siege. One remark which struck me was that English officials, including police officials, were much too trustful and would not get into the habit of carrying revolvers, so that they were often at the mercy of an assailant with whom they might easily have dealt under other conditions.

From Lucknow to Calcutta, where we stayed some days at the noble Government House with Sir Francis and Lady Jackson.

The Viceroy had meanwhile arrived at his camp and there was a great dinner in his honour. We were also invited to a Yeomanry ball at which the Viceroy and the Governor and their parties were present. Our partners were found for us beforehand, and as I did not dance I was rather sorry for mine.

The arrangements at Government House were admirable and everything was beautifully worked out: I noted particularly the 'talking list' for the Viceroy, Governor and their wives, and in fact the careful directions issued to all of us for our conduct on all occasions.

Having been merely a passer-by I cannot claim to have formed opinions worth anything about Indian politics or to have seen anything that has not been described a hundred times, so I do not propose to make any pretence about it.

From Calcutta we went on to spend a week at Secunderabad with my elder daughter, Betty Jermy Gwyn, whose husband was there with his Punjab Regiment. That was a very amusing week and we did begin to feel quite at home. Also the Nizam most kindly placed a car at our disposal so that we were able to see a good deal of the surrounding country, including Golconda, in comfort. We lunched one day with the Nizam at King Kothi, where he usually lived, the great Palace being, I believe, only used on high occasions.

We only just escaped the necessity of being inoculated for plague before going to Secunderabad as there had recently been an outbreak: some Indian magnate had been camping near my daughter's house with a household of some four hundred persons and one of his wives had died of plague, so that my daughter was prepared for the worst. However, we were lucky.

One day we lunched with the Fakir ul Mulk, an admirable host who gave us a very pleasant party. Here again I dropped a brick, for, having heard that he had had sons at Eton, and seeing the table decorated with Eton blue I guessed that he was doing honour to Eton on this occasion. It seemed that this shade of blue had been the colour of his family before Eton was thought of.

We also went to a big garden party given by an Indian host to which a great number of officials and their wives had been invited. I was much struck by the way in which the various British regiments clung together, and I was told that this was usual. In fact, everywhere in India I gathered that there was not much intermingling between military and civilians, between cavalry and infantry, or, as at Secunderabad, even between one regiment and another.

From Secunderabad our party, including my elder daughter and her husband, went on to Bombay, where we spent a day with Sir Frederick and Lady Sykes; and then on to Jamnagar, to spend Christmas with Ranjitsinhji's family, the Jam Sahib himself being in England. The honours were done by his nephews Digvijaysinhji (the present Jam Sahib), Pertab and our friend Himat, who had been a language officer in Japan. They took endless trouble to give us a good time. The programme included a good deal of shooting, for some of which we stayed at a smaller palace in the country. I was assumed to have shot two panthers and a sambhar, and may perhaps claim to have helped to shoot them. Anyhow, these expeditions were full of interest and excitement. For the sambhar we waited on one side of a deep valley while the beaters came over the top of the hill on the far side: when they had come a short way down, a panther suddenly sprang out of the bush and made a great leap across their line, happily not striking any of them. Of the panthers, one was shot from a cache, or rather caches, among the boughs of trees; the other from behind a screen of bushes. One night we spent some hour or more in a pavilion where a kid had been tied up outside to attract a panther it was desired to locate. After some time a young panther came and began the feast, but, hearing his mother approach, made off and left the remains for her.

My daughter also went out to shoot black buck with Digvijaysinhji (Digby for short).

Another day we all drove out to tea in a villa near the sea where the Jam Sahib has another shoot for small game, hares and partridges, of which there were immense quantities.   Then there was lawn tennis, as may be supposed of a very superior kind, various young relations playing who had the family genius for games, and, for that matter, the family attractiveness.

Incidentally I gathered that Ranji had done a very great deal for the development of his State in every department of administration, and we were full of admiration for all that we saw and heard.

From Jamnagar we returned to Bombay and spent two or three days at Government House.   This was very different from the splendid palaces of Delhi and Calcutta, being really a group of bungalows: we ourselves occupied a delightful bungalow close down to the sea.

One of our cheerful days at Bombay was devoted to the races in surroundings so luxurious as to make Newmarket seem almost squalid. The comfortable chairs in the Grand Stand, where we had a sort of box, the equally comfortable chairs in the paddock and the luncheon and tea arrangements were all that the most self-indulgent could desire.

At Bombay there was a good deal of talk of 'trouble,' and the police were very active, but there were no incidents during our stay.

From Bombay we sailed for Karachi and then by another boat to Basra, where we spent a day at the Consulate.   Basra, like Bangkok, rejoices in a number of small rather smelly canals, and is not a place where we had any great desire to stay.   We went on by the night train, having a coach attached to it for our use containing a sleeping-car and a dining-car: we also had our own cook for the occasion.

Next morning found us at Ur, where our coach was taken off and shunted while we went off to breakfast and spent the day with the Woolleys.

After breakfast Mr. Woolley took us off to see the excavations, and made the most dramatic guide one could imagine, talking as if he had been one of Abraham's closest companions, if not Noah's.   In one of the best houses, which had had two storeys, a big living-room downstairs, and a chapel or something corresponding to a chapel, we imagined Abraham and Sarah to have lived.   I said that I liked to think of those two sitting in their arm-chairs by the fireside, but I was afraid that was quite a false idea of their way of living.   Woolley said: "Not at all."   It seems they had not only a fire-place but arm-chairs of sorts, even stuffed chairs: so I cling to my first idea.

The surrounding scenery in Abraham's time was very different, no doubt; not sandy desert, but well-watered and fertile land.

At one point a great pit had been dug so that we could see the various strata of soil, including one which was the deposit made by Noah's flood. While we were staring at this an aeroplane swooped low down over our heads and dropped a note for Mrs. Woolley: the most dramatic contrast between new and old.

In another part of the ground some of Mr. Woolley's workers were engaged on the graves and one was carefully arranging the necklace taken from a skeleton.   Usually, it seems, the dead were buried beneath their own floor, and when the presence of too many corpses made things uncomfortable the family moved to another house.

In the evening we went back to the station and were hitched on to another train which dropped us next morning at Babylon. There we had a guide of the regular type who had learned his lesson and repeated it to us: incidentally he showed us the wall on which '*Mene mene tekel upharsin*' had been written, and told us that the inscription had been removed by German archæologists, perhaps thinking that we should swallow any tales of German wickedness. Hunting people may like to know that in the adjoining hall we found a fox.

From Babylon we continued our journey to Baghdad to stay with Sir Francis and Lady Humphries. Baghdad was in a not very beautiful phase of its metamorphosis into a capital, always a difficult process. I had the pleasure of being presented to King Feisal in his Palace, having last seen him in my own room at the Foreign Office.

We drove out to Ctesiphon and on the way saw our first and only mirage of distant trees. We also dined with Hubert Young, now Governor of Trinidad, who had worked under me in the Middle East department of the Foreign Office with what, in evangelical circles, would be called 'great acceptance' on the part of Lord Curzon.

The Residency was a pleasant house with an unexpected fountain in the hall into which strangers were apt to fall, and overlooking the Tigris.

We left Baghdad after three or four days by a 'Motorways' car to cross the desert to Damascus. Fortunately there were not many people travelling that day, so that we were able to have a car to ourselves: also we arranged to spend the night at the Rutbah rest-house instead of making the very tiring twenty-four hours' through journey. There were other cars in the convoy besides ours, but after the first hour or two we saw nothing of them; but as we saw nothing of brigands either, it did not matter.

We arrived at Rutbah in good time for dinner. The rest-house consisted of a series of bungalows round a small courtyard, the whole well fenced in with barbed wire and protected by armed guards. Some caravans and cars of sorts were parked in the middle of the court, and there was a tent or two, so that we had to pick our way rather carefully when we crossed the court to the dining-room.

We started again in the morning at six, having crossed the court for breakfast in complete darkness and fallen over some tent ropes. I suppose I was a little agitated, for when we had been driving for some hours and stopped for a picnic lunch I found that I had left my 'plate' at Rutbah. Fortunately, before we had gone much further we met a French armoured car which kindly took back a note to the manager of the rest-house and eventually one morning at Beyrout I found on the breakfast table an envelope inscribed 'Sir John Tilley's family's teeth,' a delicate way of putting it which pleased me and displeased my family.

The journey across the desert was very comfortable until we got near

Damascus, where we found the going much rougher owing, I suppose, to the greater volume of traffic, and we liked the sensation of being able to drive anywhere we chose in any direction: the sensation of travelling on a road a hundred miles wide.

Damascus we did not find very interesting, but perhaps in summer the gardens make it beautiful. We had intended to hire another 'Motorways' car to take us to Jerusalem, but the Consul had a pet garage from which a car came round for our inspection. As seen from the Consulate window on a wet day it looked all right and we agreed to the fare asked—£2 down and £3 more if we were satisfied when we reached Jerusalem.

We started next morning at the usual early hour, and very soon it began to rain. The rain drove in at the open window beside the driver: we requested him to shut it: he shook his head: we insisted: finally he pulled up the window and we saw that there was no glass left in it. Water poured into the car also through the hood, and altogether we found things most disagreeable. When we reached the Syria-Palestine frontier we requested to be taken to the house of the French official in charge of the place, the water on the road being by that time up to the axles of the wheels. I explained that I wanted, if possible, to get another car. The official offered me tea. I thanked him but said we wanted to get on and my family were still in the car. He insisted that we must all have tea, so we gave in and joined him and his family at a ten o'clock *déjeuner*. Happily, he did more than give us a second breakfast, for at his request the British frontier authorities provided a fresh car for us and we sent the Damascus car back to its home. Later on I had a letter from the Consul explaining that the driver had pointed out that the accident of a broken window was really the 'act of God,' and he suggested that we should authorize him to pay the balance of £3. I refused altogether to admit the responsibility of Providence, and as we had taken the car only a short way instead of the whole way to Jerusalem— some seven or eight hours further on—I could not agree to be generous.

Our new car did us very well except that when we got within an hour or so of Jerusalem its lights failed and we had to drive carefully in front of another car, containing a priest, and borrowing its light. We proposed, indeed, to join the priest in his car, but he explained that he could not afford to be seen with women in his car.

Eventually we reached the High Commissioner's house rather late for dinner, and with my suit-case, which had been tied on behind the car, soaked with water and half full of mud. However, Sir John and Lady Chancellor very soon made up by their kindness for any tribulations which we had experienced on the way. The weather had been so awful that we had only seen very little of the country, though we had a pleasant hour for lunch at Tiberias.

At Jerusalem again we saw everything that could be seen in a visit of a few days. An exceptional thing which we saw was an altar in the Church of the Holy Sepulchre which had been set apart for some Syrian sect; it was noticed that the picture above the altar was gradually being ruined, but it was not apparent how till the Bishop who officiated there was observed to be hacking away pieces with a penknife with a view to re-assembling them at his home town where he considered that the picture really ought to be.

We visited the Mosque of Omar in the company of a Moslem potentate with whom we were photographed, and who was, I believe, the Grand Mufti who has since made so much evil history.

We drove out one day to the Dead Sea, and another day to inspect the new Residency, which was nearly finished and looked as if it would be a success, though built on a very wind-swept spot.

From Jerusalem we drove along a road parallel with the road to Emmaus, a road along which scarlet anenomes were already (or still) in flower, in order to join the railway for Haifa. From Haifa we drove again along the shore, and thus by a good road to Beyrout, meeting with none of the brigands who were very apt to infest the district.

At Beyrout we stayed a night with Sir Harold Satow and then set out again for Baalbek. There had been heavy snow and it was only at lunch-time that the authorities announced that the road was sufficiently clear for us to make the journey.

We had the whole of the next day to devote to the glorious ruins of Baalbek and then caught the night train for Constantinople.

We had greatly looked forward to being in Constantinople again after an interval of twenty-two years, but we found something very different from what we had left. In the first place it was no longer the capital, and the departure of its glory somehow seemed very obvious. Then it had ceased to be either Eastern or mediæval: no fezzes, no yashmaks, no street dogs, nothing very queer where once everything had been queer. Luckily we were met by one of the old *kavasses* and we found the old Chancery servant still in his place.

The Embassy house was silent. Sir George Clerk, the Ambassador, had most kindly come from Ankara to entertain us, and it was a delight to meet him, as it had been any time in thirty years; but not more than one or two of the staff were to be seen where they had once been thick on the ground.

The Ambassador lent us his car and we drove out to Therapia, taking perhaps half an hour each way over an expedition to which we should once have allotted a day. The Therapia Embassy had been burned down and the other houses looked decayed. Another morning we drove across to the Walls, once also a full day's occupation.

On the whole it is perhaps a mistake ever to go back to any well-remembered place after a long absence.

From Constantinople we went to Buda Pesth to stay with the Chilstons for a few days and so back to London and the quiet life.

I can at least say this, that if I had to begin my life again I should be content to live it as I have lived it.

INDEX